Advance praise for *A System of Pleas*

"The Supreme Court has recognized that the American criminal justice system is from beginning to end a system of bargained guilty pleas. The studies presented here provide a comprehensive tour of this system from pretrial detention and the pressures it exerts though the harsh and often undisclosed collateral consequences that follow seemingly beneficial plea agreements. This book examines in depth the decisions of prosecutors, defense attorneys, and defendants (both adults and juveniles), and it documents the sentencing disparities that keep the river of guilty pleas flowing. Once you've read this book, you'll understand what makes our system of criminal justice go."

—Albert W. Alschuler, Julius Kreeger Professor of Criminal Law and Criminology Emeritus, The University of Chicago Law School

"The plea bargaining process is the silent giant without which the entire criminal justice system would grind to a halt. Yet, despite its immeasurable societal importance, the process has received scant attention from social scientists. This path breaking book remedies that glaring shortfall. The authors provide an insightful and comprehensive account of the process: the goals, incentives and constraints of the actors involved, its effect on racial minorities, juveniles and innocent defendants, and its impact on society at large. For years to come, no scholarly discussion of plea bargaining will be able to ignore this volume."

—Dan Simon, Richard L. and Maria B. Crutcher Professor of Law & Psychology, USC Gould School of Law and Department of Psychology

"With over 95% of criminal convictions in the U.S. achieved though guilty pleas, the time has come for social scientists to scrutinize the system, the process, the players, and the outcomes. With timely chapters written by active scholars, this book offers an overview of history and law; an up-to-date look at research on how prosecutors, attorneys and defendants make plea decisions; and the added challenges that confront innocents, juveniles, and minorities. Like it or not, today is the age of the plea bargain—and this book shines a critical spotlight on how it happens."

—Saul Kassin, Distinguished Professor of Psychology, John Jay College of Criminal Justice

"It has taken decades, but the disciplines of criminology, economics, psychology, criminal justice, and history now give plea bargaining the full attention it deserves. Edkins and Redlich have assembled into this one volume the interconnected insights from these disciplines to explain the plea-centered reality of criminal courts in the United States. If you're new to the work of criminal courts, you need this book. And if you're an experienced traveler in the criminal courts and need a fresh way to see daily business, you need this book."

—Ronald F. Wright, Gulley Professor of Criminal Law, Wake Forest University

A System of Pleas

American Psychology-Law Society Series

Books in the Series

Emergency Department Treatment of the Psychiatric Patient
Susan Stefan

The Psychology of the Supreme Court
Lawrence S. Wrightsman

Proving the Unprovable
Christopher Slobogin

Adolescents, Media, and the Law
Roger J.R. Levesque

Oral Arguments Before the Supreme Court
Lawrence S. Wrightsman

God in the Courtroom
Brian H. Bornstein and Monica K. Miller

Expert Testimony on the Psychology of Eyewitness Identification
Edited by Brian L. Cutler

The Psychology of Judicial Decision-Making
Edited by David Klein and Gregory Mitchell

The Miranda Ruling: Its Past, Present, and Future
Lawrence S. Wrightsman and Mary L. Pitman

Juveniles at Risk: A Plea for Preventive Justice
Christopher Slobogin and Mark R. Fondacaro

The Ethics of Total Confinement
Bruce A. Arrigo, Heather Y. Bersot, and Brian G. Sellers

International Human Rights and Mental Disability Law
Michael L. Perlin

Applying Social Science to Reduce Violent Offending
Edited by Joel Dvoskin, Jennifer L. Skeem, Raymond W. Novaco, and Kevin S. Douglas

Children Who Resist Postseparation Parental Contact
Barbara Jo Fidler, Nicholas Bala, and Michael A. Saini

Trauma, Stress, and Wellbeing in the Legal System
Edited by Monica K. Miller and Brian H. Bornstein

Psychology, Law, and the Wellbeing of Children
Edited by Monica K. Miller, Jared C. Chamberlain, and Twila Wingrove

Murder in the Courtroom: The Cognitive Neuroscience of Extreme Violent Behavior
Brigitte Vallabhajosula

Rational Suicide, Irrational Laws: Examining Current Approaches to Suicide in Policy and Law
Susan Stefan

International Perspectives on Violence Risk Assessment
Edited by Jay P. Singh, Stål Bjørkly, and Seena Fazel

Adolescence, Privacy, and the Law: A Developmental Science Perspective
Roger J.R. Levesque

The Ethical Practice of Forensic Psychology
Gianni Pirelli, Robert A. Beattey, and Patricia A. Zapf

The Jury Under Fire: Myth, Controversy, and Reform
Brian H. Bornstein and Edie Greene

The Science and Law of School Segregation and Diversity
Roger J.R. Levesque

Criminal Juries in the 21st Century: Contemporary Issues, Psychological Science, and the Law
Edited by Cynthia J. Najdowski and Margaret C. Stevenson

A System of Pleas

American Psychology-Law Society Series

Books in the Series

Emergency Department Treatment of the Psychiatric Patient
Susan Stefan

The Psychology of the Supreme Court
Lawrence S. Wrightsman

Proving the Unprovable
Christopher Slobogin

Adolescents, Media, and the Law
Roger J.R. Levesque

Oral Arguments Before the Supreme Court
Lawrence S. Wrightsman

God in the Courtroom
Brian H. Bornstein and Monica K. Miller

Expert Testimony on the Psychology of Eyewitness Identification
Edited by Brian L. Cutler

The Psychology of Judicial Decision-Making
Edited by David Klein and Gregory Mitchell

The Miranda Ruling: Its Past, Present, and Future
Lawrence S. Wrightsman and Mary L. Pitman

Juveniles at Risk: A Plea for Preventive Justice
Christopher Slobogin and Mark R. Fondacaro

The Ethics of Total Confinement
Bruce A. Arrigo, Heather Y. Bersot, and Brian G. Sellers

International Human Rights and Mental Disability Law
Michael L. Perlin

Applying Social Science to Reduce Violent Offending
Edited by Joel Dvoskin, Jennifer L. Skeem, Raymond W. Novaco, and Kevin S. Douglas

Children Who Resist Postseparation Parental Contact
Barbara Jo Fidler, Nicholas Bala, and Michael A. Saini

Trauma, Stress, and Wellbeing in the Legal System
Edited by Monica K. Miller and Brian H. Bornstein

Psychology, Law, and the Wellbeing of Children
Edited by Monica K. Miller, Jared C. Chamberlain, and Twila Wingrove

Murder in the Courtroom: The Cognitive Neuroscience of Extreme Violent Behavior
Brigitte Vallabhajosula

Rational Suicide, Irrational Laws: Examining Current Approaches to Suicide in Policy and Law
Susan Stefan

International Perspectives on Violence Risk Assessment
Edited by Jay P. Singh, Stål Bjørkly, and Seena Fazel

Adolescence, Privacy, and the Law: A Developmental Science Perspective
Roger J.R. Levesque

The Ethical Practice of Forensic Psychology
Gianni Pirelli, Robert A. Beattey, and Patricia A. Zapf

The Jury Under Fire: Myth, Controversy, and Reform
Brian H. Bornstein and Edie Greene

The Science and Law of School Segregation and Diversity
Roger J.R. Levesque

Criminal Juries in the 21st Century: Contemporary Issues, Psychological Science, and the Law
Edited by Cynthia J. Najdowski and Margaret C. Stevenson

A System of Pleas

Social Science's Contributions to the Real Legal System

Edited by

Vanessa A. Edkins

and

Allison D. Redlich

OXFORD
UNIVERSITY PRESS

OXFORD
UNIVERSITY PRESS

Oxford University Press is a department of the University of Oxford. It furthers the University's objective of excellence in research, scholarship, and education by publishing worldwide. Oxford is a registered trade mark of Oxford University Press in the UK and certain other countries.

Published in the United States of America by Oxford University Press
198 Madison Avenue, New York, NY 10016, United States of America.

CIP data is on file at the Library of Congress
ISBN 978-0-19-068924-7

To all of the great psychology and law researchers that came before us and built this field, including my mentor, Lawrence Wrightsman. Also to my husband, Trevor, for his continuing support and constant optimism, and to my sabbatical partner, Sam.

VE

To those who first inspired me to research guilty pleas. I trace it back to 2004 with a fascinating *Harvard Law Review* article by Stephanos Bibas and an enlightening PBS *Frontline* episode by Ofra Bikel. Since then, I have been fortunate to have many more inspirations, including the authors of this book.

AR

Contents

Series Foreword

This book series is sponsored by the American Psychology-Law Society (APLS). APLS is an interdisciplinary organization devoted to scholarship, practice, and public service in psychology and law. Its goals include advancing the contributions of psychology to the understanding of law and legal institutions through basic and applied research; promoting the education of psychologists in matters of law and the education of legal personnel in matters of psychology; and informing the psychological and legal communities and the general public of current research, educational, and service activities in the field of psychology and law. APLS membership includes psychologists from the academic, research, and clinical practice communities as well as members of the legal community. Research and practice is represented in both the civil and criminal legal arenas. APLS has chosen Oxford University Press as a strategic partner because of its commitment to scholarship, quality, and the international dissemination of ideas. These strengths will help APLS reach its goal of educating the psychology and legal professions and the general public about important developments in psychology and law. The focus of the book series reflects the diversity of the field of psychology and law, as we will publish books on a broad range of topics.

In the latest book in the series, *A System of Pleas: Social Science's Contributions to the Real Legal System*, Vanessa Edkins and Allison Redlich have edited a series of chapters authored by top scholars that delineate the series of influences—both positive and negative experiences—brought about by a system of plea bargaining. Influences such as private negotiations, prosecutorial discretion and power, unequal sentencing, and defendants' relinquishment of constitutional rights are explicated as readers are led through the plea bargaining process, with the psychological, economical, and sociological considerations, as well as the respective accumulation of research, outlined at each step.

Edkins and Redlich have curated a collection of 9 chapters, divided into three parts: (1) The system of pleas and its players, examining the state and history of plea bargaining, and the role of the defendant, defense attorney, and prosecutor; (2) influences in plea making, explicating the roles of race, juvenile justice, and innocence; and (3) the results of a system of pleas, delineating sentencing disparity and mass incarceration and the collateral consequences of disenfranchisement.

A System of Pleas: Social Science's Contributions to the Real Legal System presents a comprehensive and detailed analysis of issues relevant to our system of pleas. Scholars, researchers, policymakers, and practitioners will find this book integral to shaping the future of the plea bargaining process.

Patricia A. Zapf
Series Editor

About the Contributors

Shawn D. Bushway is Professor of Public Administration and Policy at the Rockefeller College of Public Affairs and Policy at the University at Albany (SUNY). He has been a member of New York State's Permanent Commission on Sentencing Reform since 2010, and his primary research interests involve criminal justice policy and the desistance process. He received the State University of New York Chancellor's Award for Excellence in Scholarship in 2014. He was also recognized as a Distinguished Scholar for the American Society of Criminology's Division on Corrections and Sentencing in 2014, and honored as a Fellow of the American Society of Criminology in 2017.

Tarika Daftary-Kapur is Associate Professor of Criminal Justice at Fairleigh Dickinson University. In her research, she addresses weaknesses in justice systems (e.g., the courts) and proposes solutions for change. She examines the role of coercion in plea bargaining, specifically related to youth. Broadly, her focus is on testing the assumptions that the legal system makes about what constitutes coercion in the plea bargain context and in identifying disparities in outcomes for youth. Professor Daftary-Kapur also studies the role of attitudes and biases in jury decision-making in various contexts, such as pretrial publicity and the death penalty.

Lucian E. Dervan is Associate Professor at Belmont University College of Law and focuses on domestic and international criminal law. He is the author of two books and dozens of book chapters and articles. He is also the founder and author of *The Plea Bargaining Blog* and a contributing editor to the *White Collar Crime Prof Blog.* In addition to his writings, he regularly lectures on criminal law and has been invited to speak before the United States House of Representatives' Judiciary Committee, the United States Sentencing Commission, and the International Criminal Tribunal for the former Yugoslavia. Prior to joining the academy, Professor Dervan served as a law clerk to the Honorable Phyllis A. Kravitch of the United States Court of Appeals for the Eleventh Circuit and practiced law with King & Spalding LLP and Ford & Harrison LLP.

Vanessa A. Edkins is Associate Professor of Psychology at Florida Institute of Technology. Her research focuses on decision-making during the plea bargaining process and on the effect of collateral consequences on plea bargains. She has also conducted research looking at employment law, and racism in the justice system. In addition to publishing in prominent psychology and law journals, her work has been featured in the *Wall Street Journal, The Economist,* and in testimony before congress. Dr. Edkins also serves as a member of the Executive Committee for the American Psychology-Law Society (Division 41 of the American Psychological Association).

Kelsey S. Henderson is Assistant Professor of Criminology and Criminal Justice at Portland State University. She received her PhD in criminology, law and society from the University of Florida in 2016. Her research examines decision-making in the legal system, specifically focusing on juror decisions about confession evidence (with and without the assistance of system variables) and plea decision-making (factors that influence true and false guilty pleas). Her work has been featured in *Law and Human Behavior.*

Rhys Hester is an Assistant Professor at Clemson University. He was formerly the Deputy Director of the Pennsylvania Commission on Sentencing and a Research Fellow in Sentencing Law and Policy at the Robina Institute of Criminal Law and Criminal Justice, University of Minnesota Law School. He studies punishment, sentencing, and decision-making. His research has appeared in *Criminology, Journal of Quantitative Criminology*, and *Crime and Justice: A Review of Research.*

Brian D. Johnson is Professor of Criminology and Criminal Justice at the University of Maryland. His areas of expertise involve social inequality in the justice system, with a particular focus on racial disparities in guilty pleas and sentencing outcomes. Dr. Johnson is the recipient of the American Society of Criminology's (ASC) Young Scholar Award as well as the ASC Division on Corrections and Sentencing Distinguished New Scholar Award. He is currently serving as co-editor of the journal *Criminology*. Dr. Johnson is also the policy expert on the Maryland State Commission on Criminal Sentencing Policy (MSCCSP). His published work has appeared in journals such as the *American Journal of Sociology, Criminology, Journal of Quantitative Criminology,* and *Justice Quarterly.*

Annmarie Khairalla is finishing her B.A. in psychology at the University of Massachusetts Lowell with minors in Arabic studies, criminal justice, and history. She plans to attend a Ph.D. program in psychology where she will continue to build a program of research in psychology and law.

Bryan C. McCannon is Assistant Professor of Economics at West Virginia University and faculty affiliate of the Center for Free Enterprise. Dr. McCannon received his Ph.D. in economics from Penn State University (2003). Dr. McCannon's research focuses on applying economic methods to issues in the criminal justice system. Notably, his research has explored the impact of prosecutor elections on the willingness to plea bargain rather than take a case to trial, the backlog of cases, and the frequency of success in appeals of felony convictions. Additionally, his research investigates how public financing constraints and judge's compensation affect case disposition.

Allison D. Redlich is Professor of Criminology, Law and Society at George Mason University. Her research centers on whether legal decision-making is knowing, intelligent, and voluntary. She examines such decision-making in vulnerable (juveniles and persons with mental illness) and non-vulnerable defendants, and across several different contexts—in the interrogation room, during the guilty plea process, and in mental health courts. Professor Redlich also studies wrongful convictions, with a particular focus on false confessions and false guilty pleas. She has published extensively on these topics and has received funding from numerous agencies and foundations in support of her research.

Rebecca Richardson is a doctoral candidate in the Department of Criminology and Criminal Justice at the University of Maryland. She is a 2017–2018 Ann G. Wylie Fellow at the University of Maryland and was awarded a Horton-Hallowell fellowship from Wellesley College in 2014. Her research interests include courts and sentencing, social inequality in criminal case processing, and evidence-based policy in the criminal justice system.

Miko M. Wilford is Assistant Professor at the University of Massachusetts Lowell. She is an applied cognitive psychologist interested in improving real-world policies and procedures, particularly in law and education. More specifically, her research has focused on ways of improving plea bargaining procedures to reduce false guilty pleas, as well as examining methods of increasing the accuracy of eyewitness testimony and identification. She is also interested in improving educational testing procedures to maximize student learning and retention.

Tina Zottoli is a New York State licensed clinical psychologist and Assistant Professor of Psychology at Montclair State University, where she also serves as director of the MA program in clinical psychology, forensic specialization. Her primary scholarship is in adolescent decision-making and legal competencies, and she is presently focused on plea deal decision-making and wrongful conviction by guilty plea. In her clinical practice, she provides consultation, forensic evaluation, and expert testimony across a range of criminal and civil domains.

Introduction

A System of Pleas

Vanessa A. Edkins and Allison D. Redlich

> In the end, petitioner's three arguments amount to one general contention: A fair trial wipes clean any deficient performance by defense counsel during plea bargaining. That position ignores the reality that criminal justice today is for the most part a system of pleas, not a system of trials. Ninety-seven percent of federal convictions and ninety-four percent of state convictions are the result of guilty pleas. . . . As explained in *Frye*, the right to adequate assistance of counsel cannot be defined or enforced without taking account of the central role plea bargaining plays in securing convictions and determining sentences.
>
> —Justice Anthony Kennedy
> *Lafler v. Cooper* (2012, p. 11, Majority Opinion)

This quote from Justice Kennedy acknowledges the fact that criminal justice in the United States today is an entirely different beast from what the founding fathers had in mind. The criminal trial is a set of checks and balances—from jury selection, to the deeming of evidence as inadmissible when its collection did not adhere to the protections afforded to us in the Fourth Amendment, to a jury of one's peers carefully weighing the case and inserting the conscience of the community into its decision. Those checks and balances—although not without their own flaws—represent a system that is open to the public and that follows clear rules and procedures intended to safeguard the constitutional rights of defendants. What we have today is not that system. Whereas discussion on juror and jury decision-making continues to expound in the field of psychology and law (e.g., see Kovera & Cutler, 2013), the processes of plea bargaining and plea decision-making have not received the same attention—that is, until recently (e.g., see Redlich, Bibas, Edkins, & Madon, 2017). We know that if a defendant is prosecuted for a crime in this country it is almost a foregone conclusion that the case will end with the entering of a guilty plea; that a conviction will be obtained with no jury in sight. Understanding the workings of the criminal justice system is understanding guilty pleas. This is the overarching aim of this book, an aim which we approach from multiple perspectives and with cutting-edge research.

To see the pervasiveness and institutionalization of plea bargaining in our justice system, one need look no further than the federal prosecution of drug crimes. According to Human Rights Watch (2013), the 97% guilty plea rate by federal drug defendants is reached through strong-arm tactics by federal prosecutors, often overcharging defendants to invoke mandatory minimum sentences that would apply if the case went to trial. Federal drug cases epitomize the impact of plea bargaining on the various players and at multiple levels of the justice system.

Consider the problem of sentence and charge bargaining. Scholars suggest that the influx of plea bargaining into the system has encouraged prosecutors to inflate charges or to threaten sentences that are much harsher than those regularly imposed (Bibas, 2012). The numbers support the contention: The average sentence length for individuals who accept a guilty plea in a federal drug case is approximately 5 years and 4 months; those who reject the prosecutor's offer and defend themselves at trial face an average of 16 years in prison (Human Rights Watch, 2013). These disparities between sentences couched in plea offers and those that result from a conviction at trial certainly influence a defendant's decision to accept a plea deal and lead to considerations of what is fair or just in the offering of a plea bargain (Bibas, 2012).

Often the reason a defendant may reject a plea bargain is based on beliefs of actual or legal innocence. For example, Darlene Eckles let her drug-dealing brother live at her house for 6 months, aware of his illegal activities (Human Rights Watch, 2013). When she was offered a 10-year sentence, the nursing assistant felt she was not guilty and put herself in that 3% minority, taking her case to trial; she received a nearly 20-year sentence upon conviction. Her brother did accept the deal he was offered—he received a sentence of 11 years and 8 months.

When a federal drug defendant faces the knowledge that 9 out of 10 individuals in his or her position who choose trial are ultimately convicted (Graham, 2012) and faces a prosecutor who threatens to file additional charges that would invoke mandatory minimum sentences, the rational choice is often to plead guilty—even if the defendant is not. Yet the ramifications of these pleas are also problematic. Automatic deportation, loss of professional licensure, inability to collect government assistance, and many other limitations are imposed on those individuals with a criminal conviction (Roberts, 2009). What begins as forfeiting one's right to a trial, ends with a forfeiture of many more rights and freedoms.

Many legal scholars have discussed the problems associated with a system built on pleas: negotiations occurring in private (Bibas, 2004), too much power and discretion on the part of prosecutors (Stuntz, 2004), encouraging defendants to forego their constitutional rights (Burke, 2007), unequal sentencing (Alschuler, 2005), among others. This book seeks to address these problems—and others—focusing on what empirical, social science research can tell us. Given that several countries have recently considered or are now considering adopting their own (partial) system of pleas (Rauxloh, 2012), examining the positive and negative experiences of plea bargaining in the United States is essential.

Social science has a great deal to offer the realm of plea bargaining, as is laid out in this volume. The goals of this book are to move the reader through the plea bargaining process, outlining the psychological, economic, and sociological considerations at each step, and the respective accumulating research. We are entrenched in a "system of pleas," as Justice Kennedy (*Lafler v. Cooper*, 2012, p. 11) called it, and we can assist legal system players—as well as students and the general public—in understanding the workings of this system.

We begin the book with the legal considerations (and history) involved in plea bargaining—think of this as a primer to the current state of our legal system. In Chapter 1, Dervan outlines how we ended up with a system of pleas and the sorts of legal issues that have arisen. The concepts of sentencing disparity and charge bargaining are discussed in this chapter, and these are concepts revisited multiple times throughout the book as the various authors discuss decision-making in the plea bargaining process, beginning with an overview of cognitive biases.

Heuristics and biases are at play in any decision that we make, and there is no reason to assume that plea negotiations are immune to these effects. In Chapter 2, Bushway addresses how a defendant's decision in a plea bargain can be affected by everything from how the offer is framed (as a "win" or a "loss") to the beliefs the defendant holds about what is fair or just in the situation. The system of pleas can only function if individuals are willing to accept what is being offered in a plea bargain. On the one hand, there is research indicating that defendants feel that plea bargains are quite fair and procedurally just (e.g., Redlich & Summers, 2012). On the other hand, states are seeing very large discrepancies between the sentences doled out after a conviction at trial and those resulting from a plea agreement (King, Soule, Steen, & Weidner, 2005), and that discrepancy may be enough to encourage a defendant to accept a plea. But what happens when the defendant feels he or she is less culpable in a crime or when a co-defendant or a similar other is receiving a different deal? Decades of research in cognitive psychology and behavioral economics highlight how rationality is often the last factor to come into play, even when the decisions are potentially life-changing, as a decision to plead guilty to a crime quite often is.

And the defendant is not the only party making these large, sweeping decisions: Henderson, in Chapter 3, discusses the plea offer and recommendation decisions by defense attorneys. As their client's main advocate and last line of protection against unfair processes or procedures, can defense attorneys overcome some of the cognitive biases to which defendants may fall prey? The research does not necessarily support that idea—and it brings into play other factors that can muddy the waters when recommending to a client that he or she accept a plea deal, such as racial biases (Edkins, 2011) or role-induced bias (Engel & Glockner, 2013).

On the other side of the adversarial aisle, turning the justice system into a system of pleas has bestowed incredibly broad (and unchecked) discretionary powers upon prosecuting attorneys. As addressed in Chapters 8 (Hester) and 9 (Edkins) in discussions of sentencing disparity and collateral consequences, these prosecutorial powers can lead to large differences in how similar cases are handled. Consider again the example of federal drug prosecutions: Two men are arrested with the same amount of drugs in their possession—one accepts a plea deal and the other refuses. While the prosecutor may not be "punishing" an individual for exercising his right to a trial, it is not uncommon for that prosecutor to use his or her discretion and tack on a charge that increases the penalty due to prior drug convictions (Human Rights Watch, 2013), and that individual convicted at trial ends up with a sentence nearly twice the length of the individual who plead guilty (King et al., 2005). In Chapter 4, McCannon discusses the effects of discretion and how the decisions made by prosecutors cannot be separated from their biases nor from their self-serving but necessary considerations inherent in a profession that relies on elections for continued employment.

The second section of the book seeks to break down influential individual factors in plea bargaining. We begin with the topic of demographic factors, with the main focus on race. While African Americans compose roughly 13% of the U.S. population and Hispanics roughly 17% (United States Census Bureau, 2014), the two groups make up 38% and 21% of prison inmates, respectively (Carson & Golinelli, 2013). This over-representation leads us to question the effects of the defendant's race—along with the race of the victim—on plea offers and sentences obtained. In Chapter 5, Johnson and Richardson paint a picture of how the impact of race in plea bargaining can contribute to the overall racial disparities in arrests, charging decisions, and sentence recommendations, thus compounding disparities observed in the system. This idea of a *cumulative disadvantage* for minorities in the justice system (Spohn, 2009)—that racial disparities will be introduced early on (targets and arrests) and will have compounding effects through charging, convictions, and sentencing—has been borne out through multiple lines of research (Kutateladze, Andiloro, Johnson, & Spohn, 2014; Sutton, 2013), which Johnson and Richardson bring together, illuminating race's influence on plea practices.

Decisions to plead also need to take into consideration the cognitive ability of the defendant and whether he or she is a member of a protected group—in this case, a juvenile. In Chapter 6, Redlich, Zottoli, and Daftary-Kapur present research supporting how juvenile justice has also turned into a system of pleas and how working with this population introduces a host of new limitations that need to be addressed when the court allows a child to plead. A large body of research exists demonstrating that juveniles have significant deficits in their legal knowledge and understanding in comparison to adults (e.g., Grisso et al., 2003). These deficits, which have been tied to immature development, have important implications for making knowing, intelligent, and voluntary plea decisions. Redlich et al. discuss the unique challenges associated with a system of pleas and youthful defendants.

Wilford and Khairalla continue the discussion in Chapter 7 with research addressing another possibly important individual variable influencing decisions to plead: actual innocence. The discussion of innocence highlights how important it is that we understand all the contributors in decisions to plead guilty. The National Registry of Exonerations (2015) looked at over 1,600 cases of individuals exonerated after conviction and found that 13% of those individuals had pleaded guilty to the crime. Studies have also replicated the phenomenon of "innocents" pleading guilty in laboratory settings (e.g., Dervan & Edkins, 2013). The common reaction to false-confession research in its nascent stages was a disbelief that someone would confess to a crime they had not committed, yet the research repeatedly showed that individuals had confessed and would confess (Kassin, 2005). A similar reaction is expected for false guilty pleas, but Wilford and Khairalla discuss how the stage is set to allow for these miscarriages of justice to occur.

The last section of the book seeks to bring us back from the piecemeal focus of individual factors and toward looking at the system as whole. The goal of this section is not to lament the state of criminal justice but to show some of the larger effects and act as a "call to arms," highlighting the areas that need further research, including research directed at policy change. Hester initiates the discussion by looking at how our system of pleas has led to an unprecedented level of disparities in sentencing and of mass incarceration that threatens to bankrupt the states and the federal system (Chapter 8). Disparities are accentuated through charge and sentence bargaining, and the focus on "governmental assistance" significantly reduces sentences in the federal system (and in most states). For example, in Darlene Eckles' federal case noted earlier, one of the reasons her drug-dealing brother was able to secure a shorter sentence than Darlene was that *he* testified against *her* at the behest of the federal prosecutor (Human Rights Watch, 2013). With regard to incarceration, many of the overly enticing bargains being offered and accepted are actually creating a possibility of "back-end" sentencing for convicts—prosecutors can offer these extreme reductions (e.g., 10 years' probation instead of 3 years in prison) with the knowledge that many individuals will violate their probation and end up serving the full prison sentence (Travis, 2007).

But disparities in penal sanctions are not the only place where we have seen the marked effects of our system of pleas. Chapter 9 looks at the current state of "collateral consequences"—the seemingly non-punitive components that are attached to criminal convictions in this country. Enticing plea deals have encouraged thousands of individuals to surrender their constitutional rights and accept a criminal conviction, not realizing that the ramifications of that decision are far-reaching and often permanent. The National Inventory of the Collateral Consequences of Conviction catalogues these consequences and has, to date, found more than 48,000 (Council of State Governments Justice Center, 2017)!

From disenfranchisement (i.e., the loss of the right to vote) to denial of student loans to ineligibility to collect welfare or food stamps to a loss of professional licenses or certifications, individuals with a criminal record are prevented from fully participating in society as equal citizens. Research in the area of collateral consequences highlights the "bait and switch" technique currently being utilized in the offer of overly enticing plea deals.

The final chapter of the book pulls all the information together and points readers forward on a path that incorporates what social science has to offer in proposed policy or legislative changes. Acknowledging that we do, indeed, operate within a system of pleas, we now need to try and change the way we approach criminal justice to reflect what we know about the most important and most powerful tool in the justice system: the plea bargain.

References

Alschuler, A. W. (2005). Disparity: The normative and empirical failure of the federal guidelines. *Stanford Law Review*, *58*, 85–118.

Bibas, S. (2004). Plea bargaining outside the shadow of a trial. *Harvard Law Review*, *117*, 2463–2547.

Bibas, S. (2012). *The machinery of criminal justice*. New York: Oxford University Press.

Burke, A. S. (2007). Prosecutorial passion, cognitive bias, and plea bargaining. *Marquette Law Review*, *91*, 183–211.

Carson, E. A., & Golinelli, D. (2013). *Prisoners in 2012*. Washington, DC: Bureau of Justice Statistics.

Council of State Governments Justice Center. (2017). *National Inventory of the Collateral Consequences of Conviction*. Retrieved from https://niccc.csgjusticecenter.org/

Dervan, L.E., & Edkins, V.A. (2013). The innocent defendant's dilemma: An innovative empirical study of plea bargaining's innocence problem. *Journal of Criminal Law and Criminology*, *103*, 1–48.

Edkins, V.A. (2011). Defense attorney plea recommendations and client race: Does zealous representation apply equally to all? *Law and Human Behavior*, *35*, 413–425. doi: 10.1007/s10979-010-9254-0.

Engel, C., & Glockner, A. (2013). Role-induced bias in court: An experimental analysis. *Journal of Behavioral Decision Making*, *26*, 272–284. doi: 10.1002/bdm.1761

Graham, K. (2012). Crimes, widgets, and plea bargaining: An analysis of charge content, pleas, and trials. *California Law Review, 100*, 1573–1630.
Grisso, T., Steinberg, L., Woolard, J., Cauffman, E., Scott, E., Graham, S., . . . Schwartz, R. (2003). Juveniles' competence to stand trial: A comparison of adolescents' and adults' capacities as trial defendants. *Law and Human Behavior, 27*, 333–364. http://dx.doi.org/10.1023/A:1024065015717
Human Rights Watch. (2013, December 13). *An offer you can't refuse: How US federal prosecutors force drug defendants to plead guilty*. Retrieved from https://www.hrw.org/report/2013/12/05/offer-you-cant-refuse/how-us-federal-prosecutors-force-drug-defendants-plead
Kassin, S. M. (2005). On the psychology of confessions: Does innocence put innocents at risk? *American Psychologist, 60*, 215–228. doi: 10.1037/0003-066X.60.3.215
King, N. J., Soule, D. A., Steen, S., & Weidner, R. R. (2005). When process affects punishment: Differences in sentences after guilty plea, bench trial, and jury trial in five guidelines states. *Columbia Law Review, 105*, 959–1009.
Kovera, M. B. & Cutler, B. L. (2013). *Jury selection*. New York: Oxford University Press.
Kutateladze, B. L., Andiloro, N. R., Johnson, B. D., & Spohn, C. C. (2014). Cumulative disadvantage: Examining racial and ethnic disparity in prosecution and sentencing. *Criminology, 52*, 514–551. doi: 10.1111/1745-9125.12047
Lafler v. Cooper, 132 U.S. 1376 (2012).
National Registry of Exonerations (2015). *The first 1,600 exonerations*. Retrieved from http://www.law.umich.edu/special/exoneration/Documents/1600_Exonerations.pdf
Rauxloh, R. (2012). *Plea bargaining in national and international law*. New York: Routledge Press.
Redlich, A. D., Bibas, S., Edkins, V., & Madon, S. (2017). The psychology of defendant plea decision-making. *American Psychologist, 72*, 339–352. doi: 10.1037/a0040436
Redlich, A. D., & Summers, A. (2012). Voluntary, knowing, and intelligent pleas: Understanding plea inquiries. *Psychology, Public Policy, and Law, 18*, 626–643. http://dx.doi.org/10.1037/a0026066
Roberts, J. (2009). Ignorance is effectively bliss: Collateral consequences, silence, and misinformation in the guilty-plea process. *Iowa Law Review, 95*, 119–194.
Spohn, C. (2009). Race, sex, and pretrial detention in federal court: Indirect effects and cumulative disadvantage. *Kansas Law Review, 57*, 879–901.
Stuntz, W. J. (2004). Plea bargaining and criminal law's disappearing shadow. *Harvard Law Review, 117*, 2548–2569.
Sutton, J. R. (2013). Structural bias in the sentencing of felony defendants. *Social Science Research, 42*, 1207–1221.
Travis, J. (2007). Back-end sentencing: A practice in search of a rationale. *Social Research, 74*, 631–644.
United States Census Bureau (2014). *QuickFacts*. Retrieved from http://www.census.gov/quickfacts/table/PST045215/00.

Section 1

THE SYSTEM OF PLEAS AND ITS PLAYERS

1

Arriving at a System of Pleas

The History and State of Plea Bargaining

Lucian E. Dervan

If you asked someone on the street to describe the typical American criminal case, you would likely hear the person tell of a courtroom trial reminiscent of those seen on television and in the movies. But the reality of the American criminal justice system is much different. Those traditional trials represent only a small portion of the total criminal docket each year.

Today, around 98% of federal convictions come not from a trial but from a plea of guilty (United States Sentencing Commission, 2012–2016). According to the United States Sentencing Commission, the plea rate at the federal level fluctuated between 96.9% and 97.3% from 2012 to 2016 (United States Sentencing Commission, 2012–2016). Often such pleas of guilty are entered into in consideration of a reduced sentence, whether through a plea bargain or because of the reductions in sentence available to those who accept responsibility under the Federal Sentencing Guidelines system. State plea rates are not far behind, at about 95% of convictions (*Padilla v. Kentucky*, 2010, p. 372).

This chapter will introduce the reader to plea bargaining. First, the chapter will discuss some of the mechanics of plea bargaining and the dominant forms of plea bargaining in the U.S. criminal justice system. In doing so, the chapter will examine the manner in which defendants engage in bargaining and the "shadow-of-trial" model of bargaining. Second, the chapter will discuss the historical rise of plea bargaining and consider whether today's plea bargains reflect the Supreme Court's vision of the system as laid down in the case of *Brady v. United States* in 1970 (*Brady v. United States*, 1970). Finally, the chapter will conclude by briefly considering several recent Supreme Court plea bargaining cases and whether a renewed focus on plea bargaining jurisprudence is materializing.

The Plea Bargaining Machine

At its simplest, plea bargaining is a contract for mutual benefits (Scott & Stuntz, 1992). In return for offering some benefit to the defendant, the government can secure a guilty plea and conviction without the formalities and costs of a potentially long and expensive trial. At the same time, the prosecution can avoid the possibility of losing at trial if the case is weak. On the other side of the table, such a plea bargain can help the defendant in avoiding the costs of proceeding to trial, which might be both financially and personally burdensome. The defendant can also often reap the benefit of a lower sentence in return for confessing guilt, particularly where the defendant provides evidence against another defendant or assists the government in its investigation. Finally, the defendant can also capture some certainty regarding the results of the case by pleading guilty.

Over time, these and other incentives have led to the evolution of four dominant forms of guilty pleas in the United States, three of which involve a bargain between the government and the defendant (Federal Rules of Criminal Procedure 11(c)(1), 2017). The first type of plea is an *open plea*, in which a defendant pleads guilty in return for no specific promise from the prosecution, but in the hopes of leniency from the court at sentencing because of a willingness to confess and accept responsibility for his or her actions. Defendants who engage in open pleas at the federal level also often receive leniency, in the form of a two- or three-point reduction in their applicable offense level under the Federal Sentencing Guidelines (see Chapter 8 in this volume for further discussion of this bargained leniency). A lower offense level results in a reduced advisory sentencing range for consideration by the judge (United States Sentencing Commission, 2016, Federal Sentencing Guidelines, Section 3E1.1). The second type of plea is a *charge bargain*. Here, the defendant pleads guilty in return for an agreement from the prosecution to drop particular charges or amend an indictment to utilize particular charges (Federal Rules of Criminal Procedure 11(c)(1)(A), 2017). This type of bargain is particularly prevalent where a defendant faces the possibility of a mandatory minimum sentence under some applicable statutes and not under others. By exercising prosecutorial discretion in selecting the charges without mandatory minimums, the defendant receives a defined benefit. The third type of plea is a *sentence bargain*, in which the defendant pleads guilty in return for an agreement from the prosecution to recommend, or, at least, to not oppose, a particular sentence in the case (Federal Rules of Criminal Procedure 11(c)(1)(B), 2017). In each of these pleas, the court retains the discretion to make the final sentencing decision, though the courts encourage plea bargaining by following the recommended or agreed-upon disposition in the vast majority of cases.

The final type of plea in the United States addresses the issue of judicial discretion at sentencing and is called a "binding plea" (Federal Rules of Criminal Procedure 11(c)(1)(A), 2017). In the binding plea setting, the prosecution and defense determine the sentence that will result from the plea of guilty and, if the court accepts the agreement, the court is bound to impose only that sentence. In the federal system, this type of plea is permitted under Federal Rules of Criminal Procedure 11(c)(1)(C), which states, "such a recommendation or request binds the court once the court accepts the plea agreement." These types of pleas are less frequent than others, because many courts reject these agreements as impermissibly intruding into the sentencing powers of the judge.

While a detailed analysis of the inner workings of the plea bargaining machine is beyond the scope of this chapter, it is worth spending a moment to consider several prevalent theories of plea bargaining's structure that have appeared in the literature over the last few decades. These theories offer an overview of some of the forces and influences that make plea bargaining such a complex system. The first theory found in some of the literature is what I have termed the "administrative theory" of plea bargaining (Dervan, 2011, p. 246). In this theory of plea bargaining, the defendant is seen as having little choice regarding the particulars of a plea offer from the government, and the process is perceived as having little of the "give and take" commonly associated with negotiations and settlement discussions in civil cases. Instead, the criminal defendant is viewed as a passive recipient of the prosecutor's determination of the appropriate punishment for the alleged offense. As an example of literature describing defendants as passive recipients of plea offers from the government, consider Donald Gifford's (1983) work entitled "Meaningful Reform of Plea Bargaining: The Control of Prosecutorial Discretion." In this piece, Gifford (1983) describes plea bargains as "not consensual agreements" but, rather, as "unilateral administrative determinations" (p. 39). In this theory, there is little bargaining; instead, prosecutors are seen as dictating the terms of a plea after assessing the case and determining on their own the defendant's culpability and the appropriate punishment for the defendant's conduct.

The second theory, which has grown to become the dominant theory of plea bargaining today, is the "shadow-of-trial" theory (see also Chapter 2 in this volume). The theory as applied to plea bargaining was discussed at length in a 1992 article by legal scholars Robert E. Scott and William J. Stuntz. Scott and Stuntz argue that plea bargaining is a system in which prosecutors and defendants bargain in the shadow of trial, which means the plea bargain is a reflection of each party's assessment of their likelihood of success at trial. Stephanos Bibas (2004) expanded on the theory by accounting for additional factors, other than simply consideration of the predicted outcome of trial based on the strength of the evidence and the anticipated punishment after conviction at trial, that might influence the outcome of plea negotiations. These additional factors include structural issues, such as the quality of lawyering and pretrial detention, and rationality considerations, such as overconfidence and risk preferences. For example, overconfidence might impede a party's ability to accurately assess the unfairness of their offer or the fairness of the offer from the other party. Applying such additional factors to a theory of plea bargaining, Bibas argued, helps explain why bargains do not always reflect the predicted outcome from a pure shadow-of-trial analysis.

Finally, Dervan (2011) expanded on the original shadow-of-trial theory by introducing the concept of a "benefit distribution theory" of plea bargaining. This theory has served to further refine our understanding of the forces that influence an eventual sentence, including the importance placed by some defendants on non-sentence benefits, such as stigma or licensing. For example, a defendant may choose to use some of his or her bargaining power to negotiate for a charge that does not result in the loss of a professional license, such as a nursing license. Where a defendant uses bargaining power for such non-sentence benefits, the negotiated sentence might be different from that which would have been predicted by a pure shadow-of-trial analysis. This theory also addresses the concepts of bilateral plea bargaining (in which the government and the defendant engage in traditional plea negotiations) versus unilateral plea bargaining (in which the defendant pleads guilty in return for no specific promise from the prosecution, but in return for benefits inherent to the system—such as the possible benefit of judicial leniency or the certain benefit of a reduced sentencing range for those found to have accepted responsibility under the Federal Sentencing Guidelines), accounting for the growing prevalence of defendants engaging in "open pleas." Finally, the benefit distribution theory reminds us that the administrative theory remains relevant, because it could be used to describe a portion of the, though not the entire, plea bargaining process.

In glimpsing these descriptions of plea bargaining, one is reminded that the study of this system remains a relatively young field with much left to discover. While many might assume that plea bargaining as it is known today is a relic of centuries-old British common law, plea bargaining is actually a phenomenon that grew from the shadows of the American criminal justice system in the nineteenth and twentieth centuries (Alschuler, 1979). To better understand plea bargaining and the importance of our continued study of this machine and the psychological forces impacting those within its bounds, one must first step back to see where this all began.

The History of Plea Bargaining

Though many U.S. attorneys might consider a country in which only 3% to 5% of convictions result from a trial as the norm, this type of criminal justice system is certainly not where America or common law began and, in fact, is a relatively recent phenomenon (Dervan, 2012).

To illustrate how far and how quickly the United States shifted perspective over time, consider as a starting point the position of the British courts as expressed in the 1783 case of *Rex v. Warickshall*. In the *Warickshall* case, the suspect was accused of knowingly receiving stolen property. When accused of the offense, Warickshall confessed after obtaining a "promise of favor"

(*Rex v. Warickshall*, 1783, p. 234). In considering the actions of the government, the British court struck down the confession as having been improperly obtained. The court stated, "[A] confession forced from the mind by the flattery of hope, or by the torture of fear, comes in so questionable a shape . . . that no credit ought to be given to it" (p. 235). Language prohibiting offers of leniency and threats of punishment also appear in early U.S. common law. For example, in the 1897 case of *Bram v. United States*, the U.S. Supreme Court said, "[The] true test of admissibility is that the confession is made freely, voluntarily and without compulsion or inducement of any sort" (*Bram v. United States*, 1897, p. 548).

One might argue that the strong language contained in these and other early cases is inapplicable to plea bargaining because these cases involved police confessions. However, up until the mid-twentieth century, both British and American courts considered a plea of guilty as merely an in-court confession (Alschuler, 1979). Concluding that these were not distinct acts, the courts applied the same law to each (Dervan, 2012).

Despite these applicable early precedents, appellate courts in the United States began seeing "plea bargain" cases around the time of the American Civil War. Given the strong language of *Warickshall*, *Bram*, and similar cases, these bargains were looked upon with disfavor by the courts. Some examples of the language used by the appellate courts during this period are informative in presenting the general attitudes toward plea bargaining at the time. One court wrote, "When there is reason to believe that the plea has been entered through inadvertence . . . and mainly from the hope that the punishment to which the accused would otherwise be exposed may thereby be mitigated, the Court should be indulgent in permitting the plea to be withdrawn" (*People v. McCrory*, 1871, p. 462). Another court said, "[Plea bargaining is] hardly, if at all, distinguishable in principle from a direct sale of justice" (*Wright v. Rindskopf*, 1877, p. 354).

Nevertheless, plea bargaining continued to operate and grow in the shadows of the American criminal justice system, for at least two reasons. First, plea bargaining was used as a tool of corruption in the early twentieth century as prosecutors, judges, and defense attorneys used bribes to secure "bargains" containing reduced sentences. This was particularly prevalent in Chicago, where "fixers" would stand in front of the courthouse and arrange deals for defendants (Alschuler, 1979).

Second, during the early part of the twentieth century, overcriminalization became a new phenomenon in the United States as a myriad of criminal laws went into effect. This was particularly true during the prohibition era (Fisher, 2003). In the face of the resulting swelling criminal dockets, many lower courts felt they had little recourse but to use legitimate forms of plea bargaining, as distinguished from the corrupt system previously described, to clear dockets and reduce caseloads.

As plea bargaining continued to grow in prominence during the early twentieth century, one might have expected the U.S. Supreme Court to directly address the issue. After all, prior precedent had admonished against the practice, yet offers of leniency and threats of punishment continued to be used to prompt guilty pleas. The court, however, hesitated to rule definitively. In the few examples where the notion of guilty pleas and bargains was discussed in opinions, the Supreme Court indicated that it was uncomfortable with the concepts (*Machibroda v. United States*, 1962; *Walker v. Johnston*, 1941). In such rulings, the court made clear that while voluntary guilty pleas were permissible, it did not favor deals that created significant incentives for defendants to admit guilt.

Given the Supreme Court's expressions of discomfort with plea bargaining in the early twentieth century and the strong historical common law language that existed, such as *Rex v. Warickshall* and *Bram v. United States*, many believed that the court would eventually rule plea bargaining was unconstitutional. In 1970, however, the court went in the opposite direction, definitively approving the use of plea bargaining in the case of *Brady v. United States* (1970).

Brady involved a defendant who pleaded guilty because the statute under which he was charged permitted the death penalty only if recommended by a jury (*Brady v. United States*, 1970). By pleading guilty, he avoided that possibility. Brady later argued that his plea should be withdrawn because the incentives were so large that his "confession" was involuntary. This argument relied, in part, on the requirements of voluntariness expressed in earlier precedent regarding confessions and pleas of guilty. In ruling on the request that the plea be withdrawn, the court determined that the defendant's plea was, in fact, voluntary and went on to state that offers of leniency and threats of punishment are permissible, as long as they do not overbear the will of the defendant.

The likely reasons the court permitted plea bargaining in the *Brady* decision, despite earlier statements and precedent, are complex and help explain the compromise that led to the decision. First, the Supreme Court justices had waited too long in definitively addressing the constitutionality of plea bargaining to have much choice in the matter. By the time of the *Brady* ruling, almost 90% of cases in the United States were being resolved through pleas of guilty, despite the earlier precedent (Dervan, 2012). With a system straining even to take 10% of cases to trial in 1970, the justices certainly realized that striking down or even severely limiting the use of plea bargaining at this time would likely mean the collapse of the entire criminal justice system.

Second, while overcriminalization had started the United States down the path of needing plea bargaining to deal with large criminal dockets, the Warren Court's due process revolution in the 1960s had only made matters more pressing (Dervan, 2012). The new rights offered to defendants during this period resulted in an even greater need for plea bargaining as trials grew more complex, costly, and lengthy. In one study, for example, it was demonstrated that the length of criminal trials almost doubled from the beginning to the end of this decade (Alschuler, 1979). Through its decision, the Supreme Court hoped to ensure that defendants with "real disputes" would be able to better use the rights handed down by the Warren Court in a system that used plea bargaining to clear dockets and free up resources.

It is important to note that while the Supreme Court approved of plea bargaining in the *Brady* decision, the court did include important limiting language as part of what looks like a compromise opinion between past precedent and current necessity. In the concluding paragraphs of the *Brady* decision, the court discussed its vision for the use of plea bargaining in the criminal justice system. The court made clear that it intended that plea bargains would assist jurisdictions in saving resources for "cases in which there is a substantial issue of the defendant's guilt or in which there is substantial doubt that the State can sustain its burden of proof" (*Brady v. United States*, 1970, p. 752). The court also continued to reiterate that bargains must be voluntary and, therefore, incentives should not be so large as to result in "overbearing the will" (p. 750) of a defendant. Finally, the court ended with a caveat. In reaching its decision, the Justices had made a significant assumption. Though cognizant of the possibility that innocents might falsely plead guilty, the court stated that it did not believe this would occur with any greater frequency because of the use of plea bargaining. Realizing this could be in error or the incentives used in plea bargaining might grow so large as to begin to capture a significant number of innocents, the court offered this final thought: "[W]e would have serious doubts about this case if the encouragements of guilty pleas by offers of leniency substantially increased the likelihood that defendants, advised by competent counsel, would falsely condemn themselves" (p. 758).

And with those parting words, the modern plea bargaining system was born. While there have been additional cases regarding plea bargaining argued before the Supreme Court since 1970, the general principles laid down in *Brady* remain. Plea bargaining is permissible, but we must be careful to ensure pleas remain voluntary. To be voluntary, incentives should not be so large as to result in "overbearing the will" of defendants.

Much of the social science plea bargaining research being conducted today speaks to the issues raised in the *Brady* decision (Redlich, Bibas, Edkins, & Madon, 2017). In particular, defendant decision-making and the related issue of innocents within the system are central to an understanding of whether the plea bargaining system in the United States today is working as envisioned by the court in 1970. Part of the recent invigoration of this line of research began with a simple query by Professor Vanessa Edkins and me in the late 2000s: What could social science tell us about the Supreme Court's pivotal assumption in 1970 that innocents would not plead guilty in significant numbers in return for the benefits of a bargain?

We know that some innocents have pled guilty in the past (see Chapter 7 for a more in-depth discussion on innocents pleading guilty). For example, in 1989, Ada JoAnn Taylor was accused with five others of killing a 68-year-old woman in Beatrice, Nebraska (Innocence Project Website, 2017). The options for Taylor were stark. If she pleaded guilty and cooperated, she would be rewarded with a sentence of 10–40 years in prison. If, however, she proceeded to trial and was convicted, she would likely spend the rest of her life behind bars. Though she initially professed her innocence, she decided to plead guilty because the risk of proceeding to trial was too great. In return for leniency, Taylor not only had to admit to committing the offense, but she had to provide evidence against the other five defendants, including testifying at trial. In the end, five defendants pleaded guilty and one was quickly convicted at trial on the basis of testimony of the others. After serving 19 years in prison, however, DNA evidence demonstrated that Taylor and the others were, in fact, innocent.

Though we know some innocent people have pleaded guilty in the past, it is very hard to ascertain exactly how many innocent people might have done something similar to Taylor and whether the number is significant enough to trigger concern regarding the Supreme Court's language in *Brady*. And this uncertainty has led to much debate over the years. Some have argued that plea bargaining has an innocence problem and such proponents have relied mainly on singular examples like the Taylor case to support their concerns. Others have argued that Taylor and others like her were rare outliers and, just as the Supreme Court stated in 1970, in almost all cases innocent defendants will not plead guilty.

This debate about innocence and its important connection to the *Brady* decision led Professor Edkins and me to approach the question in a different way. Instead of trying to look back and determine how many innocent people might have pleaded guilty in the past, we wanted to learn more about how willing an individual might be to falsely confess in the plea bargaining context. To answer this question, we created a study that tested these concepts by placing college students in the position of being accused of cheating and offered a deal for admitting guilt (Dervan & Edkins, 2013).

In our study, students were asked to participate in a research project that would compare group work to individual work (Dervan & Edkins, 2013). Unbeknownst to the students, however, the study was really a deception paradigm exploring the issue of false pleas of guilty. To examine this issue, all students who participated were accused of cheating, although, because of the use of a confederate in the room, only about half of the students actually cheated. All the students, regardless of factual guilt or innocence, were then offered a plea bargain in return for confessing to the alleged offense.

In response to our scenario, 89% of the guilty students took the offer (Dervan & Edkins, 2013). With regard to the innocent students, 56% of the participants were willing to falsely confess to an offense they had not committed in return for the benefits of the bargain. For the majority of innocent students, it appears that accepting the deal simply made more sense, just as it had for Taylor in Nebraska. This study has now been replicated in various forms numerous times as other labs work to continue exploring this and related issues in an effort to develop a broader understanding of plea bargaining. At a fundamental level, the original study and those that have come after demonstrate that the Supreme Court's assumption in 1970 was flawed. Innocent individuals *are* willing to falsely confess in the plea context; therefore, there is much work remaining to create a system of pleas that better protects the rights of the accused and more accurately reflects the vision of the Supreme Court in 1970.

While there are many ways that the current system might be amended to better protect the rights of both factually innocent and factually guilty defendants, a few important initiatives are worth brief mention here. These include limiting pretrial detention to only those cases in which it is absolutely necessary and there are no other available alternatives; ensuring counsel is available early in the process to offer guidance to defendants negotiating or considering a plea; guaranteeing that relevant evidence, especially exculpatory evidence in the hands of prosecutors, is made available to defendants before deciding whether to plead guilty; and imposing some limitations on the type and size of incentives that can be offered in return for pleading guilty to reduce the chances an innocent defendant might decide the cost of proceeding to trial is too high despite his or her innocence. Reforms such as these might help make plea bargaining more efficient by capturing less innocent defendants, while simultaneously remaining a viable mechanism for capturing guilty defendants in an overburdened system.

A New Focus on Plea Bargaining

While there was limited acknowledgment of the power of plea bargaining by the Supreme Court in the decades that followed the *Brady* decision, it appears that we have now entered a new era of jurisprudence. Today, the Supreme Court has a renewed focus on plea bargaining and, importantly, appears to have finally accepted the reality that the American criminal justice system is dominated by this machine of compromise.

The recent focus by the Supreme Court on plea bargaining began with the 2010 case of *Padilla v. Kentucky*. Padilla, who had been a lawful permanent resident of the United States for over 40 years, faced deportation as a result of pleading guilty to drug distribution charges. Padilla claimed on appeal that his attorney had failed to inform him of this potential collateral consequence of conviction, which he argued amounted to ineffective assistance of counsel under the Sixth Amendment. The Supreme Court sided with Padilla and found that the Sixth Amendment did require that a criminal defense attorney advise a client when the client's decision to plead guilty might result in deportation. While the *Padilla* decision is limited to cases involving immigration consequences, the decision is symbolic as marking the beginning of a new focus on plea bargaining by the court and, perhaps, the opening of a window to begin reshaping the jurisprudence regarding plea bargaining given all we have learned since 1970.

The Supreme Court next addressed plea bargaining in two related 2012 cases, *Lafler v. Cooper* and *Missouri v. Frye*. Both cases were similar to *Padilla* in that they involved ineffective assistance of counsel claims under the Sixth Amendment. What was different here, however, was that the defendants in *Lafler* and *Frye* had foregone plea bargains because of the alleged ineffective assistance by their attorneys. In ruling on the issue, the Supreme Court determined that plea bargaining is a "critical stage" of a criminal prosecution and, therefore, the Sixth Amendment right to effective assistance of counsel applies. In addition to the significance of this decision in extending an important right to plea bargaining, the *Lafler* and *Frye* cases also reinforced the perception that perhaps a new jurisprudential era was beginning to emerge.

While the Supreme Court had permitted plea bargaining in *Brady* in part to free up resources for trials, the Supreme Court in *Lafler* and *Frye* appeared to finally begin to understand the dwindling importance of trials in today's criminal justice system. And in a statement echoed in this volume's title, Supreme Court Justice Anthony Kennedy, in *Lafler,* wrote, "criminal justice today is for the most part a system of pleas, not a system of trials" (*Lafler v. Cooper*, 2012, p. 170). In *Frye*, Justice Kennedy elaborated on what this might mean going forward.

> Because ours "is for the most part a system of pleas, not a system of trials," it is insufficient simply to point to the guarantee of a fair trial as a backstop that inoculates any errors in the pretrial process. "To a large extent . . . horse trading [between prosecutor and defense counsel] determines who goes to jail and for how long. That is what plea bargaining is. It is not some adjunct to the criminal justice system; it is the criminal justice system." (*Missouri v. Frye*, 2012, pp. 143–144 [internal citations omitted])

In a world where the Supreme Court acknowledges the vital role of plea bargaining, perhaps opportunities exist to create a system that better protects defendants and the integrity and efficiency of the process.

In June 2017, the Supreme Court handed down yet another plea bargaining decision in the case of *Lee v. United States*. In the matter, the court considered whether a defendant who had agreed to plead guilty in reliance on his attorney's false assurances that he would not be deported should be afforded relief. In examining the issue, Justice Roberts, writing for the majority, wrote:

> But for his attorney's incompetence, Lee would have known that accepting the plea agreement would *certainly* lead to deportation. Going to trial? *Almost* certainly. If deportation were the "determinative issue" for an individual in plea discussions, as it was for Lee; if that individual had strong connections to this country and no other, as did Lee; and if the consequences of taking a chance at trial were not markedly harsher than pleading guilty, as in this case, that "almost" could make all the difference. (*Lee v. United States*, 2017, p. 12)

Having determined that Lee had been prejudiced, the court went on to reverse the lower courts' decisions denying Lee's request to vacate his conviction and withdraw his guilty plea. With each new plea bargaining case, there appears to be a growing interest in more carefully examining the protections and rights associated with plea bargaining and, therefore, an opportunity for meaningful reform exists.

Yet there is still much work to be done to educate the Supreme Court, the bar, and the public about all that has been learned, including through social science research, since *Brady* regarding the mechanics and influences of the plea bargaining system. As an indication of how much work remains, one need only look to the dissent by Justice Thomas in *Lee*. Justice Thomas wrote, "[T]he Court in *Hill* recognized that guilty pleas are themselves generally reliable. Guilty pleas 'rarely' give rise to 'concern that unfair procedures may have resulted in the conviction of an innocent defendant'" (*Lee v. United States*, 2017, p. 8 [Dissent]). Unfortunately, this statement, which relies on precedent from 1985, fails to account for all that has been learned over the last decades about the psychology of guilty pleas and the susceptibility of innocents to the powerful incentives of plea bargains. Today, we know that some significant number of innocent defendants have pleaded and will plead guilty if offered a bargain.

Fortunately, there is currently an effort underway to educate the Supreme Court in the hopes that future decisions might be informed by current research rather than past assumptions. In particular, several amicus curiae briefs filed with the Supreme Court in 2017 specifically addressed the innocence issue and included discussion of the current social science research in the area. In the case of *Class v. United States*, which was argued before the court in October 2017, the court was asked to consider whether the defendant waived his right to appeal the constitutionality of the statute under which he was convicted when he pleaded guilty to the charge pursuant to a plea bargain. In an amicus curiae filed by the Innocence Project, the Innocence Project wrote:

> The criminal justice system's reliance on pleas places pressure on all defendants to plead guilty. . . . Neither innocent nor guilty defendants want to receive the most severe punishments available under the law or endure the stress and uncertainty of trial, and their decisions to plead guilty or not are informed by these pressures. Put differently, life and liberty are often the prevailing considerations, rather than guilt or innocence. (*Class v. United States*, Brief of the Innocence Project as Amicus Curiae in Support of Petitioner, 2017, p. 6)

The brief then went on to discuss the plea bargaining research outlined here earlier (see Dervan & Edkins, 2013) and how it and other empirical studies support the proposition that defendants plead guilty to receive shorter sentences even when they may not actually be guilty (*Class v. United States*, Brief of the Innocence Project as Amicus Curiae in Support of Petitioner, 2017).

Thus, the issue of innocence and the failings of our current system to adhere to the vision of *Brady* have begun to come before the U.S. Supreme Court. How long, or if the justices will respond, is unknown, but the opportunity now presents itself for informed plea bargaining reform of all kinds as the court continues to develop this new era of jurisprudence. It is for this reason that plea bargaining research of all kinds must continue. We must ensure that we know as much as possible about the realities and risks associated with the system that has come to dominate the criminal justice system.

References

Alschuler, A. W. (1979). Plea bargaining and its history. *Columbia Law Review, 79*, 1–43. doi: 10.2307/1122051
Bibas, S. (2004). Plea bargaining outside the shadow of trial. *Harvard Law Review, 117*, 2463–2547. doi: 10.2307/4093404
Brady v. United States, 397 U.S. 742 (1970).
Bram v. United States, 168 U.S. 532 (1897).
Class v. United States, No. 16-424 (Feb. 21, 2017) (Granting Writ of Certiorari).
Class v. United States, Brief of the Innocence Project as Amicus Curiae in Support of Petitioner, Class v. United States, No. 16-424, May 19, 2017.
Dervan, L. E. (2011). The surprising lessons from plea bargaining in the shadow of trial. *Georgia State University Law Review, 27*, 239–298.
Dervan, L. E. (2012). Bargained justice: Plea-bargaining's innocence problem and the *Brady* safety-valve. *Utah Law Review, 1*, 51–97.
Dervan, L. E., & Edkins, V. A. (2013). The innocent defendant's dilemma: An innovative empirical study of plea bargaining's innocence problem. *Journal of Criminal Law & Criminology, 103*, 1–48. doi: 10.2139/ssrn.2071397
Federal Rules of Criminal Procedure 11(c)(1)(A), 11(c)(1)(B), and 11(c)(1)(C), 2017.
Fisher, G. (2003). *Plea bargaining's triumph: A history of plea bargaining*. Stanford, CA: Stanford University Press.
Gifford, D. G. (1983). Meaningful reform of plea bargaining: The control of prosecutorial discretion. *University of Illinois Law Review, 1983*, 37–98.
Innocence Project Website. (2017). *Ada JoAnn Taylor story*. Retrieved from https://www.innocenceproject.org/cases/ada-joann-taylor/
Lafler v. Cooper, 566 U.S. 156 (2012).
Lee v. United States, 582 U.S., 137 S. Ct. 1958 (June 23, 2017).
Machibroda v. United States, 368 U.S. 487 (1962).
Missouri v. Frye, 566 U.S. 134 (2012).
Padilla v. Kentucky, 559 U.S. 356 (2010).
People v. McCrory, 41 Cal. 458 (1871).
Redlich, A., Bibas, S., Edkins, V., & Madon, S. (2017). The psychology of defendant plea decision-making. *American Psychologist, 72*, 339–352. doi: 10.1037/a0040436
Rex v. Warickshall, 168 Eng. Rep. 234 (1783).
Scott, R. E., & Stuntz, W. J. (1992). Plea bargaining as contract. *Yale Law Journal, 101*, 1909–1968. doi: 10.2307/796952
United States Sentencing Commission. (2012–2016). Figure C. In *U.S. Sentencing Commission Sourcebook* (p. S-23). Retrieved from https://www.ussc.gov/sites/

default/files/pdf/research-and-publications/annual-reports-and-sourcebooks/2016/FigureC.pdf
United States Sentencing Commission. (2016). *Federal Sentencing Guidelines*, Section 3E1.1, Acceptance of Responsibility. Grand Rapids, MI: Michigan Legal Publishing.
Walker v. Johnston, 312 U.S. 275 (1941).
Wright v. Rindskopf, 43 Wis. 344, 354 (1877).

2

Defendant Decision-Making in Plea Bargains

Shawn D. Bushway

Defendants who plead guilty usually receive substantially shorter sentences than observably equivalent people who are convicted at trial (Albonetti, 1990, 1997; Bradley-Engen, Engen, Shields, Damphousse, & Smith, 2012; Dixon, 1995; Smith, 1986; Ulmer & Bradley, 2006; Ulmer, Eisenstein, & Johnson, 2010). These shorter sentences are achieved through some combination of dropped or reduced charges, and reduced sentence lengths for a given charge. One explanation for these lower sentences is that defendants receive a discount for pleading guilty—without that discount, they would not decide to plead guilty. Empirically, researchers have found that the size of this plea discount varies across individual cases (Bradley-Engen et al., 2012; Bushway & Redlich, 2012; Smith, 1986; Ulmer & Bradley, 2006; Ulmer et al., 2010). The primary theoretical model used to explain the different sizes of the discount is referred to as "bargaining in the shadow of the trial" (hereafter the "shadow" model) (Bibas, 2004; Landes, 1971; Mnookin & Kornhauser, 1979; Nagel & Neef, 1979).

This model is a rational choice-based model of defendant decision-making. The model establishes the maximum value of the potential plea or, alternatively, the minimally acceptable discount. This minimally acceptable discount is driven by the expected value of the trial outcome, which is the anticipated trial outcome discounted by the probability of being convicted at trial. For example, if the expected sentence for a conviction at trial is 5 years, and the defendant believes his probability of conviction at trial is 70%, then a plea to a sentence of no more than 3.5 years (70% of 5) represents a rational choice for a risk-neutral defendant.

Although this model has been subject to few empirical tests, there is some supporting evidence from both observational data and experiments to support the basic model (Bushway & Redlich, 2012; Bushway, Redlich, & Norris, 2014). Bushway and Redlich (2012) used case-level information from administrative records to show that the size of the discount varied with the probability of conviction, at least in the aggregate. More specifically, when estimates of probability of conviction for those who went to trial and those who pleaded guilty are compared at the aggregate level, the estimates are very similar (as predicted by the shadow-of-the trial model). However, when individual estimates are examined, Bushway and Redlich (2012) found that not all estimates are consistent with the shadow model, which is an individual, rather than aggregate, model. Bushway et al. (2014) used survey data to show that the acceptable plea offer for both prosecutors and defense lawyers for an individual case was strongly correlated with the probability of conviction. Moreover, they also showed that the probability of conviction was driven by differences in evidence. The quality of evidence is thus a major contributor to the size of the discount, as would be expected by the shadow model.

Bushway et al. (2014) also showed that the actual plea discount is generally bigger than the discount anticipated by the straightforward shadow model. This by itself is not problematic for defendant decision-making, because the model calculates the minimally acceptable plea for defendants. Prosecutors might have reasons for offering even bigger discounts, which, of course, defendants would accept. For example, prosecutors could be trying to accomplish goals other than maximizing sentence length. Prime examples include minimizing the number of trials (Alschuler, 2002) or minimizing the number of innocent people who plead guilty (Bjerk, 2007). In each scenario, the plea discounts observed in equilibrium after negotiation between the prosecution and defense may be larger than the minimum required by the defendant.

Bibas (2004) has also pointed out that that the complex institutional choices involved in bargaining could routinely lead to offers from prosecutors that are much better deals than the offers anticipated by the shadow model. For example, sentences at trial are non-continuous, meaning that they are usually given out in 6-month or yearly increments. The discrete nature of the sentences will mean that prosecutors cannot create finely tuned deals that exactly meet the upper bound predicted by the shadow model. As a result, the average plea discount will be, by definition, more than the exact minimum needed to get the defendant to plead guilty. These examples make it clear that understanding the ultimate size of the plea discount requires information about all partners in the "plea bargain," not just the defendant (see Chapter 3, this volume, for a discussion of the defense attorney's role, and Chapter 4 for a discussion of the prosecutor's role).

Bibas (2004) also suggested that these bigger discounts could be the result of non- "rational" behavior by defendants. The most likely example would involve risk-seeking behavior, demonstrated by the willingness to proceed to trial and risk a conviction with a harsher sentence. Behavioral economists and psychologists now routinely show that people, including professionals in the criminal justice system, do not act in strictly rational ways (Guthrie, Rachlinski, & Wistrich, 2001; Plous, 1993; Tversky & Kahneman, 1974).

Research in psychology on the impact of defendant's actual guilt on the defendant's decision to plead guilty also directly challenges the model of defendant decision-making represented by the shadow model. In the shadow model, actual innocence is only relevant through its impact on the probability of conviction. Holding constant the probability of conviction, the actual innocence of the defendant should not impact their decision to plead guilty. Psychologists have used experiments with mock actors and cases where the key manipulation is the innocence of the defendant. As predicted by the shadow model, results show that the "innocent" people in an experiment will, in fact, plead guilty given the "right" plea discount. However, these models have also shown that innocence seems to matter above and beyond the probability of conviction (Bordens, 1984; Dervan & Edkins, 2013; Gregory, Mowen, & Linder, 1978; Tor, Gazal-Ayal, & Garcia, 2010; see Chapter 7 this volume). This chapter will discuss the shadow model as a model of defendant decision-making and discuss possible extensions and ideas for future research that have been inspired by these apparent deviations from strictly rational behavior.

The Theory

The *shadow model* is a formal theoretical (i.e., mathematical) model of the defendant's decision-making. The outcome of the model is a clear prediction about the maximum sentence the defendant would willingly accept as part of a plea bargain. The shadow model is not a direct model of prosecutors' behavior but, as discussed, frames the prosecutors' choices. The prosecutor may want to offer a sentence above the maximum sentence acceptable to the defendant, created by the expected value of the trial, but under the shadow model, the defendant will not accept that offer. Therefore, the upper bound in the defendant's frame of reference becomes the upper bound for the offer from a rational prosecutor.

In the simplest possible version of the shadow model, the defendant faces a decision between a relatively certain outcome (the sentence after a guilty plea) and the outcome if the defendant decides not to plead guilty, which represents an uncertain mix of two outcomes—the outcome if the person is convicted at trial, and the outcome if the person is acquitted. More sophisticated models could include other possible states, including the chance that the case will be dismissed prior to trial. In probability theory, the average of all possible outcomes, weighted by the probability of each outcome occurring, is known as the *expected value*. Therefore, the choice facing the defendant is between the expected value of the plea, which is the value of the plea sentence in the simplest case, and the expected value of the trial (Eq. 1*a*). The expected value of the trial is the probability of being convicted at trial, times the outcome at trial plus the probability of being acquitted at trial, times the outcome at trial if acquitted. Given that the punishment if acquitted is zero, the expected value of the trial reduces to the sentence at trial discounted by the probability of being convicted. Using the previous example, if the sentence at trial is 5 years, and the probability of conviction is .7 (or 70%), the expected value of the trial is 3.5 years. This description is formalized in (Eq. 1*b*), where *Y* is the sentence at plea, *P* is the probability of conviction at trial, and *X* is the sentence if convicted at trial:

$$\textit{Plea value} \approx \textit{Expected value of trial} \qquad \text{(Eq. 1}a\text{)}$$

$$Y_i \approx P_i X_i \qquad \text{(Eq. 1}b\text{)}$$

The reason equivalence is not used in in Eqs. 1*a* and 1*b* is because the exact nature of the relationship will be driven by the attitude of the defendant toward risk. A defendant who is willing to accept any offer that has the same expected value regardless of the amount of uncertainty or risk is called *risk neutral*. In terms of the example just given, the risk-neutral defendant is indifferent between a plea sentence of 3.5 years and a trial with an expected value of 3.5 years. In contrast, a *risk-seeking* defendant would actually prefer to take the gamble of the trial. The fact that the trial comes with some risk adds to the utility of trial for the defendant, and he would prefer the trial if given an offer equal to the expected value of the trial. In practical terms, a proclivity for risk seeking creates a situation where a plea deal would have to be less than the expected value of the trial to convince a defendant to take the plea.

In contrast, a *risk-averse* individual prefers the certainty of the plea deal to the outcome of a trial with an uncertain outcome and would therefore be willing to accept a plea deal that is higher than the expected value of the trial. In the example, a risk-seeking defendant might need a deal of 3 years before he pleads guilty, while a risk-averse individual might plead guilty if the deal is only 4 years.

This simple model leads to some very straightforward predictions for situations where the probability of conviction is known. For example, the average probability of conviction at trial in the largest 75 counties in the United States is 75% (Cohen & Kyckelhahn, 2010). The shadow of the trial would therefore predict that the maximum average plea value would be 75% of the trial sentence. This estimate is close to some of the best current estimates of the plea discount in the literature. For example, Ulmer and colleagues (2010) estimate the plea sentence is 69% of the trial sentence, and Bushway and Redlich (2012) found an estimate of 77%.[1]

Complications in Practice

Of course, the model is, at its heart, a model of individual, not aggregate, decision-making, and findings that the model appears to work "on average"

[1] The data used in the Bushway and Redlich (2012) paper allowed for an estimate of the average probability of conviction at trial, which was also 77%.

do not prove that the model is functioning as predicted at the individual level. Indeed, Bushway and Redlich (2012) showed that the model appears to struggle to explain individual behavior, even though it appears to be predictive at the aggregate level (Bushway & Redlich, 2012; Smith 1986). Some of the problems in the Bushway and Redlich (2012) model at the individual level may not come from the model itself, but instead from challenges involved with estimation used to determine the 77% rate. In real-world cases, defendants just plead guilty—we do not know what would have happened if they went to trial. Researchers interested in using observational data to test these models need to create a model-based estimate for what would have happened if the case had gone to trial (see Smith, 1986). These models require assumptions and data—both of which could be flawed or limited.

This problem of creating comparable outcomes is not limited to researchers. Bibas (2004) pointed out that the situations for individual defendants is often far more complicated than simply facing a trial sentence with some reasonably estimated probability of conviction. Potential sentence outcomes include many other outcomes besides incarceration. It is not a simple matter to create equivalence across qualitatively different sentencing outcomes such as probation, prison, treatment, and fines. For example, consider a case where an individual accepts a plea deal for 3 years of probation when faced with a plausible threat of a 1-year jail sentence if convicted at trial. How does the researcher (or the defendant) calculate the size of the discount in this case? In the Bibas (2004) critique, the problem is not in the fundamental model, but in the practical realities of actually doing the calculus in most normal decision-making in the criminal justice system. This problem only gets more complicated in a world where collateral consequences of a conviction (e.g., barred from certain types of employment, housing options, and financial loans; see Chapter 9, this volume), which might be different for different types of pleas, become a more integral part of the sentence (O'Keefe, 2010). It is perhaps not surprising that the model has only been tested for serious cases when the defendant will receive a prison sentence whether they plead guilty or are convicted at trial (Bushway et al., 2014; Bushway & Redlich, 2012). In principal, it should be possible to create measures of equivalence across possible outcomes, but in practice this is easier said than done, for both researchers and real people (Yan, 2017).

The same can be said of additional complications that come from the contexts in which plea decisions must be made by defendants. For example, how do bail and pretrial detention play into the model? Researchers have suggested that pretrial detention increases the plea rates by making the plea more attractive (Dobbie, Goldin, & Yang, 2016). One possible reason for this is that defendants have less bargaining power when they are detained. Another possibility, however, is that offers of "time served" make the plea discount very high, given that a rational defendant would reasonably view the pretrial detention as a sunk cost. A *sunk cost* is a cost that has already been paid. Rational actors do not consider sunk costs when making decisions. Therefore, the actual cost of a plea to time served for the defendant is close to zero (at least for formal legal consequences for the incident offense), a factor which is ignored when a researcher uses time served to generate an estimate of the actual plea discount. Here again the problem is not the shadow model itself, but the complicated environment in which the model needs to be tested or identified.

More fundamentally, the shadow model in its simplest form relies on perfect information about the outcome at trial. Yet this assumption might not be realistic in a world where 95% or more of all cases are resolved through pleas. The outcome at trial, especially for less serious cases, has become like the elusive unicorn—conjectured, but never actually seen. If similar cases rarely if ever go to trial, how can defendants reasonably predict what the sentence at trial might actually be? Bushway et al. (2014) asked practicing lawyers and judges to predict the average sentence at trial for an armed robbery case in their jurisdiction. The resulting answers were highly variable, with the range covering many years, even within a given state for cases that were otherwise identical on factors that would normally determine sentencing outcomes. The standard rational choice assumption of perfect information about the outcome at trial is potentially unrealistic given the known and extensive fragmentation of the U.S. criminal justice system.

The researcher using case data to test the model can generate an estimate of the trial sentence for those who took the plea bargain only when there are actual trial outcomes for similar cases (Smith, 1986). Even then, this will only be true if the researcher is willing to make the questionable assumption that the cases that go to trial are similar to those that end with guilty pleas. Smith (1986) showed clearly that this is not the case, based only on the case factors that were observable to him (e.g., criminal history and crime severity), which, with standard case data, represents only a fraction of what the courtroom workgroup actually encounters. While this is a problem for the researcher, it again raises the question of whether the basic premise of the model for defendants is reasonable—if researchers cannot generate accurate estimates for potential trial outcomes, how can the defendant? Theoretical models that loosen the assumption of perfect information will create predicted sentences that have a great deal more imprecision than the basic model, with ranges for lower bounds, rather than point estimates. The more imprecision, the less useful the model is in practice, even though technically the model might still be empirically valid.

Another challenge for the researcher is that the observed outcomes are not just the result of defendants' decision-making—instead they reflect the outcome of interactions between defendants, defense attorneys, judges, and prosecutor. The shadow model itself only predicts the upper bound for what a rational defendant will accept. Alschuler (2002) anticipates that the actual discount will be much bigger as part of an explicit coercive effort by prosecutors with goals beyond maximizing the sentence. For example, prosecutors may want to both maximize penalties and minimize the number of trials. As a result, a rational prosecutor might lower the plea discount well below the break-even point to convince—or, more pejoratively, coerce—defendants to plead guilty quickly (see also Alschuler, 1979; Brereton & Casper, 1982; Halberstam, 1982; Nardulli, Eisenstein, & Fleming, 1988). Bibas (2004) identified fixed agency costs associated with defending or prosecuting a case as another factor that could create bigger plea discounts (see Bushway et al. [2014] for a formal model of how fixed costs could affect pleas). The claim that other factors matter by itself is not a criticism of the defendant decision-making model, but instead an observation that a full understanding of the plea discount requires an understanding of all of the actors in the system.

Criminological scholars use perspectives such as focal concerns to try to take all actors into account (Baumer, 2013; Dixon, 1995; Eisenstein, Fleming, & Nardulli, 1987; Eisenstein & Jacob, 1977; Nardulli et al., 1988; Ulmer, 1997). These perspectives emphasize that judges, prosecutors, and defense attorneys within a jurisdiction are part of an interdependent workgroup working together toward shared goals, such as disposing of cases efficiently and minimizing uncertainty (Eisenstein & Jacob, 1977). Within this framework, criminologists predict that the workgroup will establish norms, or going rates, that are less than the punishment at trial for defendants who are willing to plead guilty. These plea discounts save time and resources while simultaneously reducing uncertainty.

Over time, theorists have extended this basic framework. Dixon (1995) and Engen and Steen (2000) developed the organizational efficiency perspective that emphasizes the efficient disposition of cases. Albonetti's (1986, 1987) uncertainty avoidance theory stresses the need for heuristics and other shortcuts to help actors reduce uncertainty in the sentencing process. Steffensmeier, Ulmer, and Kramer (1998) integrated these perspectives into the focal concerns perspective, which explains how rational actors use heuristics to make sentencing decisions that try to incorporate concerns about (1) offender blameworthiness and the harm caused by the crime, (2) protection of the community, and (3) pragmatic implications such as resource constraints (Steffensmeier et al., 1998). In theory, defendants then make decisions within this context, which frames the offers they are given.

This criminological perspective is not a direct competitor to the shadow model, because it does not attempt to explain defendant behavior (Redlich, Milford, & Bushway, 2017). Instead, it is a complementary theory designed to explain the behavior of the members of the courtroom workgroup, rather than the defendant. Within that context, the idea that prosecutors might offer fixed deals that are substantially greater than what is needed for the person to actually plead guilty carries with it a potential implication from the shadow model—namely, that people who face very low probabilities of conviction might nonetheless plead guilty if given a low enough deal.

The fact that prosecutors can offer very generous plea deals well beyond the minimum discount needed to generate a plea raises the specter that individuals with very low probabilities of conviction—for example, people who are innocent or at the very least should accept the risk of conviction at trial—might instead plead guilty. Bushway et al. (2014) found evidence that judges would regularly approve fixed discounts that were well below the average probability of conviction. In the shadow model, actual guilt or innocence is not relevant for the defendant decision-making except through the influence it has on the perceived probability of conviction. Two people who face the same probability of conviction will both accept a plea offer that is below their expected value of trial, regardless of whether one is guilty and the other is factually innocent.

There is a growing awareness that innocent people do indeed plead guilty (National Registry of Exonerations, 2015; see Chapter 7, this volume). Psychological research relying on vignettes has routinely showed that some subjects who are placed in the "innocent" condition will nonetheless plead guilty (Gazal-Ayal & Tor, 2012; Norris & Redlich, 2014; Tor et al., 2010). However, psychological research has also shown that not all mock innocent people will plead guilty, and people placed in the innocent condition will plead guilty at a lower rate than people placed in the guilty condition who face the same probability of guilt (Bordens, 1984; Dervan & Edkins, 2013; Gregory et al., 1978; Tor et al., 2010). This pattern raises serious questions about the applicability of the shadow model to all defendants. The shadow model anticipates no difference in the plea rates in these scenarios. Research on this question is reviewed in more detail by Redlich et al. (2017). The psychological experiments highlight the issue that not all defendants think about trials and pleas in the same way—in these controlled experiments, the subjects all face the same constraints, and many innocent people do indeed do what the shadow model predicts. However, some do not. Figuring out what makes these defendants different could move the field beyond monolithic theories of defendant decision-making.

Future research on this topic also needs to find ways to move beyond the experimental setting to more fully understand how the phenomenon of innocence works with actual defendants, defense attorneys, and prosecutors. Anecdotally, at least, it is not uncommon to hear about defense attorneys who counsel their clients to plead guilty even when their client states that she is innocent (e.g., Frontline, 2004). In these cases, the defense lawyers are behaving according to the shadow model—but the defendants do not always follow their lead. From this perspective, defendants are ignoring the probability of conviction and working instead with asymmetric information that they have about their innocence state (i.e., they know they are innocent, while the prosecutors do not have the same information). Using asymmetric information that does not inform the expected value of the trial is clearly not rational, but it might well describe how at least some defendants think about the trials.

Theoretical models should also be expanded to include a better understanding of how defendant decision-making is itself affected by the organizational context described by focal concerns theory. Focal concerns theory suggests that the actual offer made to a defendant will be driven by a variety of factors specific to the particular courtroom workgroup. For example, researchers have shown that participants' plea decisions in hypothetical scenarios can be influenced by comparisons to the pleas offers received by similar others (Tor et al., 2010), and researchers have found that real-world defendants often refer to pressure from members of the courtroom workgroup (prosecutors or defense counsel) or family members when explaining their decision to plead guilty (Bordens & Bassett, 1985; Viljoen, Klaver, & Roesch, 2005). Theoretical models of defendant decision-making then also need to be expanded to include models of how members of the courtroom workgroup or family members might make decisions relative to the rational choice model. Bushway et al. (2014) and Pezdek and O'Brien (2014) both found that quality of evidence was the primary driving factor for both prosecutors and defense attorneys, although the effect was stronger for defense attorneys. Judges, on other hand, appeared oblivious to the quality of the evidence (Bushway et al., 2014). This suggests that some of the actors in the courtroom workgroup will be more like the defendants than others, and will therefore have recommendations that run counter to that what the defendant might derive if left to his or her own devices.

Conclusion

The shadow model represents a powerful model of defendant decision-making. As a model, it presents a compelling argument for viewing the plea bargain as evidence for a plea discount rather than trial penalty. Even if defendants are not perfectly rational, it is hard to tell a convincing story for how a defendant would agree to a plea deal that is, for the most part, certain that has the same value as an uncertain trial outcome. In the civil context, there is a consensus that settlements are driven primarily by this basic mechanism of defendant decision-making (Cooter, Marks, & Mnookin, 1982; Mnookin & Kornhauser, 1979), even if there is substantial discussion about some of the specific details (e.g., DePoorter, 2010). These details, which are similar to ones that arise in the criminal context, focus on how individual negotiators deal with uncertainty and imperfect information (Bibas, 2004; Glover, 2012).

The criminal context is further complicated, however, by two related problems. First, defendants are not negotiating over money, which is quantifiable, but, punishment, which can take many different forms. At the very least, this causes problems for researchers trying to estimate the size of the plea discount. Second, in the criminal case, the two parties are not fundamentally bargaining over the same thing. In most civil cases, the parties are both negotiating over money. What starts as the upper bound for the defendant, based on the perceived probability of losing the case, quickly becomes the lower acceptable bound for the plaintiff using the same information. As a result, in the civil case, the expected value perspective can generate a point estimate for the value of the settlement, given perfect information (DePoorter, 2010; Glover, 2012). This is not true in the criminal case, where the prosecutors may well be trying to achieve other outcomes besides maximizing punishment. The end result is that the shadow model can at best provide an upper bound for the highest punishment that the defendant will accept.

The possibility that prosecutors might be incentivized to offer very large discounts as a matter of course means that most defendants will plead guilty, even when they have a relatively low probability of conviction, which might well include the situation where they are factually innocent. This is particularly true if, as in the current U.S. context, sentences at trial have become predictably harsher through the use of determinate and mandatory sentences. The end result is a situation where not only will most cases be settled by plea, but increasing numbers of people will plead guilty (Pfaff, 2014). European reform models that seek to limit the size of the plea discount are built in part on a belief in the shadow model (Fair Trials, 2017). Discounts that cannot exceed a certain level—say 30%—should prevent rational defendants with low probabilities of conviction from pleading guilty.

Higher rates of pleas for those who are detained pretrial are also explained by the shadow model. Prosecutors who offer "time served" are essentially offering defendants an opportunity to plead with a sentence discount of 100%, given that they have already paid the cost of incarceration, reducing it to a sunk cost. As mentioned previously, a rational defendant should ignore sunk costs and focus only on the costs that they accrue in the future. Here, collateral consequences, as well as the costs of longer criminal history the next time the person is convicted, are the main costs (see Chapter 9, this volume). Each of these costs may be less transparent (or salient) to the defendant at the time he or she needs to make the decision.

Of course, there are other viable explanations for these same outcomes, and more sophisticated explanations of defendant behavior could explain some deviations from the predictions of the most straightforward version of the shadow model. These explanations are most often embedded in a more complete understanding of the social context in which defendants must make their decision, usually with the help of a defense attorney who need not have the same incentives as the defendants. Developing a better understanding of the principal agent problem between the defendant and the defense attorney might help better explain some of the observed outcomes, as well as variations across cases within a given jurisdiction in the rates of plea bargaining (see Chapter 3, this volume).

Of course, it is often far easier to develop alternative stories than it is to test possible explanations. Two paths forward appear most productive for future empirical work: (1) continued experiments with hypothetical scenarios using both defendants and members of the courtroom workgroups, and (2) increased efforts to generate estimates of plea discounts from administrative records (Redlich et al., 2017). From the perspective of the shadow model, the use of hypothetical scenarios should always include efforts to both estimate and understand the perceived probability of conviction, the lynchpin parameter of the shadow model. The use of administrative data should hinge on the continued development of plausible ways to estimate reasonable counterfactuals for how cases might have been resolved at trial. More broadly, future empirical work would benefit from more explicit linkage to the specific and direct predictions of the formal mathematically derived shadow model. The fact that the real world is more complex (Bibas, 2004) does not by itself render the shadow model powerless to render more insight. Bushway and colleagues (2014) demonstrated clearly that even the simplest form has some real ability to explain behavior. Furthermore, simple explanations can sometimes help frame more sophisticated explanations.

References

Albonetti, C. A. (1986). Criminality, prosecutorial screening, and uncertainty: Toward a theory of discretionary decision making in felony case processings. *Criminology*, *24*, 623–644.

Albonetti, C. A. (1987). Prosecutorial discretion: The effects of uncertainty. *Law and Society Review*, *21*, 291–313.

Albonetti, C. A. (1990). Race and the probability of pleading guilty. *Journal of Quantitative Criminology*, *6*, 315–334.

Albonetti, C. A. (1997). Sentencing under the federal sentencing guidelines: An analysis of the effects of defendant characteristics, guilty pleas, and departures, 1991–1992. *Law and Society Review*, *31*, 601–634.

Alschuler, A. W. (1979). Plea bargaining and its history. *Columbia Law Review*, *79*, 1–43.

Alschuler, A. W. (2002). Straining at gnats and swallowing camels: The selective morality of Professor Bibas. *Cornell Law Review*, *88*, 1412.

Baumer, E. (2013). Reassessing and redirecting research on race and sentencing. *Justice Quarterly*, *30*, 231–261.

Bibas, S. (2004). Plea bargaining outside the shadow of trial. *Harvard Law Review*, *117*, 2463–2547.

Bjerk, D. (2007). Guilt shall not escape or the innocence sufer? The limits of plea bargainin when defendant guilt is uncertain. *American Law and Economics Review*, *9*, 305–329.

Bordens, K. S. (1984). The effects of likelihood of conviction, threatened punishment, and assumed role on mock plea bargaining decisions. *Basic and Applied Social Psychology*, 5, 59–74. doi: 10.1207/s15324834basp0501_4

Bordens, K. S., & Bassett, J. (1985). The plea bargaining process from the defendant's perspective: A field investigation. *Basic and Applied Social Psychology*, *6*, 93–110. doi: 10.1207/s15324834basp_0602_1

Bradley-Engen, M., Engen, R. L., Shields, C., Damphousse, K. R., & Smith, B. L. (2012). The time penalty: Examining the relationship between time to conviction and trial vs. plea disparities in sentencing. *Justice Quarterly*, *29*, 829–857.

Brereton, D., & Casper, J. D. (1982). Does it pay to plead guilty? Differential sentencing and the functioning of criminal courts. *Law and Society Review*, *16*, 45–70.

Bushway, S. D., & Redlich, A. D. (2012). Is plea bargaining in the 'shadow of the trial' a mirage? *Journal of Quantitative Criminology, 28*, 437–454.
Bushway, S. D., Redlich, A. D., & Norris, R. J. (2014). An explicit test of plea bargaining in the "shadow of the trial." *Criminology*, 52, 723–754. doi: 10.1111/1745-9125.12054
Cohen, T. H., & Kyckelhahn, T. (2010). *Felony defendants in large urban counties, 2006*. Washington, DC: U.S. Department of Justice, Bureau of Justice Statistics.
Cooter, R., Marks, S., & Mnookin, R. (1982). Bargaining in the shadow of the law: A testable model of strategic behavior. *Journal of Legal Studies, XI*, 225–251.
DePoorter, B. (2010). Law in the shadow of bargaining: The feedback effect of civil settlements *Cornell Law Review, 95*, 957–988.
Dervan, L., & Edkins, V. (2013). The innocent defendant's dilemma: An innovative empirical study of plea bargaining's innocence problem. *The Journal of Criminal Law and Criminology, 103*, 1–48.
Dixon, J. (1995). The organizational context of criminal sentencing. *American Journal of Sociology, 100*, 1157–1198.
Dobbie, W. Goldin, J., & Yang, C. (2016). *The effects of pre-trial detention on conviction, future crime and employment: Evidence from randomly assigned judges*. Princeton, NJ: Princeton University Economics working paper.
Eisenstein, J., Fleming, R., & Nardulli, P. (1987). *The contours of justice: Communities and their courts*. Boston: Little, Brown.
Eisenstein, J., & Jacob, H. (1977). *Felony justice: an organizational analysis of criminal courts*. Boston: Little, Brown.
Engen, R. L., & Steen, S. (2000). The power to punish: Discretion and sentencing reform in the war on drugs. *American Journal of Sociology, 105*, 1357–1395.
Fair Trials. (2017). *The disappearing trial: What does justice mean in a world with more guilty pleas and fewer trials?* London: Fair Trials International.
Frontline (2004). *The plea*. Public Broadcasting System. Season 22 Episode 14.
Gazal-Ayal, O., & Tor, A. (2012). The innocence effect. *Duke Law Journal, 62*, 339–401.
Glover, J. M. (2012). The federal rules of civil settlement. *New York University Law Review 87*, 1713–1778.
Gregory, W., Mowen, J., & Linder, D. (1978). Social psychology and plea bargaining: Applications, methodology, and theory. *Journal of Personality and Social Psychology, 36*, 1521–1530.
Guthrie, C., Rachlinski, J., & Wistrich, A. (2001). Inside the judicial mind. *Cornell Law Review, 86*, 777.
Halberstam, M. (1982). Towards neutral principles in the administration of criminal justice: A critique of Supreme Court decisions sanctioning the plea bargaining process. *Journal of Criminal Law and Criminology, 73*, 1–49.
Landes, W. M. (1971). An economic analysis of the courts. *Journal of Labor Economics, 14*, 61–107.
Mnookin, R. H., & Kornhauser, L. (1979). Bargaining in the shadow of the law: The case of divorce. *Yale Law Journal, 88*, 950–997.
Nagel, S. S., & Neef, M. (1979). *Decision theory and the legal process*. Lexington, MA: Lexington Books.
Nardulli, P., Eisenstein, J., & Fleming, R. (1988). *The tenor of justice: Criminal courts and the guilty plea process*. Urbana: University of Illinois Press.

The National Registry of Exonerations (2015). *Innocents who pled guilty*. The National Registry of Exonerations Newsletter.

Norris, R., & Redlich, A. (2014). Seeking justice, compromising truth? Criminal admissions and the Prisoner's Dilemma. *Albany Law Review*, *77*, 1005–1038.

O'Keefe, K. (2010). Two wrongs make a wrong: A challenge to plea bargaining and collateral consequences statutes through their integration. *Journal of Criminal Law and Criminology*, *100*(1), 243–276.

Pezdek, K., & O'Brien, M. (2014). Plea bargaining and appraisals of eyewitness evidence by prosecutors and defense attorneys. *Psychology, Crime, & Law*, *20*, 222–241. doi: 10.1080/1068316X.2013.770855

Pfaff, J. (2014). Escaping from the standard story: Why conventional wisdom on prison growth is wrong, and where we can go from here. *Federal Sentencing Reporter*, *265*, 26.

Plous, S. (1993). *The psychology of judgment and decision-making*. New York: McGraw-Hill.

Redlich, A., Wilford, M., & Bushway, S. (2017). Understanding guilty pleas through the lens of social science. *Psychology, Public Policy, and Law*, *23*(4), 458–471.

Smith, D. A. (1986). The plea bargain controversy. *Journal of Criminal Law and Criminology*, *77*, 949–968.

Steffensmeier, D., Ulmer, J., & Kramer, J. (1998). The interaction of race, gender, and age in criminal sentencing: The punishment cost of being young, black, and male. *Criminology*, *36*, 763–798.

Tor, A., Gazal-Ayal, O., & Garcia, S. M. (2010). Fairness and the willingness to accept plea bargain offers. *Journal of Empirical Legal Studies*, *7*, 97–116.

Tversky, A., & Kahneman, D. (1974). Judgment under uncertainty: Heuristics and biases. *Science*, *185*, 1124.

Ulmer, J. T. (1997). *Social worlds of sentencing: Court communities under sentencing guidelines*. Albany: State University of New York Press.

Ulmer, J. T., & Bradley, M. S. (2006). Variation in trial penalties among serious violent offenses. *Criminology*, *44*, 631–670.

Ulmer J. T., Eisenstein, J., & Johnson, B.D. (2010). Trial penalties in federal sentencing: Extra-guidelines factors and district variation. *Justice Quarterly*, *27*, 560–592.

Viljoen, J. L., Klaver, J., & Roesch, R. (2005). Legal decisions of preadolescent and adolescent defendants: Predictors of confessions, pleas, communication with attorneys, and appeals. *Law and Human Behavior*, *29*(3), 253–277. doi: 10.1007/s10979-005-3613-2

Yan, S. (2017). Search for the hidden punishments: An alternative approach to studying alternative sanctions. *Journal of Quantitative Criminology*, *33*, 21–44.

3

Defense Attorneys and Plea Bargains

*Kelsey S. Henderson**

As discussed in the introduction of this book, guilty pleas comprise the vast majority of criminal convictions in the United States; in the 2013 fiscal year, 97% of felony defendants convicted in U.S. district courts pleaded guilty before or during trial (U.S. Department of Justice Executive Office for United States Attorneys, 2013). Criticisms of the high percentage of cases adjudicated through guilty pleas revolve around possible infringements of defendants' rights and a lack of adversarial system safeguards. One such issue involves the quality of lawyering and what constitutes effective lawyering in plea bargaining (Alschuler, 1986). Much of the legal precedent guiding the attorney's role focuses on the attorney's responsibilities at trial. However, as the majority of cases never see a trial, greater attention should be directed toward the attorney's role and involvement in the plea bargaining process.

Attorneys act as a translator of the criminal justice system to their clients, guiding them through the adjudication process. In one of the landmark cases on the right to counsel, *Powell v. Alabama* (1932), Justice Sutherland stated, "The right to be heard would be, in many cases, of little avail if it did not comprehend the right to be heard by counsel. . . . He [the defendant] requires the guiding hand of counsel at every step in the proceedings against him" (pp. 68–69). The U.S. Supreme Court (USSC) has upheld this right throughout the years (albeit at times interpreted differently; see later discussion). Following this perspective, the right to counsel is viewed as a primary safeguard of fairness in the plea bargaining process (Alschuler, 1975).

Despite this important role, public perception of the legal profession and lawyers is not as highly regarded as many other professions in society. An American Bar Association consumer survey found only 19% of respondents reported they were "extremely" or "very" confident in the legal profession/

---

* The author wishes to thank Reveka Shteynberg for her thoughtful comments and suggestions on an earlier draft of this chapter.

lawyers, and over two-thirds felt lawyers were greedy and more interested in money than serving their clients (American Bar Association, 2002). In a survey administered to clients of public defenders, roughly 53% were overall satisfied with their public defender, 32% were dissatisfied, and 15% were indifferent (Campbell, Moore, Maier, & Gaffney, 2015). These data suggest that attorneys, and more specifically public defenders, may suffer a lack of legitimacy and a strained relationship with clients. Exploring the complex relationship between client and counsel is an important and necessary component of understanding plea decision-making and working to improve these decisions within the legal system.

The purpose of this chapter is to present an overview of the role of the defense attorney in the plea bargaining process, while acknowledging the context in which plea decisions occur and how various factors must be considered in thinking about rational decision-making. In the following sections, I begin with a brief overview of legal decisions and professional guidelines regarding the attorney's role. Then, a discussion of legal factors that affect defense attorneys' decisions follows, along with an outline of how a rational plea decision model could be expanded to account for various structural influences and psychological biases that arguably also affect attorney decisions and recommendations (Bibas, 2004). Much of the empirical evidence presented in this chapter was collected using various forms of experimental studies (hypothetical scenarios, deception-based experiments, surveys, etc.), one of the more often-used methods for examining factors that affect decision-making within certain controlled environments. This chapter will conclude with a discussion of the information presented and possible directions for future research on the role of defense attorneys in plea bargaining.

What Is the Attorney's Role in Plea Bargaining?

Before delving into a discussion of factors that affect attorneys' level of involvement and decision-making within plea bargaining, it is important to frame both the legal and professional standards regarding the defense attorney's role. Following is a review of cases and professional guidelines that have played a crucial part in shaping the defense attorney's role in our criminal justice system and, more specifically, within the plea bargaining context.

In the 1963 landmark decision of *Gideon v. Wainwright*, the USSC extended the right of court-appointed counsel for indigent defendants charged with serious felonies to state courts (overturning the earlier decision in *Betts v. Brady*, 1942; extending the federal-court-only rule in *Johnson v. Zerbst*, 1938, and capital-crime-only rule in *Powell v. Alabama*, 1932). In this decision, the Court interpreted a defendant's right to counsel (appointed if need be) as fundamental to fairness, relevant to the due process clause of the Fourteenth Amendment (*Gideon v. Wainwright*, 1963). This right was later extended to defendants charged with a misdemeanor offense carrying potential loss of liberty (*Argersinger v. Hamlin*, 1972). At the time of the *Gideon* decision and today, a large percentage of defendants are indigent (43% in 1962 and over 80% more recently; Silverstein, 1965, as cited by Stuntz, 1997; Harlow, 2000).

Following the *Gideon* decision, the legal profession expanded rapidly: Within the 10-year period following *Gideon*, the number of individuals enrolled in law school increased by roughly 114% (49,552 in 1963–1964 to 106,102 in 1973–1974; American Bar Association, n.d.). To serve the growing number of individuals now guaranteed counsel under law, many states established public defender offices. As of 2013, 28 states have a statewide public defender program, and in the remaining states, public defender systems are county based, administered at a local level, and funded through a mix of county or state funds (Strong, 2017). Type of indigent defense representation varies (Strong, 2017): governmental public defender offices, non-governmental public defender offices (written contract involving governmental entity and non-profit), contract (with attorneys or law firms operating for profit), and assigned systems (the judge, or an appointed administrator, assigns attorneys or law firms on a case-by-case basis). *Gideon* was the wide-sweeping decision propelling the use of counsel in criminal proceedings; later decisions would further solidify the role of counsel in our criminal justice system.

Although *Gideon* established the right to counsel for indigent, felony defendants (later extended to juveniles in *In re Gault*, 1967), the Court did not provide guidance as to what constitutes "effective assistance" of counsel until years later in *Strickland v. Washington* (1984). In *Strickland*, the Court established a two-prong test for demonstrating ineffective assistance of counsel. Under this standard, the defendant must prove (1) his or her attorney's performance fell below a reasonable standard (deficient performance) and (2) that performance prejudiced the outcome (i.e., if not for counsel's performance at trial, the outcome would have been different). The bar was set high to prevail in an ineffective assistance of counsel claim on appeal. For examples of cases that did not pass the *Strickland* standard, but could arguably be considered poor lawyering, see *Muniz v. Smith* (2011) and *People v. Badia* (1990).

When applying the *Strickland* standard to plea bargaining, the USSC ruled in the 1985 *Hill v. Lockhart* case that a defendant would need to prove that if not for counsel's advice, he or she would have insisted on going to trial (rather than accepting a guilty plea). In this case, the Court addressed the issue of whether counsel's deficient performance *caused* the defendant to accept a guilty plea (*Hill v. Lockhart*, 1985). However, as in the *Strickland* decision, the Court did not address what necessarily constitutes ineffective assistance of counsel. Some 25 years later, the USSC took on the issue of counsel in plea bargaining in a series of decisions. In *Lafler v. Cooper* (2012), the Court held that counsel referenced an incorrect legal rule in giving advice; as a result, the respondent lost the opportunity to accept a more favorable plea offer. In *Missouri v. Frye* (2012) the respondent's counsel did not notify the defendant of the prosecutor's plea offer before the offer expired (referred to as an "exploding plea"). The Court concluded that respondent's counsel should have notified him of the plea offer, but also counsel's performance prejudiced the respondent in that he later pleaded guilty to a felony rather than the original misdemeanor charge. And in *Padilla v. Commonwealth of Kentucky* (2010) the Court ruled that Padilla's counsel failing to advise him, a non-citizen, of the risk of deportation resulting from his conviction constituted ineffective assistance of counsel. It remains to be seen if the *Padilla* ruling will be extended to ineffective assistance of counsel claims regarding notification of other collateral consequences (for more on collateral consequences see Chapter 9, this volume).

It has only been within the last decade that the USSC concluded ineffective assistance of counsel in plea bargaining could potentially encompass failing to inform a client of a plea offer (*Missouri v. Frye*, 2012), giving a client flawed advice (*Lafler v. Cooper*, 2012), or failing to advise a client of immigration and deportation risks as a result of accepting a guilty plea (*Padilla v. Commonwealth of Kentucky*, 2010). Beyond that, there exists little guidance as to what constitutes *effective* assistance of counsel in plea bargaining. As Justice Kennedy acknowledged, bargaining is an individual skill and talent, and defining defense attorneys' duties and responsibilities in plea bargaining is not practical, nor prudent (*Missouri v. Frye*, 2012). These recent cases suggest a shifting focus to a largely ignored area—the defense attorney's role in plea bargaining.

Regarding professional standards, the American Bar Association (2015) lists key standards that defense attorneys should meet in regard to plea bargaining: The defense attorney should keep the defendant advised of developments (a failure in *Missouri v. Frye*, 2012), aid the defendant in reaching a decision, not knowingly make false statements regarding law or fact (a failure in *Lafler v. Cooper*, 2012), explore diversion possibilities, and advise clients of possible collateral consequences (a failure in *Padilla v. Commonwealth of Kentucky*, 2010). Also included in the defense function standards (American Bar Association, 2015), after informing the client properly of rules of law, the attorney should advise the accused with complete honesty about all aspects of the case, including probable outcomes. He or she should not intentionally over- or understate the risks or prospects of the case to unduly influence the client's plea decision. To understand how attorneys make judgments about the "value" of a case (i.e., value of the plea in relation to probable outcomes at trial), it is important to consider factors that affect attorney decisions.

Legal Factors Affecting Defense Attorney Decision-Making

The "shadow of the trial" framework posits that the *rational* individual will use information available regarding the likelihood of conviction based on the strength of evidence, and possible sentence if convicted at trial, to weigh the option of accepting a guilty plea versus going to trial (Mnookin & Kornhauser,

1979; see Chapter 2, this volume). For the defendant, the most likely source of information regarding the strength of evidence, likelihood of conviction, and possible sentencing options is his or her attorney. There may be a number of situations in which there is evidence to support a rational plea decision. One of the attorney's jobs is then to point out the strength of evidence against the defendant and how that will likely affect his or her outcome at trial (Bibas, 2004).

The influence of legal factors on defense attorneys' plea decisions has been well documented (Kramer, Wolbransky, & Heilbrun, 2007; McAllister & Bregman, 1986). In one study, as sentence severity and the defendant's probability of conviction increased, defense attorneys became more willing to advise a guilty plea (McAllister & Bregman, 1986). Defense attorneys were least willing to advise a guilty plea when the defendant faced 2 years with a 20% probability of conviction and most willing when the defendant faced 5 years with an 80% probability of conviction. Defense attorneys rated the likelihood of the defendant's conviction and the value of the plea based on the potential sentence if convicted at trial as the most important factors in their plea decision (McAllister & Bregman, 1986).

One of the strongest determinants of the strength of evidence is the type of evidence (e.g., confession, scientific, and eyewitness evidence). In two separate experimental studies, hypothetical case materials were sent to legal actors to participate in a plea decision-making task (Pezdek & O'Brien, 2014; Redlich, Bushway, & Norris, 2016). The presence of confession evidence, DNA evidence, and a positive eyewitness identification positively increased defense attorneys' willingness to accept a guilty plea (Redlich et al., 2016). Defense attorneys were also cognizant of variations in eyewitness evidence and factors that contribute to reliable identifications (e.g., factors that influence fair line-up procedures; Pezdek & O'Brien, 2014). Defense attorneys rated the defendant's likelihood of guilt higher in same-race identifications than cross-race identifications (i.e., when the eyewitness and the defendant were of the same race, rather than different races) and were more likely to recommend their client accept a guilty plea in conditions in which the eyewitness had prior contact with the defendant (familiar) than when the eyewitness was unfamiliar with the defendant (Pezdek & O'Brien, 2014). These results suggest defense attorneys are sensitive to variations in evidence strength and quality and would likely use that information in making legally justified recommendations to their client.

In the Redlich et al. study (2016; see also Bushway, Redlich, & Norris, 2014), participants were presented with 31 case folders containing different information and instructed to open folders they would normally consider; the folders contained defendant characteristics, evidentiary factors, and non-evidentiary factors. Defense attorneys and prosecutors were more likely than judges to open folders containing evidentiary information. In addition, defense attorneys were more likely than prosecutors and judges to open folders containing non-evidentiary information and information regarding characteristics of the defendant (Redlich et al., 2016). Given the defense attorney's relationship with and responsibility to their client, it is understandable that they would be interested in both defendant characteristics and non-evidentiary information. However, this suggests defense attorneys use extralegal factors in their decision-making, in addition to legal factors.

Expansion of the Shadow of the Trial Framework

While the shadow of the trial framework best incorporates legal factors that influence plea decisions, it has been considered simplistic. Specifically, Bibas (2004) has argued for an expansion of the theoretical model to account for psychological processes and structural influences that likely influence plea decision-making. Structural influences such as the courtroom workgroup, lawyers' self-interests, bail rules, and pretrial detention likely affect decision-making (Bibas, 2004). Research supports the influence of these factors on plea decisions. For example, individuals noted incompetence of their attorney as an influencing factor of their self-reported false guilty plea (Redlich, Summers, & Hoover, 2010). Psychological processes such as overconfidence, self-serving biases, and risk preferences also likely affect decision-making (Bibas, 2004). Even if structural influences and psychological processes do not hinder the efficacy of plea bargaining, they likely skew the fairness of punishments (Bibas, 2004). Some individuals who pleaded guilty included those who might have otherwise gone to trial, those who went to trial when they should have pleaded guilty to avoid a harsher punishment, and those who accepted plea offers inferior to those of their counterparts.

The Importance of Structural Influences

While Bibas (2004) acknowledges many structural influences that affect rational decision-making, in fitting with the scope of this chapter, I focus here exclusively on some of those issues relating to the defense attorney and effective bargaining.

Courtroom Workgroup

The courtroom workgroup stresses the importance of cooperation over conflict and creates an atmosphere of "court regulars" (i.e., public defenders, prosecutors, judges) and "outsiders" (i.e., the defendant and privately retained counsel; Blumberg, 1967). The courtroom workgroup phenomenon suggests public defenders and prosecutors (also referred to as assistant or deputy district attorneys, etc., depending on jurisdiction) work together on a frequent basis, and because of this, public defenders might be able to generate better case outcomes for their clients than privately retained attorneys. Examining the effects of the courtroom workgroup relationship (and type of counsel) is important considering public defenders or appointed counsel represent 66%

of federal felony defendants and 82% of state felony defendants in large urban jurisdictions (Harlow, 2000).

There may be benefits for defense attorneys who operate within the courtroom workgroup, such as knowing the "going rate" for plea offers for a particular crime, which judges are more or less "friendly" toward certain crimes, and possibly having a more approachable relationship with prosecutors in a jurisdiction. Public defenders typically manage a high volume of cases, which could result in more experience with certain types of cases and greater accuracy in estimating the defendant's probability of conviction at trial and possible sentence. Public defenders may be able to systematically "choose their battles" and might consider implicit trade-offs of some cases for another (e.g., a concession in Case A for a harsher punishment in Case B; see Bibas, 2004). Furthermore, mandatory sentencing guidelines have incentivized cooperation with the government (e.g., dropped charges or sentencing outside the mandatory guidelines for the individual who helps "break" the case, feeds the government information, or testifies against others; Bibas, 2004). Prosecutors may be more willing to engage in these concessions with public defenders, whom they work with frequently, and public defenders may feel pressure to maintain a relationship of reciprocity with the district attorney's office.

However, it is possible that clients with privately retained attorneys may fare better in plea negotiations considering the structural constraints of the working environment of public defenders (e.g., lack of funding and resources, high caseloads). Prosecutors may perceive they have to offer a more desirable plea deal to clients of private counsel (Bibas, 2004). In one study, prosecutors were asked if a plea agreement would differ depending on whether the defendant was represented by private counsel or a public defender (Champion, 1989). Of those who responded a public defender would make a difference in plea negotiations, 86% reported the difference would be *less* favorable to the defendant. Of those who responded a private attorney would make a difference, 96% reported the difference would be *more* favorable to the defendant (Champion, 1989). In general, these results highlight that prosecutors perceive clients of public defenders at a disadvantage in plea bargaining negotiations.

Case Outcomes

But do these possible advantages or disadvantages translate to disparities in case outcomes? A wealth of research has been conducted exploring differences in case outcomes as a function of type of defense attorney, and the results are mixed (a few of these studies are highlighted here). Some research has demonstrated no effect of type of counsel on key outcome measures. Plea acceptance rates are similar for defendants of court-appointed counsel (75 largest counties, 71%; U.S. district courts, 87.1%) compared to those of privately retained counsel (75 largest counties, 72.8%; U.S. district courts, 84.6%; Harlow, 2000). Other research found no direct effect of type of counsel on case processing decisions (bail, primary charge reduction, sentenced to prison, and mean sentence length; Hartley, Miller, & Spohn, 2010). Rather, legally relevant variables were the strongest predictor of decisions (some context-specific effects were found; Hartley et al., 2010).

When there are differences in case outcomes, the research has been inconsistent regarding which type of defender is more beneficial for the client. For example, in a sample of Kentucky, Tennessee, and Virginia cases, 48% of the cases involving private attorneys were dropped compared to 11.3% of cases involving public defenders (Champion, 1989). In state courts, convicted defendants represented by court-appointed lawyers were more likely to be incarcerated (71.3%) than those represented by privately retained lawyers (53.9%); however, of those sentenced to serve time, defendants with court-appointed lawyers received shorter sentences than those with privately retained lawyers (Harlow, 2000). Other work has compared different types of indigent representation (Roach, 2014). Public defenders generated more favorable outcomes for their clients than did assigned counsel. Defendants of assigned counsel were more likely to be convicted of the most serious offense, receive longer expected sentences, and suffered a longer wait period from arrest to adjudication than those of public defenders (see Roach, 2014, for a discussion of accounting for possible selection bias of cases when assigned counsel is used). These conflicting results are likely context specific and dependent on a range of factors such as geographical region, court type, and sentencing guidelines; however, these results highlight that in some contexts, type of counsel may affect key outcomes.

Source of Funding

One of the main factors influencing defense representation is funding source (Bibas, 2004)—a key difference between privately retained and court-appointed counsel, and a caveat of the possible benefits of working within the courtroom workgroup. Funding for court-appointed lawyers is likely fixed at a certain amount, regardless of the hours devoted to each case (e.g., public defenders are salaried employees, appointed counsel may be working pro bono or receive a fixed fee). Comparatively, private attorneys typically charge an hourly fee and may be in a better position to devote more time and resources to each case. However, it is also worth noting that some private attorneys follow a flat-fee structure, in which a quick bargain might be more desirable. That is, regardless of how much time is spent on any one case, the defense attorney receives the same amount, which arguably creates incentive to invest less time.

Funding issues exacerbate differences between public defenders and prosecutors, the latter typically being well resourced (this discrepancy could be related to the fact that prosecutors' offices may handle civil cases in addition to criminal cases). According to the U.S. Bureau of Justice, there are over 25,000 attorneys in state prosecutors' offices compared to 15,000 attorneys in public defender offices; annual funding for prosecutors' offices totaled

$5.8 billion compared to $2.3 billion in expenditures for public defender offices (Langton & Farole, 2010; Perry & Banks, 2011).

Recent cuts to indigent defense budgets have drawn public attention to the funding issues plaguing public defender offices, which are overburdened with cases and underwhelmed with funding. In some jurisdictions, these cuts have resulted in furloughed or laid-off lawyers and staff, less funding for expert testimony and case investigative work, and attorneys handling more cases than professional standards recommend (Cooper, 2017; Nixon, 2013). Because of high caseloads, public defenders may be able to devote only minutes to individual cases (Giovanni & Patel, 2013). In New Orleans, public defenders stopped working with defendants charged with certain felonies because they lacked the time and resources needed to defend their clients properly (Cooper, 2017). At one point, 52 public defenders represented over 22,000 cases. This resulted in standards of representation not in line with attorney code of ethics or constitutional and professional standards, according to the chief public defender of the area (Cooper, 2017). And in 2013, the Florida Supreme Court ruled public defenders could withdraw as counsel on the basis of excess caseloads, work restrictions, or inadequate funding (*Public Defender, Eleventh Judicial Circuit of Florida, et al. v. State of Florida*, 2013). While the issue of funding for indigent defense services has received significant attention, even those defense attorneys not serving as public defenders are subject to financial pressures, which can hinder their ability to mount a strong defense for individual cases. It is possible that plea bargaining becomes almost inevitable in these cases, given the limited availability of time and resources, where preparing each case (or even a greater majority of cases) for trial is not a feasible option.

Informational Deficit

The shadow of the trial framework assumes defense attorneys can properly estimate the value of the plea and their client's likely probability of conviction at trial. Attorneys' overconfidence in their abilities, and deficits in information, can affect the accuracy of this calculation. Defendants who are, for example, innocent, under the influence of substances at the time of the crime, mentally ill, or simply not forthcoming with their attorney exacerbate the problem of the informational deficit for attorneys (Bibas, 2004). In general, defense attorneys are at an informational deficit compared to prosecutors, who at the early stages of proceedings typically have access to a full police report, interview statements, and evidence (Rakoff, 2014). Defense attorneys might not have many opportunities to meet with their clients before a plea decision is made (e.g., only 31% of juveniles in a sample met with their attorney on more than three occasions before accepting a guilty plea; Zottoli, Daftary-Kapur, Winters, & Hogan, 2016).

Furthermore, evidence disclosure rules, established in *Brady v. Maryland* (1963), are not consistently held in plea bargaining. While it is true that the

Supreme Court has affirmed suppression of *Brady* materials violates the knowing and voluntary components of the defendant's plea decision (*Boykin v. Alabama*, 1969; *Miller v. Angliker*, 1988), they have also ruled that the prosecutor does not have to disclose the same types of evidence (i.e., impeachment evidence) prior to a defendant accepting a guilty plea as they would be required to before trial (*United States v. Ruiz*, 2002). Evidence disclosure rules are not clear-cut or consistent when applied to plea bargaining (see Heumann, 1981 for a discussion of discovery "norms" between prosecutors and defense attorneys). Thus, attorneys may not have all the information necessary to make an educated calculation of their client's chances at trial and, thus, an informed recommendation to their client.

Psychological Processes and the "Debiaser" Role

One shortcoming of the shadow of the trial framework is it assumes a rational thought process, devoid of emotions and biases (Bibas, 2004). Individuals generally make decisions in difficult environments, with complex motives, and a multitude of social factors that affect processing and perception of new information (Hollander-Blumoff, 2008). It has been proposed that attorneys' experience and expertise put them in the best position to counteract some of the biases and heuristics of the defendant and to assist the defendant in making a rational choice (Bibas, 2004). Thus, the defense attorney may act as a "debiaser" for their client. This relies on the assumption that defense attorneys themselves are not subject to these heuristics and biases. However, attorneys are human and not totally free from biases; thus they may not fit within a rational actor paradigm in their interactions with clients and negotiations with prosecutors (Hollander-Blumoff, 2008). In the following sections, I focus on a few psychological processes and biases that have been shown to affect defense attorney decision-making.

Loss Aversion and Risk Behaviors

Loss aversion, as a psychological construct, refers to individuals making a decision and weighing the loss of something as more influential than the gain of an equal value (Kahneman & Tversky, 1979). Applying this framework to plea bargaining decisions, the plea is a trade of a certain loss (conviction and punishment) versus the possibility of no loss (acquittal) or an even greater loss at trial (conviction and a harsher punishment; Covey, 2007). In line with the endowment effect (i.e., the tendency for people to assign more value to a good they possess than on those they do not; Thaler, 1980; Tversky & Kahneman, 1981), defendants may place a high value on their right to trial and be reluctant to "give it up," and the plea discount—the difference between the sentence/sanction offered in the plea and the typical sanction imposed upon conviction—will then need to be of a certain value to induce the defendant to relinquish this right (Covey, 2007). However, trial represents risk and the possibility of loss, and some defendants may prefer the known plea outcome to engaging in any risky behavior, even if there are potential gains (for a greater discussions of prospect theory, see Kahneman & Tversky, 1979; specific to defendant plea decision-making, see Redlich, Wilford, & Bushway, 2017). These decisions are subjective to the individual, and one's willingness to "gamble" in these situations likely rests on one's aversion to loss and/or willingness to take risks.

An individual's risk propensity (some may be more risk seeking or risk averse) and risk perception influence behavior (Bibas, 2004). Past experiences, such as having successfully taken risks, and information and recommendations from others, affect an individual's perception of risk. When thinking of risk behaviors and plea bargaining, the real gambler is the defendant. However, it is important to consider the defense attorney's risk behavior as well, as he or she is the defendant's most likely source of information. The attorney's level of optimism about acquittal at trial or improved future plea offers likely affects the defendant's perception of his or her case and final outcome decision. Two important considerations come to mind regarding risk preferences: advising an innocent defendant (and how that may differ from advising a guilty individual) and when preferences do not align between the defendant and the defense attorney.

Advising the Innocent Defendant

In making key legal decisions, innocent individuals tend to be more risk seeking and prefer trial over accepting a guilty plea, in part because the concept of being convicted for a crime you did not commit seems too unfair (Tor, Gazal-Ayal, & Garcia, 2010). While accepting a guilty plea may be rational for the guilty defendant, the assumption is that rational, innocent individuals would not accept a guilty plea. However, innocent individuals do accept guilty pleas (albeit at lower levels than guilty individuals; Dervan & Edkins, 2013; Tor et al., 2010). Roughly 11% of individuals exonerated with the help of the Innocence Project falsely pleaded guilty (Innocence Project, n.d.). Furthermore, the USSC has ruled that proclaiming innocence does not preclude an individual from accepting a guilty plea (*North Carolina v. Alford*, 1970).

Innocent individuals may have an unrealistic level of optimism regarding acquittal at trial (i.e., view their chances as higher than an objective standard; Shepperd, Waters, Weinstein, & Klein, 2015). It may be difficult for defense attorneys to advise clients in these types of situations. It is also possible that attorneys will work hard to counteract these risk-seeking behaviors and innocent individuals may be more likely to yield to their attorney's recommendations. Research suggests an advocate's recommendation influences innocent individuals' decisions to plead guilty (Henderson & Levett, 2018). The effect of advocate recommendation on plea decisions was only marginally significant for guilty individuals. It seems that innocence, the resulting risk aversion, and reliance on an advocate's advice create a paradigm that might not fit so well within a rational model of decision-making.

Differences in Preferences

Defendants' and their attorney's preferences (trial or accepting a guilty plea) and risk behavior also may not align. Both the defendant and the attorney likely have a preconceived opinion or preference about the best resolution for the case (although ultimately, it is the defendant's decision). For example, the defendant may be risk seeking and want to go to trial, and the defense attorney, having more experience and possibly a lower level of unrealistic optimism in acquittal, may be more risk averse than the defendant. In one vignette study, defense attorneys generally recommended their client accept a guilty plea, even against the client's stated wishes (Kramer et al., 2007). This effect was most pronounced in conditions in which there existed strong evidence against the defendant (Kramer et al., 2007). While attorneys seek to offset any irrationality on the defendant's part, which likely means assigning considerable weight to legal variables in calculating outcomes and decisions, issues might arise when the defendant's and attorney's preferences are different.

Self-Serving Assessments of Fairness and Overconfidence

In general, plea bargaining involves a negotiation in which each party's perception of the "best possible outcome" might look slightly different (although in some cases and jurisdictions the "going plea rate" for a particular charge might limit negotiation). Conflict resolution and negotiation are complex; the resulting ambiguity allows for multiple and differing interpretations of fairness (Thompson & Loewenstein, 1992). Self-serving assessments of fairness may cause individuals to combine what is fair in a given situation with what benefits themselves; that is, people often arrive at judgments of fairness and equity that are biased in the direction of their own interests (Babcock & Loewenstein, 1997). Self-serving biases in assessment and interpretation are commonly referred to as egocentrism (for an in-depth discussion see Bazerman, Curhan, & Moore, 2001). Possible explanations for egocentric interpretations of fairness are that individuals encode information in a biased manner, selectively recall facts and information favoring their position, and weight factors that favor their own position as more important and influential (Thompson & Loewenstein, 1992).

In the context of plea bargaining, each side thinks it deserves a better deal than what the other side believes is warranted based on the evidence, case facts, and law (Bibas, 2004). The nature of our adversarial system often results in the defense and state portraying the significance of or interpreting evidence in a greatly different manner. Each side may come to

distort "fairness" in a given situation to be more in favor of their own side's interest. It is possible there exists a prosecutorial bias in favor of plea bargaining and defense attorney bias against plea bargaining (McAllister & Bregman, 1986), and prior research consistently shows defense attorneys are less willing to accept a guilty plea than prosecutors are to offer one (Pezdek & O'Brien, 2014; Redlich et al., 2016). Furthermore, on average, prosecutors perceive a higher plea sentence as more reasonable than do defense attorneys (Pezdek & O'Brien, 2014). This could be related to prosecutors' confirmation biases regarding the defendant's guilt, as they are more likely to believe the defendant is guilty than defense attorneys are (Pezdek & O'Brien, 2014), and is likely intertwined with the structural components of plea bargaining (i.e., prosecutors seek convictions). Thus, prosecutors and defense attorneys may be biased toward diverging outcomes and may interpret the same set of factors and evidence in line with their differing perspectives.

Defense attorneys and prosecutors could fail to compromise on a plea deal because they feel they deserve better resolutions than the other side believes is warranted. Both defense attorneys and prosecutors may look at the evidence, or their arguments, and consider it to be more persuasive to a judge or jury than the opposing side's evidence or arguments. Inflating the value of a case may result in disillusionment regarding fair and appropriate plea offers, which could affect defense attorney recommendations to their client. A defense attorney may advise his or her client to reject a plea offer because the attorney believes the prosecutor's offer to be unfair, believes a better offer will come along, and/or is overly optimistic regarding the chances of prevailing at trial.

According to the American Bar Association's (2015) defense function standards, the defense attorney should not under- or overstate the risks and prospects of a case, assuming implicitly that defense attorneys can accurately estimate the probable outcome for each case and accurately relay that information to their client. Undermining the validity of this assumption, research suggests attorneys routinely overestimate their chances of being successful at trial (Goodman-Delahunty, Granhag, Hartwig, & Loftus, 2010). For instance, Goodman-Delahunty and colleagues (2010) compared final case outcomes with prior case predictions for over 450 lawyers. They found that lawyers tended to be overconfident in their case predictions. This overconfidence may affect the plea bargaining counseling phase, when defense attorneys communicate to their client the possible risks and benefits associated with accepting or rejecting a guilty plea. Others found that defense attorneys rate their likelihood of winning at trial lower than do prosecutors (Pezdek & O'Brien, 2014). This may be a consequence of the high conviction rates at trial. Self-serving assessments of fairness may hinder effective, rational bargaining and contribute to overconfidence in one's chances of prevailing at trial.

Implicit Biases and Heuristics

Implicit biases are deeply ingrained attitudes or stereotypes that affect understanding, decisions, and actions in an involuntary, unconscious manner (for a review, see Andersen, Moskowitz, Blair, & Nosek, 2007). These attitudes and biases may become activated and affect judgments and decisions when exposed to various cues (e.g., exposure to a certain racial group). In the discussion that follows, I include a selection of research examining the effects of implicit biases regarding race/ethnicity on decision-making; for an overview of implicit bias in the courtroom, see Kang et al. (2012).

Examining the effects of implicit biases and attitudes in plea decision-making is an important consideration in light of extensive research suggesting that African American defendants fare worse than white defendants at various criminal justice decision-making points. For example, one study found that the state was more likely to upgrade homicide cases involving a white victim than those involving an African American victim (the effect was most pronounced in cases involving a white victim and African American defendant; Radelet & Pierce, 1985). In another study, when told death was the maximum potential sentence, jurors were more likely to convict black defendants (80%) than white defendants (55.1%; Glaser, Martin, & Kahn, 2015). It is possible these disparities are the result of conscious decisions, but also unconscious processes, implicit stereotypes, and prejudice that affect decisions.

Individuals may use stereotypes about African Americans and involvement in criminal behavior as a heuristic in making decisions. For example, participants in one study held implicit associations between "black" and "guilty" and these associations predicted probative values for evidence against a black defendant (Levinson, Cai, & Young, 2014). Other research using an implicit association test suggests trial judges harbor racially implicit attitudes, much like the larger public (Rachlinski, Johnson, Wistrich, & Guthrie, 2009). However, when aware of the need to suppress these biases, judges are motivated and appear to be able to do so (Rachlinski et al., 2009). While more research has explored prosecutorial, juror, and judicial decision-making, these effects likely influence defense attorneys' recommendations and decisions as well.

In one study assessing defense attorneys' judgments about a hypothetical case, defense attorneys encouraged accepting guilty pleas that were less favorable for their African American clients than for white clients under equal conditions (Edkins, 2011). Although attorneys viewed the white client to be slightly guiltier than the African American client, having an African American client increased the odds of imprisonment by roughly three times (Edkins, 2011). Edkins noted that attorneys may be acting in good faith, fearing African American clients will suffer at trial, a rational concern considering research on juries and racial biases. However, this concern for their defendant being convicted at trial should have been evidenced by higher likelihood of conviction rates, which were not found (Edkins, 2011). These results suggest defense attorneys are also subject to biases in decision-making, similar to those reported for other legal actors. Overall, greater attention should be given to the psychological processes and biases that affect plea decision-making, specifically focusing on the defense attorney as well.

Conclusions

This chapter, while not exhaustive, presents an overview of information central to exploring the role of defense attorneys in plea bargaining. While much is known regarding legal actors' roles in our criminal justice system, there remains work to be done in defining the defense attorney's role in plea bargaining and untangling factors that influence plea negotiation and advising. The defense attorney plays a critical role in a defendant's decision-making process. Research suggests that attorneys influence defendants' willingness to accept a guilty plea (Viljoen, Klaver, & Roesch, 2005), but very little existing research addresses precisely *how*. Conflicting findings and areas of underdeveloped research leave a path for researchers interested in further exploring the role of defense attorneys in plea bargaining.

For example, more information is needed on the negotiation phase of plea bargaining and how egocentric interpretations of fairness contribute to legal actors' decision-making processes and related outcomes. What influences the "give and take" in these decisions (e.g., reciprocity within the courtroom workgroup)? Does prosecutorial overcharging exacerbate the issues related to fair negotiation? Does overconfidence influence these decisions? Goodman and colleagues (2010) found attorneys overestimate their chances; however, the majority of these cases were civil cases (70% civil versus 30% criminal). Future research should explore and attempt to disentangle the complex motivations within plea bargaining negotiations for each legal actor involved.

In this chapter, I discussed the role of defense attorneys from a legal and professional standpoint, challenging the assumptions behind these guidelines. I also addressed issues plaguing the work of defense attorneys (e.g., information deficit, lack of secure funding, advising the innocent client). These structural influences and psychological processes likely color effective representation. The intent is not to imply these factors take away from the work and role of defense attorneys, but rather they are important considerations in understanding plea advising and decision-making. For the criminal defendant, the decision to waive one's rights and accept a guilty plea versus take their case to trial is a decision of paramount importance and likely carries considerable, and potentially lifelong, consequences. The defendant must make this decision knowingly, voluntarily, and intelligently (*Boykin v. Alabama*, 1969). Because the relationship between client and counsel is unique and privileged, attorneys are the most likely source of information for defendants and can assist the defendant in making rational, informed, and intelligent decisions. As they are an important source of influence, understanding the defense attorney's role is a central component of evaluating plea decision-making.

References

Alschuler, A. W. (1975). The defense attorney's role in plea bargaining. *Yale Law Journal, 84*(6), 1179–1315. doi: 10.2307/795498

Alschuler, A. W. (1986). Personal failure, institutional failure, and the Sixth Amendment. *New York Review of Law and Social Change, 14*, 149–156. Retrieved from http://chicagounbound.uchicago.edu/cgi/viewcontent.cgi?article=2002&context=journal_articles

American Bar Association. (n.d.). *Enrollment and degrees awarded.* Retrieved from https://www.americanbar.org/content/dam/aba/administrative/legal_education_and_admissions_to_the_bar/statistics/enrollment_degrees_awarded.authcheckdam.pdf

American Bar Association. (2002). *Public perception of lawyers consumer research findings. Section of litigation.* Retrieved from http://www.americanbar.org/content/dam/aba/migrated/marketresearch/PublicDocuments/public_perception_of_lawyers_2002.authcheckdam.pdf

American Bar Association. (2015). *ABA criminal justice standards for the defense function* (4th ed.). Retrieved from https://www.americanbar.org/groups/criminal_justice/standards/DefenseFunctionFourthEdition.html#1.2

Andersen, S. M., Moskowitz, G. B., Blair, I. V., & Nosek, B. A. (2007). Automatic thought. In A. W. Kruglanski & E. T. Higgins (Eds.), *Social psychology: Handbook of basic principles* (2nd ed., pp. 138–175). New York: Guilford Press.

Argersinger v. Hamlin, 407 U.S. 25 (1972).

Babcock, L., & Loewenstein, G. (1997). Explaining bargaining impasse: The role of self-serving biases. *Journal of Economic Perspectives, 11*(1), 109–126. doi: 10.1257/jep.11.1.109

Bazerman, M. H., Curhan, J. R., & Moore, D. A. (2001). The death and rebirth of the social psychology of negotiation. In G. J. Fletcher & M. S. Clark (Eds.), *Blackwell handbook of social psychology: Interpersonal processes* (pp. 196–228). Malden, MA: Blackwell Publishing.

Betts v. Brady, 316 U.S. 455 (1942).

Bibas, S. (2004). Plea bargaining outside the shadow of a trial. *Harvard Law Review, 117*, 2463–2547. doi: 10.2307/4093404

Blumberg, A. (1967). The practice of law as a confidence game: Organizational cooptation of a profession. *Law and Society Review, 1*(2), 15–40. doi: 10.2307/3052933

Boykin v. Alabama, 395 U.S. 238 (1969).

Brady v. Maryland, 373 U.S. 83 (1963).

Bushway, S. D., Redlich, A. D., & Norris, R. J. (2014). An explicit test of plea bargaining in the "shadow of the trial." *Criminology, 52*(4), 723–754. doi: 10.1111/1745-9125.12054

Campbell, C. M., Moore, J., Maier, W., & Gaffney, M. (2015). Unnoticed, untapped, and underappreciated: Clients' perceptions of their public defenders. *Behavioral Sciences and the Law, 33*(6), 751–770. doi: 10.1002/bsl.2182

Champion, D. J. (1989). Private counsels and public defenders: A look at weak cases, prior records, and leniency in plea bargaining. *Journal of Criminal Justice, 17*, 253–263. https://doi.org/10.1016/0047-2352(89)90031-7

Cooper, A. (2017, April 16). Inside NOLA public defenders' decision to refuse felony cases. *CBS 60 Minutes*. Retrieved from http://www.cbsnews.com/news/inside-new-orleans-public-defenders-decision-to-refuse-felony-cases/?ftag=CNM-00-10aab5j&linkId=36566717

Covey, R. (2007). Reconsidering the relationship between cognitive psychology and plea bargaining. *Marquette Law Review, 91*, 213–247. Retrieved from http://scholarship.law.marquette.edu/cgi/viewcontent.cgi?article=1133&context=mulr

Dervan, L., & Edkins, V. (2013). The innocent defendant's dilemma: An innovative empirical study of plea bargaining's innocence problem. *Journal of Criminal Law and Criminology, 103*(1), 1–48. doi: 10.2139/ssrn.2071397

Edkins, V. A. (2011). Defense attorney plea recommendations and client race: Does zealous representation apply equally to all? *Law and Human Behavior, 35*(5), 413–425. http://dx.doi.org/10.1007/s10979-010-9254-0

Gideon v. Wainwright, 372 U.S. 335 (1963).

Giovanni, T., & Patel, R. (2013). *Gideon at 50: Three reforms to revive the right to counsel*. Brennan Center for Justice. Retrieved from http://www.brennancenter.org/sites/default/files/publications/Gideon_Report_040913.pdf

Glaser, J., Martin, K. D., & Kahn, K. B. (2015). Possibility of death sentence has divergent effect on verdicts for black and white defendants. *Law and Human Behavior, 39*(6), 539–546. http://dx.doi.org/10.1037/lhb0000146

Goodman-Delahunty, J., Granhag, P. A., Hartwig, M., & Loftus, E. F. (2010). Insightful or wishful: Lawyers' ability to predict case outcomes. *Psychology, Public Policy, and Law, 16*(2), 133–157. http://dx.doi.org/10.1037/a0019060

Harlow, C. W. (2000). *Defense counsel in criminal cases. Bureau of Justice Statistics Special Report*. Retrieved from https://www.bjs.gov/content/pub/pdf/dccc.pdf

Hartley, R. D., Miller, H. V., & Spohn, C. (2010). Do you get what you pay for? Type of counsel and its effect on criminal court outcomes. *Journal of Criminal Justice, 38*, 1063–1070. http://dx.doi.org/10.1016/j.jcrimjus.2010.07.009

Henderson, K. S., & Levett, L. M. (2018). Investigating predictors of true and false guilty pleas. *Law and Human Behavior*. Advance online publication. http://dx.doi.org/10.1037/lhb0000297

Heumann, M. (1981). *Plea bargaining: The experiences of prosecutors, judges, and defense attorneys*. Chicago: University of Chicago Press.

Hill v. Lockhart, 474 U.S. 52 (1985).

Hollander-Blumoff, R. (2008). Social psychology, information processing, and plea bargaining. *Marquette Law Review, 91*(1), 163–182. Retrieved from http://scholarship.law.marquette.edu/cgi/viewcontent.cgi?article=1131&context=mulr

Innocence Project. Website at http://www.innocenceproject.org

In re Gault, 387 U.S. 1 (1967).

Johnson v. Zerbst, 304 U.S. 458 (1938).

Kahneman, D., & Tversky, A. (1979). Prospect theory: An analysis of decision under risk. *Econometrica, 47*, 263–291. doi: 10.2307/1914185

Kang, J., Bennett, M., Carbado, D., Casey, P., Dasgupta, N., Faigman, D., . . . Mnookin, J. (2012). Implicit bias in the courtroom. *UCLA Law Review, 59*(5), 1124–1186. Retrieved from https://www.uclalawreview.org/pdf/59-5-1.pdf

Kramer, G. M., Wolbransky, M., & Heilbrun, K. (2007). Plea bargaining recommendations by criminal defense attorneys: Evidence strength, potential sentence, and defendant preference. *Behavioral Sciences and the Law*, *25*, 575–585. doi: 10.1002/ bsl.759

Lafler v. Cooper, 132 S. Ct. 1376 (2012).

Langton, L., & Farole, Jr. D. (2010). *State public defender programs, 2007*. U.S. Department of Justice, Office of Justice Programs, Bureau of Justice Statistics. Retrieved from https://www.bjs.gov/content/pub/pdf/spdp07.pdf

Levinson, J. D., Cai, H., & Young, D. (2014). Guilty by implicit racial bias: The guilty/not guilty implicit association test. *Ohio State Journal of Criminal Law*, *8*, 187–207. doi: 10.1371/journal.pone.0092365

McAllister, H. A., & Bregman, N. J. (1986). Plea bargaining by prosecutors and defense attorneys: A decision theory approach. *Journal of Applied Psychology*, *71*, 686–690. doi: 10.1037/0021- 9010.71.4.686

Miller v. Angliker, 848 F.2d 1312, 1320–21 (2d Cir. 1988).

Missouri v. Frye, 132 S. Ct. 1399 (2012).

Mnookin, R. H., & Kornhauser, L. (1979). Bargaining in the shadow of the law: The case of divorce. *Yale Law Journal*, *88*, 950–997. doi: 10.2307/795824

Muniz v. Smith, 647 F.3d 619 (2011)

Nixon, R. (2013, August 23). Public defenders are tightening belts because of steep federal budget cuts. *New York Times*. Retrieved from http://www.nytimes.com/2013/08/24/us/public-defenders-are-tightening-belts-because-of-steep-federal-budget-cuts.html

North Carolina v. Alford, 400 U.S. 25 (1970).

Padilla v. Commonwealth of Kentucky, 559 U.S. 356 (2010).

People v. Badia, 159 A.D.2d 57 (1990).

Perry, S. W., & Banks, D. (2011). *Prosecutors in state courts, 2007—Statistical tables*. U.S. Department of Justice, Office of Justice Programs, Bureau of Justice Statistics. Retrieved from https://www.bjs.gov/content/pub/pdf/psc07st.pdf

Pezdek, N., & O'Brien, M. (2014). Plea bargaining and appraisals of eyewitness evidence by prosecutors and defense attorneys. *Psychology, Crime, & Law*, *20*(3), 222–241. http://dx.doi.org/10.1080/1068316X.2013.770855

Powell v. Alabama, 287, U.S. 45 (1932).

Public Defender, Eleventh Judicial Circuit of Florida, et al. v. State of Florida, Nos. SC09-1181 and SC10-1349 (2013).

Rachlinski, J. J., Johnson, S. L., Wistrich, A. J., & Guthrie, C. (2009). Does unconscious racial bias affect trial judges? *Notre Dame Law Review*, *84*, 1195–1246. http://dx.doi.org/10.2139/ssrn.999490

Radelet, M. L., & Pierce, G. L. (1985). Race and prosecutorial discretion in homicide cases. *Law & Society Review*, *19*, 587–621. doi: 10.2307/3053422

Rakoff, J. S. (2014, November 20). Why innocent people plead guilty. *New York Review of Books*. Retrieved from http://www.nybooks.com/articles/2014/11/20/why-innocent-people-plead-guilty/

Redlich, A. D., Bushway, S. D., & Norris, R. J. (2016). Plea decision-making by attorneys and judges. *Journal of Experimental Criminology*, *12*, 537–561. doi: 10.1007/s11292-016-9264-0

Redlich, A. D., Summers, A., & Hoover, S. (2010). Self-reported false confessions and false guilty pleas among offenders with mental illness. *Law and Human Behavior*, *34*, 79–90. doi: 10.1007/s10979-009-9194-8

Redlich, A. D., Wilford, M. M., & Bushway, S. (2017). Understanding guilty pleas through the lens of social science. *Psychology, Public Policy, and Law, 23*(4), 458. http://dx.doi.org/10.1037/law0000142

Roach, M. A. (2014). Indigent defense counsel, attorney quality, and defendant outcomes. *American Law and Economics Review, 16*(2), 577–619. doi: 10.1093/aler/ahu003

Shepperd, J. A., Waters, E. A., Weinstein, N. D., & Klein, W. M. (2015). A primer on unrealistic optimism. *Current Directions in Psychological Science, 24*(3), 232–237. doi: 10.1177/0963721414568341

Silverstein, L. (1965). *Defense of the poor in criminal cases in American state courts: A field study and report.* Chicago: American Bar Association.

Strickland v. Washington, 466 U.S. 668 (1984).

Strong, S. M. (2017). *State-administered indigent defense systems, 2013.* U.S. Department of Justice, Office of Justice Programs, Bureau of Justice Statistics. Retrieved from https://www.bjs.gov/content/pub/pdf/saids13.pdf

Stuntz, W. J. (1997). The uneasy relationship between criminal procedure and criminal justice. *Yale Law Journal, 107*(1), 1–76. doi: 10.2307/797276

Thaler, R. (1980). Toward a positive theory of consumer choice. *Journal of Economic Behavior & Organization, 1*(1), 39–60. https://doi.org/10.1016/0167-2681(80)90051-7

Thompson, L., & Loewenstein, G. (1992). Egocentric interpretations of fairness and interpersonal conflict. *Organizational Behavior and Human Decision Processes, 51*, 176–197. https://doi.org/10.1016/0749-5978(92)90010-5

Tor, A., Gazal-Ayal, O., & Garcia, S. (2010). Fairness and the willingness to accept plea bargain offers. *Journal of Empirical Legal Studies, 7*(1), 97–116. doi:10.1111/j.1740-1461.2009.01171.x

Tversky, A., & Kahneman, D. (1981). Loss aversion in riskless choice: A reference-dependent model. *Quarterly Journal of Economics, 106*(4), 1039–1061. https://doi.org/10.2307/2937956

U.S. Department of Justice Executive Office for United States Attorneys. (2013). *United States Attorneys' annual statistic report: Fiscal report 2013.* Retrieved from https://www.justice.gov/sites/default/files/usao/legacy/2014/09/22/13statrpt.pdf

United States v. Ruiz, 536 U.S. 622 (2002).

Viljoen, J., Klaver, J., & Roesch, R. (2005). Legal decisions of preadolescent and adolescent defendants: Predictors of confessions, pleas, communication with attorneys, and appeals. *Law and Human Behavior, 29*(3), 253–277. doi: 10.1007/s10979-005-3613-2

Zottoli, T. M., Daftary-Kapur, T., Winters, G. M., & Hogan, C. (2016). Plea discounts, time pressures, and false guilty pleas in youth and adults who pleaded guilty to felonies in New York City. *Psychology, Public Policy, and Law, 22*(3), 250–259. http://dx.doi.org/10.1037/law0000095

4

Prosecutors and Plea Bargains

Bryan C. McCannon

In the U.S. criminal justice system, the prosecutor is the lynchpin. Prosecutors are endowed with a substantial amount of discretion. They can choose which charges and how many to file. They are free to dismiss charges, seek alternative resolutions, and recommend sentences. The decisions they make are impactful. Not only do they affect the accused, the victim, and their families, but their decisions spill over onto society through the impact on public finances and crime's deterrence. (For discussion of the depths of prosecutors' discretion and power see Bibas [2004] and Wright and Miller [2010].)

At the nexus of prosecutorial discretion and its impact is plea bargaining. A system of pleas, as noted throughout this volume, has been established. Plea bargaining circumvents the jury trial process, enhancing the prosecutor's primacy in the criminal justice system. In the criminal justice system, there is a significant amount of heterogeneity, both across jurisdictions and over time. Also, as policymakers actively adjust these institutions (e.g., through statutory interventions regarding sentencing guidelines or mandatory minimums, or changes in electoral rules), they adjust the relative power of the prosecutor and his or her accountability to the public. Consequently, research on the prosecutor's role in plea bargaining provides the opportunity to have a meaningful societal impact.

The purpose of this chapter is to connect prosecutors to the plea bargaining process. While plea bargaining dominates the U.S. criminal justice system (see Chapter 1, this volume), modern commentators document its growing spread, in various forms, around the world (Thaman, 2010b). Plea bargaining relieves resource constraints, acts as a screening mechanism partially separating the guilty from the innocent, and mitigates uncertainty, which is valuable to those involved. Prosecutors' search for pretrial alternatives can be found throughout history. In Ancient Athens, for example, an accidental murderer's prosecution allowed for the perpetrator to negotiate with the prosecutor representing the victim's family. A mutually agreed-upon monetary payment substituted for a formal court hearing that had capital punishment as the prescribed sanction (McCannon, 2010). For less serious crimes, the accused was allowed to counterpropose a lesser sanction for a jury of 500 to consider as an alternative (McCannon, 2011). Society's search for intermediate sanctions is a core element of democratic institutions. (See Thaman [2010a] for a more in-depth discussion of the spread of plea bargaining around the modern world and the various forms and adaptations that exist.)

In this chapter, research on prosecutor behavior is organized to provide a simple, theoretical framework as the foundation for studying plea bargaining. With this framework, the prosecutor's role within it can be analyzed. The model can be used to both organize past research on the prosecutor's role within a system of pleas and guide future investigations.

A Rational Choice Model

Numerous actors are involved in the plea bargaining process. It is not just the interaction between an individual accused of a crime and a prosecutor. It involves the family of the accused, the victim, and, of course, the accused's legal representation. The prosecutor works within an institutional system that includes judges, juries, parole boards, and others, all of whom may influence outcomes through the incentives created. Hence, a unifying framework is needed to guide systematic analysis of the plea bargaining process.

The framework needs to balance generalizability, precision, and flexibility. Ideally, to address the issue of how prosecutors utilize and influence the plea bargaining process, a model that can be used to form testable hypotheses is valuable. A rational choice model is a prominent method for doing so (see Chapter 2, this volume for discussion on the defendant as a rational actor).

Therefore, I start with the simplest framework possible. Consider the interaction between two parties. One is the defendant, denoted as *D*. Of course, in practice the defendant is not alone. The defendant will have a family (e.g., parents, spouse, children, etc.) and, obviously, professional defense representation is a crucial part of the team (see Chapter 3, this volume). With the goal of maintaining a simple framework, I condense all of these individuals into one hypothetical agent, *D*, and treat that agent as a single decision-maker. Once the basic framework is established, one can explore how to incorporate and differentiate the various team members who make up the defense.

D interacts with the prosecution, *P*, who will again be assumed to be a single actor making decisions. Of course, this is a simplifying assumption. Prosecutors can work as teams with other prosecutors and support staff. Prosecution decisions can be made in conjunction with a more senior member of the prosecutor's office, or within an organizational structure with policies and rules governing decision-making, although some research suggests much of it occurs in a vacuum, without adequate knowledge of how other prosecutors are proceeding (Wright, 2017). Again, I have built the foundation with P as a single decision-maker, but the framework, once established, can be expanded to separate the various decision-makers.

Hence, at the core of the plea bargaining process is the interaction between D and P. This interaction is nested within a social, economic, and political system that involves additional actors who contribute to and, at times, directly intervene in the process. Law enforcement makes investigatory investments. Forensic specialists, experts, and witnesses provide information. Judges have the ability to contribute directly in the negotiations or indirectly through "veto" power and sentencing. Parole boards, legislative bodies, and bureaucratic committees such as sentencing commissions all lurk in the background potentially influencing this bilateral interaction. All of these additional individuals will be treated as part of the institutional environment within which the two main actors, D and P, are interacting. With this framework, the ways in which institutional factors affect the guilty plea can be examined.

I first consider a dichotomous decision: whether to accept a plea bargain or refuse it and take a case to trial. Of course, in reality the action space is substantially richer. Again, the insights from a simple model can be extended later to more robust decision problems. The "action" is denoted as a_d for D's choice and a_p for P's choice.[1] Consequently, $a_i = B$ is the action of accepting a plea bargain (where the subscript i denotes the actor, either $i = D$ or $i = P$). Also, $a_i = T$ is the action of going to trial.

Since the presumed default outcome of an unsuccessful plea bargaining process is a jury trial, we can assume that if either actor opts for trial, then a jury trial occurs. A plea bargain arises if, and only if, both actors opt for the plea bargain.[2]

The third component to a rational actor model is to define the individual's objectives. Among the numerous things the individual may care about, the sanction that arises at trial and the sanction that comes out of the plea bargaining process can be expected to be at the top of the list of concerns (Bibas, 2004). We can denote s and b as these outcomes, respectively. It may be convenient to think of both as prison sentences, using a common unit of measurement such as months, but this is not necessary. All that is assumed is that greater values of s and b represent more severe outcomes for D.[3]

---

1 For readers familiar with game theory, I avoid the term *strategy* and instead use *action*. A strategy implies a full-contingency plan of an actor within a game; a strategy defines the choice to be made in every situation that may arise. Plea bargaining could involve offers and counteroffers over time as evidence becomes available. Therefore, the potentially complex strategies to be employed are condensed to the simplified action of going to trial or accepting a guilty plea.

2 Since the focus of this chapter is on prosecutors, I do not extend the framework to the distinction between bench and jury trials, along with judge versus jury sentencing. See Lundberg (2016) for a theoretical model attempting to do so.

3 Thus, the assumption is that all possible outcomes can be ordered, or, rather, D's preferences are complete and transitive. If given any two options, D can compare them, picking the one he or she prefers (i.e., completeness) and when bringing

The two actors have preferences over the outcomes. For example, it may be a reasonable assumption that *D* prefers *s* and *b* to be as small as possible with values of 0 being best. The utility received need not be linear. For example, being able to get *P* to agree to one less month of incarceration may be more valuable on a 4-month sentence than a 40-year sentence. Consequently, let $u_d(b)$ and $u_d(s)$ denote the utility received by *D* when receiving a plea bargain sanction of *b* and a trial sanction of *s*, respectively. The function u_d maps the sanction to the utility derived from that sanction. Similarly, *P* has preferences over the case outcomes. Let $u_p(b)$ and $u_p(s)$ denote the utility received by *P* when agreeing to a plea bargain sanction of *b* and a trial sentence of *s*, respectively.

A second, crucial element of the plea bargaining process is cost. One of the primary arguments in favor of plea bargaining is that jury trials are costly (Landes, 1971). A jury trial uses public resources (e.g., judge's and other personnel's salary), takes up the time of the jury members, creates additional legal fees for the defense (or takes up the time of the public defender that could have been devoted to other cases), and creates opportunity costs to the prosecutor (again, through lost time that could have been devoted to other cases; see Landes [1971] for an early, seminal contribution to the role of plea bargaining as a resource conservation tool).

Therefore, let c_p and c_d denote the costs incurred by *P* and *D*, respectively, when the case goes to trial. For simplicity, assume plea bargaining has a zero cost. Of course, pretrial deliberations are costly for both parties and the costs have been shown to affect outcomes systematically (see Stevenson [2016] for a recent example of the effect of pretrial detention). What is important is that going to trial is more costly for both parties. Therefore, one can interpret c_p and c_d as the additional cost of trial.

A third, crucial component to plea bargaining is uncertainty. Outcomes of jury trials are difficult to predict accurately. While the trial process may act to clarify some of the uncertainty to a degree (Bjerk, 2007), the decision-making of the jury can still be expected to experience occasional errors (i.e., incorrect convictions and erroneous acquittals). A guilty plea, while not able to guarantee an absence of errors (see Chapter 7, this volume, for a discussion of innocents pleading guilty), mitigates the uncertainty inherent in jury trials. It does not necessarily eliminate it, as judicial sentencing, parole decisions, and appellate court choices can still influence actual time served. In fact, as initially articulated by Grossman and Katz (1983) and further explored by Bjerk (2008), with risk-averse defendants, plea bargaining can take on an insurance role, as it provides a relatively more certain outcome that risk-averse individuals are willing to "pay" a premium for.

together multiple binary comparisons, the logical chain of transitivity is satisfied (i.e., if Option A is preferred to Option B, and Option B is preferred to Option C, then it must be that Option A is preferred to Option C).

Consequently, let p_d and p_p be the probability the sanction s arises in the jury trial as assessed by D and P, respectively. As with any probability in a discrete environment, p_d and p_p must be between zero and 1 and I assume this to be the case. A value of p_i equal to 1 (zero) means that a conviction (acquittal) is certain. Assume the outcome of plea bargaining is certain, or for an alternative interpretation, p_i denotes the difference in the certainty between the two actions.

To begin with, I will focus on three important components to the outcome of the interaction that D and P care about. There are more, but for the time being, I will first consider these three; a researcher who wants to build additional considerations into the objective function of either party should be able to easily add them to this foundational framework.

Given this environment, a behavioral assumption must be imposed. As is common in economics and political science, *rationality* is assumed. While controversial, the definition of rationality used here is quite narrow. Rationality in such an environment means that the actor chooses an action that maximizes its payoff given the knowledge, beliefs, and preferences it holds. Preferences may be abnormal, knowledge may be imperfect, and beliefs may be biased,[4] but taking them as given, the individual acts to select the action that maximizes his or her payoff. In decision-making under an uncertainty context, the actor is assumed to maximize the expected payoff.[5]

Therefore, the payoff D receives from accepting a plea bargain offer, $\pi_d(B)$, is

$$\pi_d(B) = u_d(b). \tag{1}$$

Alternatively, the payoff D receives from going to trial is either $\pi_d(T \mid \text{conviction}) = u_d(s) - c_d$ if convicted or $\pi_d(T \mid \text{acquittal}) = u_d(0) - c_d$. As a consequence, the expected payoff is

$$E\pi_d(T) = p_d u_d(s) + (1 - p_d) u_d(0) - c_d. \tag{2}$$

---

[4] Hence, rationality defined here should be distinguished from the concept of rational expectations. In differing contexts, rational expectations has various operationalizations, but a common element is that beliefs need to be properly updated to the information received (according to Bayes' rule, for example). Much of the discussion to follow will explore divergent beliefs, including those violating rational expectations. Rationality, here, requires optimization given the beliefs and does not impose rational formation of beliefs.

[5] It is common in rational actor models to use the terms *utility* and *payoff* interchangeably. Here, for convenience, *utility* is used to describe the benefit or loss, depending on the actor, from the sanction. The payoff aggregates this utility with the disutility associated with the costs.

On the other hand, for P, the payoff received from accepting a guilty plea is

$$\pi_p(B) = u_p(b), \tag{3}$$

and the expected payoff to going to trial is

$$E\pi_p(T) = p_p u_p(s) + (1 - p_p) u_p(0) - c_p. \tag{4}$$

Consequently, applying the behavioral assumption of rationality, an actor will prefer to plea bargain when $\pi_i(B) > E\pi_i(T)$. With this setup established, I will explore the role of the prosecutor in plea bargaining and the related literature by exploring and exploiting this framework.

The Conundrum of Trials

The law and economics field has focused attention on one perplexing result: trials should not occur (e.g., Landes, 1971). To see this conundrum, let's first suppose that both actors (i) care only about the resulting sentence and (ii) have rational expectations regarding the outcome of the jury trial. An unexpected outcome arises in this environment.

While I explore alternatives to (i) in the following section, a common assumption is that D's utility is strictly decreasing in the sanction obtained, $u_d(x) = -x$, and P's utility is strictly increasing in the sanction obtained, $u_p(x) = x$. These assumptions can be justified. Regarding D, once the case has made it to the jury trial stage, it seems reasonable to presume the defendant is willing to take whichever action reduces the number of months in prison. It is more controversial with respect to the assumption on P's preferences, since one can interpret it as assuming that the prosecutor's goal is to maximize sentence length. If one argues that case screening has already occurred, so that questionable cases (from the prosecutor's perspective) have been dismissed, then the assumption may be a correct one. If, additionally, we consider that the decision problem is limited to only three outcomes s, b, and 0, it is more reasonable to assume that, given all of the uncertainties and imperfections present, P simply believes the s is a more appropriate outcome than b, and that b is more appropriate than 0. For example, if P believes that the sentencing guidelines reflect societal preferences with sufficient accuracy, then, as a public servant, obtaining a sentence closer to those outlined in the guidelines is preferred.

Regarding (ii), one can argue that both parties form expectations regarding the same event, using relatively the same information, employing professionals with legal knowledge and experience. Rulings such as *Brady v. Maryland* (1963), in which the Supreme Court held that the prosecution must *at least* turn over any exculpatory evidence to the defense team, contribute to a common appreciation of the facts of the case. If parties are incentivized to share information in the hopes of resolving uncertainty and mitigating the possibility of the costly trial, then these two parties, forming expectations based on the same evidence, should be able to form similar assessments regarding the potential outcome of the trial. Therefore, a common assumption is that $p_p = p_p = p$.

These two assumptions have been commonly used not just in law and economics but also in criminology, where they have also been debated (Bushway & Redlich, 2012). For example, Bushway, Redlich, and Norris (2014) designed an experimental test using actual judges, prosecutors, and public defenders as research subjects to investigate what type of information these actors use and what expectations they have regarding the outcome to assess whether a "bargaining in the shadow of the trial" framework is appropriate (see Chapter 2, this volume, for more detail about this framework).

Applying these two arguments to the rational choice framework identified, *D* prefers to plea bargain when the expression in (1) is greater than (2). This arises when $-b \geq -ps - c_d$, or rather, when

$$b < ps + c_d. \tag{5}$$

Alternatively, *P* prefers to plea bargain when the expression in (3) is greater than (4). This occurs when $b > ps - c_p$, or rather,

$$b > ps - c_p. \tag{6}$$

Since costs exist, both inequalities hold. That is, there exist plea bargains, *b*, such that the plea bargaining process always finds at least one mutually agreeable outcome. In other words, bargaining should be successful and trials should not exist. The ability to resolve a dispute via pretrial negotiations exists regardless of the stakes (e.g., time of incarceration), type of crime (e.g., felony versus misdemeanor), and costs involved (low-cost versus high-cost legal representation).

There is a counterintuitive irony to the result. If both parties form similar expectations, even if they are highly inaccurate assessments, trials should not arise. The question is not, then, why is plea bargaining so prevalent but, rather, why are trials as frequent as they are?

The framework developed can provide a guide to answering this question and specifically focus on how prosecutors contribute to the frequency of trials. Continuing, for simplicity, with the assumption that $u_d(x) = -x$ and $u_p(x) = x$, *D* prefers the plea bargain when $b \leq p_d s + c_d$ and *P* prefers the plea bargain when $b \geq p_p s - c_p$. If the right-hand side of the former is less than the right-hand side of the latter, then there will not exist any value of *b* that satisfies the two inequalities. Therefore, if $p_d s + c_d < p_p s - c_p$, which simplifies to

$$(p_p - p_d)s > c_p + c_d, \tag{7}$$

then jury trials arise. From this expression, it becomes clear that the source of plea bargaining failures is the divergence in expectations between the two parties regarding the potential outcome if the case went to trial, $p_p - p_d$.

Second, predictions regarding the factors that influence the rate of plea bargaining become apparent. A plea bargain is more likely to arise when at least one of the following conditions arise:

(1) Expectations are similar.
(2) Stakes are lower.
(3) Trial costs are higher.

Prosecutors and Expectations

How can expectations between prosecutors and defendants diverge? One simple answer is inaccuracies. Optimism bias, amateurism, and irrationality can be the culprits. Optimism bias can be expected to manifest itself (Chortek, 2013) and can then contribute to plea bargaining's failure. Optimism bias in this framework is defined as arising when *D*'s anticipated probability of conviction at trial is less than the "true" probability, $p_d < p$, and when P's expectations exceed this level, $p_p > p$. One may expect, for example, that a neophyte prosecutor would be more susceptible to this bias than an experienced attorney. Farmer and Pecorino (2002) investigated the role of self-serving bias in plea bargaining and reached the conclusion that an increase in self-serving bias on either the part of the defendant or the prosecutor will increase the likelihood of a case proceeding to trial.

There is reason to believe that professional representation may correct for inaccurate expectations (Bibas, 2004; see Chapter 3 for a more detailed discussion of the impact and import of the defense attorney). Since accused criminals almost always have legal defense, evidence from other types of legal disputes is needed. Farmer and Tiefenthaler (2001) considered divorce disputes. They provided evidence that the primary determinant on how well a woman does in the asset-division problem is her use of an attorney. Professional representation mitigates continued legal disputes.

In a seminal contribution to the impact of divergent beliefs within bargaining in the legal system, Priest and Klein (1984) developed a theoretical model to understand the selection mechanism by which which disputes find their way to trial. In their framework, each side to the dispute observes the true probability (whether it is a conviction at a criminal trial or a ruling favoring the plaintiff in a civil lawsuit), p, with an error term. Hence, $p_d = p + \varepsilon_d$ and $p_p = p + \varepsilon_p$. The error terms ε_d and ε_p are drawn from distribution functions with means of zero, so that, on average, disputants are correct (i.e., there is no systematic bias), but the noise can either overassess or underassess *D*'s probability of winning at trial. In this framework, a negotiation can fail if the randomly arising error parameters are large. The insight of their framework is that the divergence that arises due to noise in expectations is magnified for those cases with p near ½. The logic is straightforward. If the evidence overwhelmingly favors guilt, then the dispute is far from the threshold required for a jury to convict, and it is unlikely that the noise of the assessments will include acquittal as a reasonable possibility. Thus, cases with strong evidence favoring guilt will be settled. Similarly, for cases where the evidence is extremely weak, the noise associated with divergent expectations needs to be substantial to reach the point that one party believes a jury trial conviction is reasonable. Thus, again, a mutually agreeable settlement arises (which may very well be the dismissal of charges). Under this model, it is only those cases with moderate evidence and an uncertain outcome that proceed to trial.

Since jury trials are socially inefficient and costly, then P has the incentive to mitigate erroneous beliefs. This is especially true with false negatives—wrongful acquittals. It is reasonable to presume that the prosecutor wants to convict culpable individuals, not wanting to see a guilty individual escape punishment. The dilemma arises with regard to false positives—innocent individuals being punished. Whether the prosecutor has the incentive to mitigate these concerns is unclear. While "justice" is a noble objective, one can be worried that obtaining prosecutions is an objective, even if it increases error rates (McCannon, 2013). Numerous court cases have dealt with prosecutors unwilling to share exculpatory evidence, centered on the landmark Supreme Court case *Brady v Maryland* (1963) mentioned previously. Therefore, whether the prosecutor chooses to take actions, such as sharing information, to mitigate divergent beliefs depends crucially on his or her objective function, explored in further detail in the upcoming section.

A limitation of the divergent-beliefs literature is that it relies on either mistakes (e.g., Priest & Klein, 1984) or optimism (e.g., Burke, 2007). In other words, it relies on a breakdown in rational expectations. Therefore, a related literature has investigated theoretical environments where structural/institutional limitations lead to divergence in beliefs that can cause the bargaining process to fail.

Building off of early theoretical contributions (Baker & Mezzetti, 2001; Reinganum, 1988), plea bargaining's failure is treated like other market failures. A common cause for imperfections is asymmetric information. Just as informational limitations may cause imperfections in labor markets or corporate governance, as two examples, it can also affect the prosecutor's ability to successfully negotiate a guilty plea. There are many dimensions to the plea bargaining environment, such as the quality of the evidence, the willingness to negotiate, and extralegal factors. It is quite common for one party to have relevant information the other side does not have.

To keep the analysis simple, suppose there are two "states of the world." In one circumstance the probability of conviction is high, which I will denote as p^1, and in the other situation it is low, p^2 ($<p^1$). Many applications can arise. Parties could have asymmetric information on the availability and quality of some evidence (Reinganum, 1988), the willingness of the prosecutor to bargain, or the defendant's willingness to negotiate as impacted by, for example, risk aversion (Farmer & Pecorino, 1994). The asymmetry is modeled here to affect the probability of conviction, but the model can be easily augmented to

have uncertainty in the sanction (e.g., judge sentencing preferences or parole board choices) or costs.

Suppose *P* knows the true conviction probability, but *D* only has imperfect beliefs, p_d. If *P* offers a plea bargain equal to the expected sanctions at trial, then trials would not arise.

What would stop a prosecutor, interested in getting a stiffer sanction, from offering $b^1 = p^1 s$ (the larger sanction) to *D* when the true conviction probability is only p^2? *P* could take advantage of his or her informational superiority and extract a more severe punishment when, for example, there is actually only weak evidence of guilt. *D* always accepting an offer of b^1 (or rather, using the terminology of game theory, accepting an offer as a pure strategy) is not an equilibrium best response. Consequently, the settlement rate drops below 100% and, hence, plea bargaining fails.[6]

Therefore, jury trials can arise without the need to assume irrationality in the actors. The distinction between the two environments is important for evaluating prosecutorial conduct. Under divergent beliefs, the prosecutor may act to mitigate the divergence or intentionally choose not to (see Farmer & Pecorino, 2013, for an investigation of the incentive of parties to disclose information in a legal dispute). In an asymmetric information environment, the prosecutor seeks institutional solutions to facilitate screening. Importantly, then, policy that alters criminal justice institutions can spill over onto the plea bargaining process.

The asymmetric-information environment can be reversed to consider the situation where *D* has private information. For example, Reinganum (2000) considered the situation of plea bargaining when the defendant knows the severity of the offense and can make plea bargaining offers. Her objective was to evaluate how sentencing guidelines affect the prosecutor's willingness to avoid trial. In this case, *P* must assess how *D*'s decisions convey (or signal) information about the underlying guilt. Similarly, Baker and Mezzetti (2001) included a resource allocation decision (i.e., how much to spend on prosecution) to an environment where *D* is privately informed of guilt or innocence.[7]

Finally, Daughety and Reinganum (2016) considered an alternative dimension to asymmetric information that can affect the prosecutor's plea bargaining behavior. They considered an environment where "outside," nonstrategic observers can impose sanctions on either *P* or *D*. One can think of

---

6 In Bayesian game theoretic models, it is common for *P*'s offer to involve a mixed strategy in which a probability distribution over a set of offers is chosen. Alternatively, if *D* is the informed party, his or her acceptance strategy involves agreeing to a plea bargain with a probability between zero and 1.

7 Farmer and Pecorino (2010) extended this general framework to contrast the unilateral payoff relevance and bilateral payoff relevance of asymmetric information. A fascinating and troubling issue here is that an innocent defendant can rationally enter a guilty plea when the informational constraints lead it to being the wise decision. See Chapter 7, this volume, for a discussion of this problem.

these observers as those who care about criminals being adequately punished and innocent individuals not being harmed. Daughety and Reinganum (2016) have argued that a prosecutor being viewed as "soft on crime" or "not up to the task" can affect the prosecutor's career via lost appointments, re-elections, or lost opportunities in private law firms. By taking actions, such as being more zealous in his or her prosecution decisions, *P* can influence society's beliefs, which cycles back and influences *P*'s expected payoffs to taking a case to trial.

Prosecutors and Stakes

The rational choice model predicts that plea bargaining should be more prevalent when the stakes are lower, and this conforms to the data that exist. For example, Yan and Bushway (2017) evaluated plea bargaining in New York State and found that murder, clearly a serious crime, makes up approximately 13% of the sample of jury trial convictions but only 1% of plea bargains. At another extreme, drug possession makes up only 5% of jury convictions but 12% of plea bargains. In fact, using the data presented, Figure 4.1 maps out the sample distributions across the five crime levels, with Class A felonies being the most severe and Class E felonies being the least.

As one can see, as the crimes decrease in seriousness, the proportion of guilty pleas that fall within that class increases, while the proportion of jury trial convictions decreases. This is consistent with the predictions derived from (7).

How can prosecutors influence the stakes? One obvious way is to recommend a lower sanction. Typically, in a jurisdiction with sentencing guidelines a judge has a range of potential sentences to pick from. It is even possible to deviate from the guidelines, and jurisdictions differ in terms of how "costly" these deviations are. Regardless, there is a range of potential sanctions that can

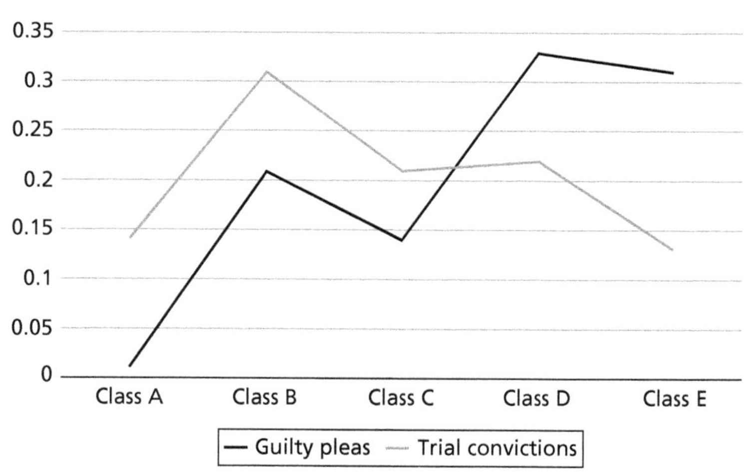

Figure 4.1 Proportion of the samples falling with each crime class.
Source: Table 2, Yan and Bushway (2017).

be made. A prosecutor may negotiate with the defense where the agreement requires the prosecutor to make a sentencing recommendation for the judge to choose the lowest sentence within the guidelines, for example. This is the practice known as *sentence bargaining* (Bibas, 2004).

Alternatively, the prosecutor can adjust the charges. If, for example, first-degree assault is downgraded to second-degree assault, then, even without changes in the expectations of conviction, the lower stakes should increase the chance that the defendant is willing to enter a guilty plea. This refiling to a lesser offense as part of a negotiated agreement is known as *charge bargaining* (Bibas, 2004). Empirical investigations have documented the prevalence of this form of plea bargaining and noted that the impact of charge bargaining varies. In comparing a state with presumptive sentencing guidelines to one with voluntary guidelines, Piehl and Bushway (2007) provided evidence that the impact of charge bargaining on sentences is greater in the former, which is consistent with differences in prosecutorial power in the two jurisdiction types (see Chapter 8, this volume, for further discussion of charging practices and sentence disparities).

In another practice prosecutors are accused of, known as *charge stacking* or *overcharging* (Caldwell, 2011), the prosecutor adds charges so as to increase the expected disutility of going to trial. When negotiating, the prosecutor can remove the additional charge, lowering the stakes and encouraging a guilty plea. Fully incorporating this practice into the rational choice model in a convincing manner is difficult, though. The presumption of the model is that s can be lowered without affecting the probability of conviction or, more accurately, affecting the divergence in the beliefs about the likelihood of being convicted at trial. If a second count is added, and both D and P know there is only a very low probability of a jury actually convicting D of the new charge, then the prevalence of plea bargaining is unaffected.

These are two obvious ways for a prosecutor to affect the stakes. They have taken the variable s as literally the sentence handed down by the judge. The interpretation of s can be expanded to consider alternatives. For example, from D's perspective s is anything that lowers his or her utility. A prominent example of harm that can influence the disutility from conviction comes from the collateral consequences attached to that conviction (Olivares, Burton, & Cullen, 1996; Chapter 9, this volume). *Collateral consequences* is a broad name capturing losses the defendant can incur just by being convicted of a felony. For example, in some states voting rights are lost. In other states, access to welfare services is affected. Frequently, individuals must disclose whether they have a felony conviction on a job application. States vary in the number of collateral consequences that arise (see https://niccc.csgjusticecenter.org), but such consequences can certainly be considered as additional sanctions. If charge bargaining can also have the impact of reducing collateral consequences (e.g., moving from a low-level felony to a misdemeanor), then the impact on the willingness to plea bargain can be substantial. This is just one example of sanctions other than incarceration that could influence the plea bargaining process and can be manipulated by the prosecutor.

On the other side of the bargaining table is the prosecutor's payoff. Again, the variable s generically captures the benefits received from obtaining the conviction at trial. While putting the "criminal behind bars" is a reasonable goal of someone who has made a career of prosecuting accused criminals, other considerations may affect this decision.

Prominent among these extralegal factors is career concerns. Salary, promotions, and external labor market opportunities should be expected to affect a prosecutor as it would affect an individual in any other line of work. The field of public choice, which sits at the intersection of economics and political science, focuses on considering the objectives of those in law-making and bureaucratic positions to appreciate the public sector, rather than make naïve assumptions about benevolent public servants. As outlined later, a growing literature has begun to document how these public choice considerations spill over into the outcomes of the criminal justice system.

The institutional environment within which the prosecutor is operating becomes, then, crucial as it provides the incentive structure. Sharp distinctions arise between the federal court system and the state courts as the selection and retention mechanisms differ. In 46 states, local prosecutor offices are led by chief prosecutors who are selected by popular election using plurality voting (Wright, 2009).[8] Voters, then, serve as the primary accountability mechanism for these prosecutors. How might voters influence prosecutor's choices when engaged in plea bargaining?

Gordon and Huber (2002) provided the first analysis related to this question. One can think of two distinct resource-allocation problems to be made within a prosecutor's office. In one dimension, number (and identity) of staff can be shifted among the various cases to be processed. Additionally, the effort exerted by the prosecutors on the cases they handle needs to be incentivized—often referred to as the *principal-agent problem*. These are two classic dimensions to any labor management application. Gordon and Huber focused on the problem of encouraging effort. Exerting time and effort is costly; therefore, absent external incentives, lower levels of effort will be preferred by the prosecutor. They argued that by rewarding incumbent prosecutors who obtain convictions with retention incentives, the investments are incentivized. At the plea bargaining table, then, the benefit to the trial court conviction, s, is composed of two distinct components: the utility derived from the actual sanction, s^*, and the extralegal benefit of improving the incumbent's chances of being re-elected, r. Hence,

$$s = s^* + r. \tag{8}$$

[8] If only two individuals run for an office, plurality voting is equivalent to majority voting. When three or more candidates run for election, plurality voting installs the individual who receive the most votes, which may not necessarily constitute a majority.

If voters' attention is concentrated in the period immediately preceding re-election, then *s* is greater during the re-election season than outside of it. As a consequence of the rational choice model developed, plea bargaining should be less prevalent.

A similar framework was developed by Bandyopadhyay and McCannon (2013, 2014, 2015). The distinction is that in their work, rather than thinking of the prosecutor as trying to avoid exerting effort, they built a framework of asymmetric information. The fundamental problem voters are trying to solve is to identify the skills and abilities of the candidates. These authors argued that it is reasonable to presume that some individuals are higher-quality prosecutors who have the intelligence, education, and experience to do the job better than others. Voters benefit from having high-quality individuals in the public position, as such a person can, for example, secure convictions of the guilty, more accurately screen out the innocent, and properly manage public finances, as a few examples. Voters are imperfectly informed on the quality of the incumbent but can use outcomes of court cases as signals of the underlying skill.

These signals could be quite imprecise, and the incumbent could distort these signals by choosing how to proceed with the prosecution of a case, thereby masking the difference between high- and low-quality prosecutors. In another study by Bandyopadhyay and McCannon (2015), the issue of how voters take in signals from case outcomes was explored. Voters could, for example, expect a good prosecutor to be able to win a high percentage of the cases taken to trial (i.e., have a high "batting average") and/or voters may expect a high-quality prosecutor be able to obtain longer sentences. The authors explored these alternatives and showed in a Bayesian game theoretical model that distortions to the prosecution decisions can be expected, but the direction of the distortion depends crucially on how voters choose to evaluate the output of the prosecutor's office. If voters focus on the conviction rate, then, theoretically, low-quality prosecutors could pull back the number of cases taken to trial, only prosecuting the more certain cases, to mimic what a high-quality prosecutor could obtain. Alternatively, to distinguish herself, a high-quality prosecutor could further pull back the number of cases taken to trial to make it impossible for a low-quality person to mimic the extremely high conviction rate. Regardless of which equilibria arise in practice, prosecutor elections should coincide with increases in plea bargaining and reductions in trials. Alternatively, Bandyopadhyay and McCannon (2015) found that if voters focus on convictions *and* sentences, the opposite predictions are made: The margin reduces so that more cases are taken to trial to avoid the plea discount needed to facilitate a guilty plea. Again, this can arise either by a low-quality incumbent attempting to mimic, or a high-quality prosecutor trying to differentiate herself. Bandyopadhyay and McCannon (2013) showed theoretically that even if it is socially optimal for every case to be plea bargained, the potential for elections to distort plea bargaining exists.

The question becomes whether plea bargaining a case during the re-election season improves s (or rather, $r > 0$) or lowers s ($r < 0$). To address this question, Bandyopadhyay and McCannon (2014) considered a panel data set of prosecution outcomes across the prosecutorial districts in North Carolina. They documented that the proportion of convictions that arise from jury trials increases when the incumbent prosecutor is running for re-election, and there is a further escalation in the trial rate when the incumbent is challenged. Alternatively, in districts where incumbents do not face contested elections, plea bargaining is substantially more prevalent. These results are consistent with the framework that obtaining a jury trial conviction during the election season provides an additional bump to the prosecutor's payoff, adjusting the plea bargaining decision-making for *P*.

Whether driven by costly effort or asymmetric information, decision-making by state-level prosecutors has been shown to vary in a predictable way with the election cycle. While the focus here is on plea bargains, these career concerns have spillover effects. For example, in one study I (McCannon, 2013) asked whether the decisions made are accurate. Of course, accuracy is difficult to assess. Taking a modest approach, I measured an outcome as inaccurate if an appellate court, reviewing an appealed conviction, decided to either modify the sentence or reverse the conviction. Using data on appeals of felony convictions in New York State, I connected the original case to the incumbent prosecutor's election cycle. I documented that appeals of felony convictions are much more likely to be successful if the original conviction occurred during the 6-month period prior to the prosecutor's re-election. Therefore, not only is the prosecution decision more zealous, but potentially more inaccurate.

The stakes can include other career-related concerns. For example, Boylan (2004) has provided evidence that U.S. attorneys' salaries affect turnover decisions. When salary is higher, relative to private labor markets for attorneys, a U.S. attorney is less likely to depart from his or her job. Boylan (2004) also provided evidence that experience correlates with a number of important output variables. The more years of experience a U.S. attorney has, the higher the conviction rate, the more prison months that are obtained, and the higher the plea bargaining rate.

In a complementary study, Boylan (2005) investigated the subsequent careers of U.S. attorneys after they leave their position. Convictions, measured as prison months obtained, was strongly correlated with becoming a federal judge, but conviction rates and number of indictments were not. A similar finding arose when considering the likelihood a U.S. attorney becoming a partner in a large law firm.

Similar evidence arises with assistant U.S. attorneys. Boylan and Long (2005) presented evidence that a case is more likely to be taken to trial by an assistant U.S. attorney when private market salaries are higher. They argued that this is consistent with prosecutors using jury trials to gain experience that is valuable in the private sector. Therefore, as illustrated in each of these studies, future employment opportunities increase the benefit of getting the conviction, *r*.

Prosecutors and Costs

The trial condition provided in (8) also suggests that costs affect the plea bargaining rate. Unlike beliefs, it is the aggregate costs that matter. That is, both the costs incurred by *P* and *D* influence plea bargaining.

It is common to interpret c_p and c_d as the monetary costs, such as legal expenditures. In an economic model, though, the costs capture any factor that lowers the utility of the decision-maker. Therefore, non-monetary disutility is included. An important example is opportunity costs. A cost to making a decision to pursue X is that Y must be given up. For the prosecutor on an annual salary, this means giving up time and effort for other cases. Alternatively, public choice considerations may mean that devoting more time and effort on a case comes at the expense of personal leisure and free time.

Landes (1971) provided the first analysis of prosecutors' cost management and plea bargaining. If a chief prosecutor is facing a binding budget constraint, then plea bargaining a case provides an additional benefit of allowing the office's resources to be redeployed to another case. Presumably, then, there is an interrelationship between *P*'s costs for one case, c_p, and the benefits received on a different case. If the evidence is cut and dried so that similar expectations form, then there is a benefit to the prosecutor by being able to shift resources to another case where the time, effort, and manpower can have a larger marginal impact.

In an important contribution to the role of cost in prosecutor decision-making, Rasmusen, Raghav, and Ramseyer (2009) built a theoretical model considering a resource-constrained prosecutor. *P* has two margins to influence: the *extensive margin*—how many cases to pursue a conviction with, and the *intensive margin*—how much to expend on the prosecution of those pursued. The focus of their analysis was to appreciate how expanding the prosecutor office's resources affects the prosecution decisions. Importantly, they contrasted the environment where *P* is interested in pursuing societal welfare with a public choice environment where *P* also gains from the unused resources, which would include reduced workloads. Analyzing a cross-sectional data set of local prosecutor offices in the United States, Rasmusen et al. provided evidence that increased funding expands both margins.

A similar investigation was conducted by Detotto and McCannon (2017a, 2017b). These authors evaluated the prosecutorial production function—that is, the deployment of the prosecutor's office resources (e.g., support staff, investigators, and assistant prosecutors) as inputs into the "production" of outcomes (e.g., number of jury trials, cases disposed, and convictions obtained). Using a programming method known as data envelopment analysis, first applied by Gorman and Ruggiero (2009), Detotto and McCannon estimated the productive efficiency of prosecutor offices. In other words, they analyzed how the costs are allocated within an office. In the first study (Detotto & McCannon, 2017a), variation in the quality of the prosecution's efficiency across states was considered, and it was shown that states with higher average efficiency are also states that have more effective policies (both fiscal and regulatory) in areas outside of criminal justice.[9]

In the subsequent study (Detotto & McCannon, 2017b), the consolidation of prosecutor offices was evaluated. While it is common for local prosecutor offices to be a county-level office, in 23 states counties are merged into larger prosecutorial districts. For example, the 100 counties in North Carolina are organized into 43 prosecutorial districts. Detotto and McCannon showed that prosecutorial efficiency is higher in those areas of the country that have consolidated prosecutor offices than in comparable counties, and provided evidence that the improved efficiency is not due to a change in plea bargaining rates but rather to a more effective use of office resources, allowing for more to be accomplished with fewer inputs. Thus, there is a "returns to scale" being taken advantage of, where more "output" is achieved with only modest increases in the use of "inputs." Additionally, Detotto and McCannon provided evidence that the returns to scale identified accompanied increased use of investigator services. Consolidated offices were more likely to have the budget to hire investigators. Therefore, the improved cost management could potentially come with improved accuracy as additional investigative investments should improve distinguishing the innocent from the guilty.

The Role of the Prosecutor on the Plea Discount

The previous discussion addressed the issue of how many cases will be resolved via plea bargaining, or the "quantity" of plea bargaining. The complementary dimension to a negotiation to be considered, then, is the "price" paid. Since the plea bargaining process negotiates for administered sanctions (either directly through sentence bargaining or indirectly through charge bargaining), I now turn to discuss the role the prosecutor plays in driving the value of b (the plea bargain) in the model presented.

Returning to the theoretical model developed, rather than treat b as a fixed parameter, suppose it is variable, determined by a negotiation. An agreement of b is mutually agreeable when both (5) and (6) are satisfied. Consequently, when the trial condition presented in (8) fails to hold, there exists a range of

---

[9] Specifically, they used the Economic Freedom of North American Index, produced by the Fraser Institute, which measures regulations (e.g., labor market restrictions), taxation (e.g., income, sales, and property tax levels), and government spending (e.g., debt).

possible negotiated pleas that are mutually agreeable. Using (5) and (6), any value of b within

$$[p_p u_p(s) - c_p, p_d u_d(s) + c_d] \tag{9}$$

can potentially arise. This range is commonly referred to as the *bargaining zone* (Loewenstein & Moore, 2004).

A common simplification in the literature is that bargaining in the shadow of the trial should lead to $b = ps$ (Bushway et al., 2014). Even from this simple framework, it is clear that a number of additional assumptions are made to reach this prediction. First, costs must be driven to zero (or made equal to one another) and the preferences of P and D must be linear. Furthermore, importantly, assumptions regarding the bargaining mechanism must be made.

First, regarding the bargaining mechanism, it is not necessarily clear what assumption is best. For example, suppose we consider a framework where P makes a take-it-or-leave-it offer to D. In this case, there is little reason for P to offer anything other than

$$b = p_p u_p(s) - c_p, \tag{10}$$

the lower bound of the bargaining zone. Nobel laureate Thomas Schelling wrote extensively on bargaining tactics. His work was focused on international negotiations, conflict, and nuclear war. In his seminal contribution, *The Strategy of Conflict* (1960), he refers to this bargaining tactic as *final offer bargaining*, emphasizing that one "wins" at a negotiation if one is able to convince the other side that the current offer on the table is the best he or she will receive and that one is willing to walk away if it is not accepted. And, in fact, this is not an uncommon scenario in plea bargaining. Consider the use of *time-limited* or *exploding offers* by prosecutors (Caldwell, 2011; Gross, 2015); these are plea deals that supposedly expire within a short window of time, pressuring the defendant to accept it quickly, and insinuating that rejection will lead to a trial. Additionally, research with the District Attorney of New York offices shows that here prosecutors operate by a "first best" approach, explicitly stating that any future plea offers will not be as beneficial to D as the first offer (Kutateladze, Andiloro, & Johnson, 2016). Adopting this tactic at the plea bargaining table, then, one would expect the plea bargain to be driven by D's expected payoff if going to trial. Therefore, the prosecutor's ability to influence D's perceptions of a jury trial conviction, the disutility associated with the trial sanction, and D's cost to going to trial drive the negotiated sanction.

An alternative, popular bargaining mechanism to employ is the Nash bargaining solution (Nash, 1950). Nobel laureate John Nash proposed a solution concept to be applied to any negotiation. Nash famously proved that there is a unique outcome that satisfies a number of desirable properties. In his solution, the default outcomes are of upmost importance to predicting the outcome of the bargaining process. The gap between the minimum sanction that P will accept and the maximum sanction that D will accept rather than go to trial is the "gains from trade" to be divided. The Nash bargaining solution is to divide equally these gains. In the plea bargaining environment considered, the gains from trade is the "length" of the bargaining zone and, therefore, the equilibrium is its midpoint. Rather,

$$[p_p u_p(s) + p_d u_d(s) + c_d - c_p]/2 \tag{11}$$

Therefore, for example, the bargaining in the shadow-of-trial framework arises if (i) the Nash bargaining solution is applied, (ii) trial costs are the same for P and D, and (iii) utility is linear and strictly increasing (decreasing) for P (D). With these three assumptions, $b = ps$.

The important difference between these two bargaining mechanisms is whether the plea bargain is driven by only D's preferences for going to trial or by a combination of D's and P's preferences for going to trial.

But how can the prosecutor influence the plea bargaining outcome? Interestingly, it follows from (11) that the same factors that influence the prevalence of plea bargaining affect the plea discount: expectations of conviction, utility when a conviction arises, and the costs of going to trial.

While bargaining failure is driven by the divergence in expectations, the outcome when plea bargaining is successful is driven by the size of the expectations. Any action the prosecutor can take to increase p_d should lead to a greater sanction. This then justifies the concern that the prosecutor is motivated to present evidence supporting conviction, but may not necessarily be motivated to share information that lowers the assessment of a jury trial conviction, as it reduces D's willingness to accept a plea and, consequently, increases the plea discount.

The utility associated with the sanction provided if convicted at trial matters for the plea bargain as well. It is important to emphasize that the prosecutor's ability to increase sentences depends on how D views the sanction. For example, risk aversion is a concern (Grossman & Katz, 1983). A risk-averse defendant experiences greater disutility with the uncertain, severe sentence arising from a trial. This increases the defendant's willingness to negotiate, which results in a less generous plea bargain. Disparities in sentencing, then, can be driven by differences in risk preferences rather than by culpability or harm caused.

Relatedly, the extralegal factors that influence P can spill over into the plea bargains. Career concerns, as previously discussed, increase the utility derived from a jury conviction. When prosecutors are negotiating at the bargaining table, they present higher sanctions when these career concerns are present. Evidence supporting this theoretical prediction exists in McCannon's (2013) evaluation of appeals of felony convictions: When prosecutors are up for re-election, appealed convictions are more likely to be successful. The effect is not in wrongful convictions that necessitate reversals but rather in sentence modifications. From these findings, one could conclude that appellate courts systematically view sanctions obtained during prosecutor re-elections as being too harsh.

Finally, cost matters. For the prevalence of plea bargaining, it is the aggregate costs that matter, (8); for the size of the plea bargain, it is the discrepancy in the costs, (10). When in a position of bargaining power, where going to trial is relatively less costly for *P*, greater sanctions can be obtained. An important cost driver is pretrial detention. Reaching a negotiated plea not only provides the opportunity to experience a shorter prison time, for example, but also provides an immediate outcome, avoiding the wait of going to trial. If this pretrial period is spent in jail, then costs to defending oneself at trial escalate. Not only should higher costs lead to an increased plea bargaining rate, but they should also lead to less generous offers and longer sentences. This is precisely what Stevenson (2016) found when considering differences in pretrial detention and resulting outcomes. Looking at data from Philadelphia's criminal system, she determined that pretrial detention increased the likelihood of conviction, mainly through increasing the chances that the detained individual would accept a guilty plea.

Relatedly, one can think of the fact that underneath this framework is an individual consumption decision-making problem: *D*'s payoff function, $-c_d$. Income and resources spent on lawyers reduce *D*'s well-being, as this expenditure reduces the number of other consumption goods that can be enjoyed. Time spent at trial takes away time for income-earning activities or leisure activities. In other words, the cost is the *relative price* of buying defense. Consequently, the relative price of trial may be different for an individual with a higher income than for someone with a lower income. The expenses of trial might be relatively small for a higher-income individual who is better able to afford the costs. As a consequence, the prosecutor can be expected to agree to a lower sanction. This provides an explanation for sentencing disparities correlated with wealth/income and, in part, racial sentencing disparities (Schanzenbach & Yaeger, 2006; see Chapters 7 and 8, this volume).

Conclusion

In this chapter I have built a formal, rational choice framework to guide analysis of the prosecutor's role in the plea bargaining process. The model is general enough to incorporate numerous considerations that are hypothesized to influence outcomes, such as risk preferences and income disparities.

Importantly, by focusing the analysis on the bilateral interaction between the prosecutor and the defendant/defense, the motivations of the two parties becomes central. Consequently, the influences affecting prosecutors drive the discussion. This chapter can best be thought of as an attempt to emphasize the public choice of the legal system.

Public choice involves study of the incentives of the decision-maker in considerations of policy and public outcomes. The field of public choice, pioneered by Nobel laureate James Buchanan, who focused attention on constitutions (Buchanan & Tullock, 1962), has received only limited attention in criminal justice. Prominent examples include Judge Posner's evaluation of the motivations of judges (Posner, 1993, 2008) and the extensive body of research on how extralegal factors influence judicial decision-making (Lim, 2013; Shepherd, 2009). Put simply, prosecutors respond to incentives. The institutional environment in which prosecutors operate creates the influences expressed in the system of pleas that exists in the United States. Considering one without the other results in an incomplete analysis.

Future work on the criminal justice system in the United States must focus on the plea bargaining process, as it dominates convictions and sentencing. Consequently, the prosecutor, as the primary decision-maker endowed with substantial discretion, is at the center of the institution. As a result, future work should continue to focus on the motivations of prosecutors and, specifically, the institutional framework within which they operate.

References

Baker, S., & Mezzetti, C. (2001). Prosecutorial resources, plea bargaining, and the decision to go to trial. *Journal of Law, Economics, and Organization*, *17*, 149–167. doi: 10.1093/jleo/17.1.149

Bandyopadhyay, S., & McCannon, B. C. (2013). Re-election concerns and the failure of plea bargaining. *Theoretical Economics Letters*, *3*, 40–44. doi: 10.4236/tel.2013.35a2007

Bandyopadhyay, S., & McCannon, B. C. (2014). The effect of the election of prosecutors on criminal trials. *Public Choice*, *161*, 141–156. doi: 10.1007/s11127-013-0144-0

Bandyopadhyay, S., & McCannon, B. C. (2015). Prosecutorial retention: Signaling by trial. *Journal of Public Economic Theory*, *17*, 219–256. doi: 10.1111/jpet.12107

Bibas, S. (2004). Plea bargaining outside the shadow of trial. *Harvard Law Review*, *117*(8), 2463–2547. doi: 10.2307/4093404

Bjerk, D. (2007). Guilt shall not escape or innocence suffer? The limits of plea bargaining when defendant guilt is uncertain. *American Law and Economics Review*, *9*(2), 305–329. doi: 10.1093/aler/ahm010

Bjerk, D. (2008). On the role of plea bargaining and the distribution of sentences in the absence of judicial system frictions. *International Review of Law and Economics*, *28*(1), 1–7. doi: 10.1016/j.irle.2007.12.005

Boylan, R. T. (2004). Salaries, turnover, and performance in the federal criminal justice system. *Journal of Law and Economics*, *47*, 75–92. doi: 10.1086/378695

Boylan, R. T. (2005). What do prosecutors maximize? Evidence from the careers of U.S. attorneys. *American Law and Economics Review*, *7*, 379–402. doi: 10.1093/aler/ahi016

Boylan, R. T., & Long, C. X. (2005). Salaries, plea rates, and the career objectives of federal prosecutors. *Journal of Law and Economics*, *48*(2), 627–651. doi: 10.1086/429854

Brady v. Maryland, 373 U.S. 83 (1963).
Buchanan, J. M., & Tullock, G. (1962). *The calculus of consent: Logical foundations of constitutional democracy*. Ann Arbor: University of Michigan Press.
Burke, A. S. (2007). Prosecutorial passion, cognitive bias, and plea bargaining. *Marquette Law Review*, *91*, 183–211.
Bushway, S. D., & Redlich, A.D. (2012). Is plea bargaining in the "shadow of the trial" a mirage? *Journal of Quantitative Criminology*, *28*(3), 437–454. doi: 10.1007/s10940-011-9147-5
Bushway, S. D., Redlich, A. D., & Norris, R. J. (2014). An explicit test of plea bargaining in the "shadow of the trial." *Criminology*, *52*, 723–754. doi: 10.1111/1745-9125.12054
Caldwell, H. M. (2011). Coercive plea bargaining: The unrecognized scourge of the system. *Catholic University Law Review*, *61*, 63–96.
Chortek, M. (2013). The psychology of unknowing: Inadmissible evidence in jury and bench trials. *Review of Litigation*, *32*, 121–145.
Daughety, A. F., & Reinganum, J. (2016). Informal sanctions on prosecutors and defendants and the disposition of criminal cases. *Journal of Law, Economics, and Organization*, *32*, 359–394. doi: 10.1093/jleo/ewv0202
Detotto, C., & McCannon, B. C. (2017a). Economic freedom and public, non-market institutions: Evidence from criminal prosecution. *Economics of Governance*, *18*, 107–128. doi: 10.1007/s10101-016-0183-3
Detotto, C., & McCannon, B. C. (2017b). Consolidation of prosecutor offices. Unpublished manuscript.
Farmer, A., & Pecorino, P. (1994). Pretrial negotiations with asymmetric information on risk preferences. *International Review of Law and Economics*, *14*, 273–281. doi: 10.1016/0144-8188(94)90043-4
Farmer, A., & Pecorino, P. (2002). Pretrial bargaining with self-serving bias and asymmetric information. *Journal of Economic Behavior and Organization*, *48*, 163–176. doi: 10.1016/s0167-2681(01)00236-0
Farmer, A., & Pecorino, P. (2010). Pretrial bargaining with asymmetric information: Unilateral versus bilateral payoff relevance. *Southern Economic Journal*, *77*, 369–384. doi: 10.4284/sej.2010.77.2.369
Farmer, A., & Pecorino, P. (2013). Discovery and disclosure with asymmetric information and endogenous expenditures at trial. *Journal of Legal Studies*, *42*, 223–247. doi: 10.1086/667932
Farmer, A., & Tiefenthaler, J. (2001). Conflict in divorce disputes: The determinants of pretrial settlement. *International Review of Law and Economics*, *21*, 157–180. doi: 10.1016/s0144-8188(01)00054-0
Gordon, S. C., & Huber, G. A. (2002). Citizen oversight and the electoral incentives of criminal prosecutors. *American Journal of Political Science*, *46*, 334–351. doi: 10.2307/3088380
Gorman, M. F., & Ruggiero, J. (2009). Evaluating U.S. judicial district prosecutor performance using DEA: Are disadvantaged counties more inefficient? *European Journal of Law and Economics*, *27*, 275–283. doi: 10.1007/s10657-008-9093-3
Gross, S. R. (2015, July 24). The staggering number of wrongful convictions in America. *Washington Post*. Retrieved from https://www.washingtonpost.com/opinions/the-cost-ofconvicting-the-innocent/2015/07/24/260fc3a2-1aae-11e5-93b7-5eddc056ad8a_story.html

Grossman, G. M. & Katz, M. L. (1983). Plea bargaining and social welfare. *American Economic Review, 73*, 749–757.
Kutateladze, B. L., Andiloro, N. R., & Johnson, B. D. (2016). Opening Pandora's box: How does defendant race influence plea bargaining? *Justice Quarterly, 33*, 398–426. doi: 10.1080/07418825.2014.915340
Landes, W. M. (1971). An economic analysis of the courts. *Journal of Law and Economics, 14*, 61–107. doi: 10.1086/466704
Lim, C. (2013). Preferences and incentives of appointed and elected public officials. *American Economic Review, 103*, 1360–1397. doi: 10.1257/aer.103.4.1360
Loewenstein, G., & Moore, D.A. (2004). When ignorance is bliss: Information exchange and inefficiency in bargaining. *Journal of Legal Studies, 33*, 37–58. doi: 10.1086/382581.
Lundberg, A. (2016). Sentencing discretion and burdens of proof. *International Review of Law and Economics, 46*, 34–42. doi: 10.1016/j.irle.2015.12.002
McCannon, B. C. (2010). Homicide trials in classical Athens. *International Review of Law and Economics, 30*, 46–51. doi: 10.1016/j.irle.2009.08.003
McCannon, B. C. (2011). The median juror and the trial of Socrates. *European Journal of Political Economy, 26*, 533–540. doi: 10.1016/j.ejpoleco.2010.03.005
McCannon, B. C. (2013). Prosecutor elections, mistakes, and appeals. *Journal of Empirical Legal Studies, 10*, 697–715. doi: 10.1111/jels.12024
Nash Jr., J. F. (1950). The bargaining problem. *Econometrica, 18*, 155–162. doi: 10.2307/1907266
Olivares, K. M., Burton Jr., V. S., & Cullen, F. T. (1996). The collateral consequences of a felony conviction: A national study of state legal codes 10 years later, *Federal Probation, 60*, 10–16.
Piehl, A. M. & Bushway, S. D. (2007). Measuring and explaining charge bargaining. *Journal of Quantitative Criminology, 23*, 105–125. doi: 10.1007/s10940-006-9023-x
Posner, R. A. (1993). What do judges and justices maximize? (The same thing everybody else does). *Supreme Court Economic Review, 3*, 1–41. doi: 10.1086/scer.3.1147064
Posner, R. A. (2008). *How judges think*. Cambridge, MA: Harvard University Press.
Priest, G. L., & Klein, B. (1984). The selection of disputes for litigation. *Journal of Legal Studies, 13*, 1–55. doi: 10.1086/467732
Rasmusen, E., Raghav, M., & Ramseyer, M. (2009). Convictions versus conviction rates: The prosecutor's choice. *American Law and Economics Review, 11*, 47–78. https://doi.org/10.1093/aler/ahp007
Reinganum, J. F. (1988). Plea bargaining and prosecutorial discretion. *American Economic Review, 78*, 713–728.
Reinganum, J. F. (2000). Sentencing guidelines, judicial discretion, and plea bargaining. *RAND Journal of Economics, 31*, 62–81. doi: 10.2307/2601029
Schanzenbach, M., & Yaeger, M. (2006). Prison time, fines, and federal white-collar criminals: The anatomy of a racial disparity. *Journal of Criminal Law and Criminology, 96*, 757–794.
Schelling, T. C. (1960). *The strategy of conflict*. Cambridge, MA: Harvard University Press.
Shepherd, J. (2009). The influence of retention politics on judges' voting. *Journal of Legal Studies, 38*, 169–206. doi: 10.1086/592096

Stevenson, M. (2016). Distortion of justice: How the inability to pay bail affects case outcomes. Unpublished manuscript. Retrieved from http://dx.doi.org/10.2139/ssrn.2777615

Thaman, S. C. (2010a). A typology of consensual criminal procedures; An historical and comparative perspective on the theory and practice of avoiding the full criminal trial. In S. C. Thaman (Ed.), *World plea bargaining: Consensual procedures and the avoidance of full criminal trial* (pp. 297–396). Durham, NC: Carolina Academic Press.

Thaman, S. C. (2010b). *World plea bargaining: Consensual procedures and the avoidance of full criminal trial*. Durham, NC: Carolina Academic Press.

Wright, R. F. (2009). How prosecutor elections fail us. *Ohio State Journal of Criminal Law, 6*, 581–610.

Wright, R. F. (2017). Prosecutor institutions and incentives. *Criminology, Criminal Justice, Law & Society, 18*(3), 85–100.

Wright, R. F., & Miller, M. L. (2010). The worldwide accountability deficit for prosecutors. *Washington and Lee Law Review, 67*, 1587–1620.

Yan, S., & Bushway, S. D. (2017). Estimating and explaining the magnitude of pleas of plea bargaining in New York State. Unpublished manuscript.

Section 2

INFLUENCES ON PLEA DECISION-MAKING

5

Race and Plea Bargaining

Brian D. Johnson and Rebecca Richardson

Historical treatments of criminal punishment routinely focus on the pivotal role that race and ethnicity play in criminal case outcomes in American courtrooms. This, in part, reflects the unique historical legacy of racism in the United States as well as evidence of social inequality in various aspects of criminal case processing. To some extent, racial and ethnic differences are a product of both the differential involvement in serious crime (Hindelang, 1978) and the potentially disparate impact of discretionary decisions in the criminal justice system (Walker, Spohn, & DeLone, 2004). On any given day, African American males are more than five times as likely as white males to be incarcerated (Bureau of Justice Statistics, 2016), and Latino males are more than 2.5 times as likely to be behind bars. Demographic estimates suggest that one in three black men and one in six Latino men can expect to go to prison at some point during their lifetime (Bureau of Justice Statistics, 2003), and among high school dropouts, black men have a cumulative risk of imprisonment greater than 50% (Western, 2006). Given this stark racial disproportionality, it is not surprising that criminologists, psychologists, sociologists, and legal scholars have long sought to understand the foundations of racial inequality in the justice system.

Traditionally, empirical research has focused on disparities in sentencing (Baumer, 2013; Spohn, 2000; Ulmer, 2012). Although studies of this ilk provide many valuable insights, they fail to account for the consequential ways that plea negotiations shape punishment outcomes in the halls of justice. Roughly 95% of all U.S. criminal convictions are the result of guilty pleas (Reaves, 2013), yet relatively few checks and balances have been instituted to ensure fairness and equality in plea bargaining. Surprisingly little theoretical or empirical work focuses on the determinants of guilty pleas or the potential for racial and ethnic disadvantage in plea deals (Johnson, King, & Spohn, 2016). For individual defendants, the decision to enter a guilty plea is highly consequential. It can substantially reduce one's punishment, but it also comes with other legal ramifications such as foregoing one's right to appeal their sentence. Notably, some argue that this right takes on "added significance as a safeguard in a system that depends so heavily upon plea-based convictions" (Dyer & Judge, 1989–1990, p. 670).

Legal scholars have long debated the relative advantages and disadvantages of a system of pleas (Alschuler, 1981; Feeley, 1979/1992), but limited research attempts to understand the guilty plea decision itself. This void is the product of several factors, including an absence of publicly available data on plea bargains, a lack of formal oversight and legal review procedures during charging and plea bargaining, and a reticence on the part of court actors to open themselves up to academic scrutiny. Recently, though, a number of scholars have called for greater attention to unwarranted disparities in plea bargaining (Johnson et al., 2016; Kutateladze, Andiloro, & Johnson, 2016; Shermer & Johnson, 2010). In part, this reflects the growing recognition that, as Justice Anthony Kennedy opined (and as the title of this volume references), plea bargaining "is not some adjunct to the criminal justice system, it is the criminal justice system" (*Missouri v. Frye*, 2012, p. 10-444).

The chapter reviews contemporary theoretical explanations for racial differences in plea bargaining, drawing on a range of interdisciplinary perspectives. It appraises the current state of research on race and plea bargaining and identifies limitations in existing scholarship. We consider racial differences in who pleads guilty along with the various factors that shape charging and plea negotiations. We also discuss ways that guilty pleas can contribute to broader patterns of cumulative disadvantage—to understand fully the consequences of plea disparity it is necessary to place it in the broader context of related case outcomes. Finally, we conclude with a discussion of fruitful directions for future research and reflect on current policy debates related to one of the most consequential and overlooked processes in the American court system: the negotiated guilty plea.

Theoretical Perspectives on Race and Plea Bargaining

To understand racial disparities in plea bargaining it is useful first to consider the various theoretical perspectives that help to explain how race might shape the guilty plea process. Distinct theories have evolved across disciplines, and by integrating their insights, we can paint a more complete picture of how and why the race of a defendant matters in plea bargaining.

Traditional perspectives on guilty pleas conceptualize them as the result of repeated interactions among multiple members of a courtroom workgroup, which is characterized by interdependent relationships, shared workloads, and a local court culture complete with organizational goals that include pursuing justice, group cohesion, and efficient case processing (Eisenstein & Jacob, 1977). From this perspective, plea bargaining serves several shared organizational goals, even though members of the courtroom workgroup may differ in their individual goals. Thus, plea bargaining entails a multifaceted negotiated process in which multiple court actors seek to identify a package of criminal sanctions that all parties will accept.

A number of different perspectives provide insights into how and why the race of the defendant might affect this negotiated process. We begin by reviewing sociolegal perspectives on plea bargaining before turning to additional insights from the fields of psychology and economics. Adopting an interdisciplinary perspective is useful for broadening our understanding of the various social forces that may contribute to social inequality in the guilty plea process.

Sociolegal Perspectives on Plea Bargaining

Traditional sociolegal approaches to racial disparity draw from conflict theory and critical race perspectives, which contend that racism is deeply embedded in the rule of law (Chambliss & Seidman, 1971). As such, the criminal justice system reinforces existing racial hierarchies in America. Richard Quinney (1970), for example, observed that the people in power create the law to favor powerful groups in society. From this perspective, the law is used to subjugate racial and ethnic minority groups who are viewed as a threat to the established racial order. Although scholars have long applied critical race perspectives to various aspects of criminal case processing, they have proved difficult to test (Hagan, 1989), so they have been largely integrated into more recent perspectives such as causal attribution and focal concerns theory.

Causal attribution theory offers an alternative to systemic explanations for racial disparity. It posits that court actors are subject to heuristic decision-making processes that result in race and ethnicity exerting subtle and unintentional influences on criminal case outcomes (Albonetti, 1987, 1991). Because prosecutors, defense attorneys, and judges are all subject to time and information constraints, they cannot make perfectly rational decisions. Instead, they rely on cognitive shortcuts rooted in experience, cultural norms, and societal stereotypes to make the punishment process more efficient. Racial stereotypes link certain categories of criminal defendant to perceptions of future risk, shaping plea bargaining outcomes in consequential ways. Racial identity can also intersect with other stereotypical attributions, such as those tied to defendant age and gender. For instance, young, male, minority defendants may be particularly disadvantaged because causal attributions link them to "membership in social groups thought to be dangerous and crime prone" (Steffensmeier, Ulmer, & Kramer, 1998, p. 768).

Recent work in the focal concerns tradition builds on these ideas, arguing that racial stereotypes affect court actor assessments of various case-processing considerations. In its original formulation, it suggested sentencing judges have three primary concerns: offender blameworthiness; protection of the community; and practical constraints, which include a variety of individual and organizational factors such as institutional resource availability (Steffensmeier et al., 1998). From this perspective, racial disparities are the result of differential perceptions of blameworthiness, dangerousness, or the likelihood of future recidivism, along with assessments of certain practical considerations such as one's ability to "do time" in prison. According to the theory, minority defendants are often judged to be more culpable, dangerous, and/or likely to reoffend (Kramer & Steffensmeier, 1993; Steffensmeier et al., 1998), resulting in harsher criminal justice outcomes for minority defendants.

Despite its frequent use, focal concerns theory has been subjected to limited formal testing or empirical verification, especially in the area of negotiated guilty pleas. Research seldom includes direct measures of the focal concerns, relying instead on coarse proxies such as offense severity or prior record to infer the attribution process. As Hartley, Maddan, and Spohn (2007) argued, the "focal concerns concepts have not been fully operationalized" (p. 63) and the role of guilty pleas in particular "has been consistently under-evaluated" (p. 74). Some recent work, however, extends this perspective to prosecutorial decision-making (Shermer & Johnson, 2010; Spohn, Beichner, & Davis-Frenzel, 2001). Prosecutors are theorized to maintain similar stereotypical attributions as judges; however, their mental calculus includes additional concerns, such as the likelihood of obtaining a conviction in the case, which may also contribute to racial disparities in plea bargaining. If prosecutors predict that jurors or judges will be less sympathetic to minority defendants at trial, for instance, they may be inclined to offer less generous plea deals to defendants in those cases (Frohmann, 1997; Spohn et al., 2001).

Although plea bargaining is often explained as the natural product of courtroom elites seeking to dispose of cases efficiently (Dixon, 1995; Eisenstein & Jacob, 1977), the process depends fundamentally on a defendant's willingness to plead guilty. As Alschuler (1983) explains, one of the more powerful determinants of case disposition is defendants' expectations about their treatment during criminal justice processing. Defendants who have greater faith in the justice system may be more willing to engage in plea bargaining because they assume court actors will treat them fairly. Notably, the research indicates that there are clear racial differences in perceptions of fairness in the criminal justice system (Bobo & Thompson, 2006; Hagan & Albonetti, 1982; Unnever, Gabbidon, & Higgins, 2011). Hagan and Albonetti (1982), for example, found that black individuals were more likely to feel that the courts violate defendants' constitutional rights during plea bargaining. These differential perceptions may increase preference among black defendants for trial, where juries can scrutinize case facts more closely. Albonetti (1990) has argued that "black defendants exhibit less confidence in a system in which bargains are struck in the dark," a system that is "replete with uncertainty and ambiguity for the accused" (p. 329), and Frenzel and Ball (2008) posit that high trial rates for black defendants also reflect greater distrust in the system.

Psychological Perspectives

Insights from the field of psychology complement sociolegal theorizing on race and plea bargaining. The burgeoning discourse on implicit bias in decision-making represents one promising avenue (Banaji & Greenwald, 2016; Kang et al., 2012). Implicit bias, which signifies "the attitudes or stereotypes that affect our understanding, actions, and decisions in an unconscious manner" (Staats, 2013, p. 6), may occur involuntarily and without awareness, making it a markedly insidious source of racial inequality. Implicit racial bias has been linked to multiple decisions in the criminal justice system, including police use of deadly force (Correll, Park, Judd, & Wittenbrink, 2002) and both judicial (Rachlinski, Johnson, Wistrich, & Guthrie, 2009) and juror (Kang et al., 2012) decision-making.

Although research has not empirically linked implicit bias directly to plea outcomes, some scholars have cogently argued its importance. Smith and Levinson (2011), for instance, discuss a variety of ways in which prosecutors' implicit racial biases might affect pretrial strategies, including their willingness to offer quality plea deals to minority defendants. Because plea bargaining is a widespread and largely unregulated phenomenon, it may be an especially fertile ground for implicit bias. Although less attention has been devoted to defense attorneys, they may be susceptible to similar biases that affect their ability to advocate for racial minority clients (Edkins, 2011; Eisenberg & Johnson, 2003).

Implicit bias is particularly important in light of research that suggests court actors are often overconfident about their ability to remain fair and impartial (Irwin & Real, 2010). Multiple studies find that judges overestimate their own objectivity; when asked to rank their capacity to avoid racial prejudice, 97% categorize themselves in the top 50% (Guthrie, Rachlinski, & Wistrich, 2009), and work from other fields indicates that decision-makers who believe they are objective are actually more likely to act on personal biases. Uhlmann and Cohen (2007), for example, found that priming decision-makers with a sense of objectivity increased gender discrimination in hiring decisions. When judges believe they are immune to bias, they may actually be more susceptible to it. Although we are unaware of equivalent work that focuses specifically on guilty pleas, the same logic may apply to prosecutors and defense attorneys during plea negotiations.

Psychological perspectives also contribute to our understanding of how defendants shape their own case outcomes. Research indicates that whites relative to blacks are more likely to believe they have the power to control their own life outcomes (Tashakkori & Thompson, 1991). Survey research similarly suggests that whites have higher levels of self-efficacy and perceived control (Gurin, Gurin, & Morrison 1978), which may contribute to racial disparity in both the willingness to negotiate and the types of concessions defendants are willing to accept. White defendants who maintain confidence in their ability to determine their own outcomes may be more aggressive in plea bargaining and expect more favorable outcomes, whereas minority defendants may feel powerless in the plea bargaining process and either refuse to engage or accept lesser concessions, believing they will not be able to obtain fair plea deals regardless.

Economic Perspectives

Looking at plea bargaining through an economics lens is also beneficial (see Chapter 4, this volume). Economic approaches to plea research typically begin with assumptions about courtroom actor and defendant rationality, followed by efforts to model decision-making. The most popular economic approach to plea bargaining is arguably the shadow-of-the-trial model (Bibas, 2004; Bushway, Redlich, & Norris, 2014; Landes, 1971), which purports that rational defendants aim to minimize their punishment, while prosecutors attempt to maximize it. Court actors and defendants negotiate plea outcomes with explicit consideration of expected trial outcomes; both parties weigh the relative costs and benefits of a certain plea outcome against an uncertain trial. According to the theory, a rational defendant will never accept a plea deal that is more than the expected punishment at trial given the possibility of acquittal, and a rational district attorney will never offer a plea deal that is less than this adjusted trial sentence (see Chapter 4 this volume for a more in-depth treatment). Although there are limitations to this conceptualization of plea bargaining (Bibas, 2004), it provides a clear and testable prediction about the expected size of a plea discount (Bushway & Redlich, 2012). To date, though, few discussions of the shadow model explicitly focus on racial disparities.

Some scholars have applied another economic approach, known as game theory, more directly to plea disparities. This perspective treats the plea negotiation as a series of strategic interactions between prosecutors, defense attorneys, and defendants (Reinganum, 1988). Savitsky (2012), for instance, envisioned plea bargaining as a collective action problem, in which defendants must collectively buck the system and go to trial in order for the group to obtain the best outcomes. Every plea deal made is a success for the prosecutor, who achieves a conviction and saves resources that ensure a stronger bargaining position in future cases. This game may generate poorer outcomes for black defendants, who typically have fewer resources to mount a defense, reducing the transaction costs necessary for prosecutors to pursue trial. Minority perceptions of the justice system as harsh and unfair may also make them more risk averse, which puts them in a worse bargaining position as well.

Other economic approaches are also useful for informing race and plea bargaining research. Harris and Springer (1984) portray plea bargaining as a simple two-player game with prior criminal record serving as the most important consideration. Defendants with long criminal records have less incentive to plea bargain because they are still likely to receive significant prison sentences, and prior work indicates that minority defendants tend to have longer criminal histories (Kutateladze, Lawson, & Andiloro, 2015). Harris and Springer (1984) found evidence consistent with this perspective. They suggest that racial disparity in plea bargaining may be related to differences in plea incentives produced by prior record. Similar work shows that cooperation is typically greater, and joint negotiation payoffs larger, among people of the same race (Oore, Gagnon, & Bourgeois, 2013). Given that the vast majority of U.S. prosecutors are white, racial dissimilarity may be a barrier to minority defendants negotiating favorable plea deals (Ward, Farrell, & Rousseau, 2009).

Power disparities between black and white individuals outside the domain of the criminal justice system might also affect the negotiation process. Scholars have identified racial differences in a variety of real-world bargaining situations. For example, audit studies of discrimination indicate that black consumers fare worse during transactions (Ayres & Siegelman, 1995; Yinger, 1998). One study of car dealerships found that black individuals paid higher auto financing charges (Gillis & Alexander, 2004), and a large survey of over 3,000 new hires reported that ethnic minorities negotiated substantially lower starting salaries than whites (Seidel, Polzer, & Stewart, 2000). Patterns of differential negotiation may extend to the criminal justice system and leave minority defendants at a disadvantage in the plea process. Notably, this is consistent with early sociological work that argues the favorability of a plea bargain is directly related to the political and economic power of the defendant, with indigent and minority-group members routinely disadvantaged (Chambliss & Seidman, 1971).

Empirical Research on Race and Plea Bargaining

Empirical studies of race, ethnicity, and punishment are legion (Baumer, 2013; Johnson & Lee, 2013; Ulmer, 2012); yet, surprisingly few analyses focus on racial disparity in plea bargaining. In part, this reflects the fact that there are no national data on guilty pleas, and collecting original data on plea bargaining is time and resource intensive. Most existing scholarship has been narrowly focused on racial differences in who pleads guilty, has their case dismissed or diverted, or receives favorable charge reductions. In general, reviews of this work find little evidence of widespread and systematic overt racial discrimination in guilty plea processes, though a number of individual studies report evidence of significant inequalities in specific stages of case processing (Johnson et al., 2016; Kutateladze, Lynn, & Liang, 2012). We summarize key findings from this body of empirical work in the sections that follow.

Racial Disparity in Guilty Pleas and Plea Bargaining

Although most empirical examinations of racial disparity in plea bargaining focus on the plea decision as an isolated outcome, in reality guilty pleas are situated within a larger web of interdependent criminal justice processing decisions. Decisions that precede plea negotiations can significantly influence guilty plea outcomes. At the same time, the choice to plead guilty can itself shape later punishment determinations. As such, it is important to consider the broad impact of earlier case decisions on the racial dynamics of guilty pleas, as well as the ways that guilty pleas shape other downstream decisions in the criminal justice system.

First, police arrest decisions may shape racial disparity in plea outcomes. As Spohn (2013) discusses, arrest decisions largely determine the pool of cases eligible for a guilty plea. If there are racial or ethnic disparities in the decision to arrest, then those disparities will be incorporated into cases forwarded for prosecution (Tomic & Hakes, 2008). This muddies interpretations of racial disparity in guilty pleas and makes it difficult to isolate the unique effects of defendant race. For example, some work suggests that police officers are more likely to arrest racial-minority than white suspects (Kochel, Wilson, & Mastrofski, 2011), which could contribute to differences in the types of cases eligible for prosecution. If evidence is weaker in minority arrests, this may contribute to racial differences in who pleads guilty, though little empirical work examines this issue.

In a similar vein, initial screening decisions made by prosecutors could also result in a selected sample of cases being eligible for plea bargaining. Kutateladze et al. (2012) note that most prior studies focus on initial screening or dismissal decisions. These authors conclude that although the effects of race and ethnicity are inconsistent, "the preponderance of the research" suggests that "race and ethnicity matter" at early stages of prosecution (Kutateladze et al., 2012, p. 7). Wu's (2016) meta-analysis of race and prosecution similarly finds that race and ethnicity matter, especially at initial screening. Overall, though, little research examines racial disparity in prosecution, and very little work explicitly considers how initial screening decisions shape subsequent plea negotiations. Some research finds that high rates of case acceptance are associated with high dismissal or plea bargaining rates (Eisenstein & Jacob, 1977; Kutateladze et al., 2012), but we clearly need more work that focuses on how the multiple stages of charging are related to one another and how they jointly shape racial disparities in punishment.

There is also convincing evidence that pretrial detainment is highly consequential in fashioning guilty plea outcomes. Research in this area identifies notable disadvantages for minority defendants, with black and Hispanic defendants less likely to be released pretrial (Demuth, 2003; Kutateladze, Andiloro, Johnson, & Spohn, 2014; Wooldredge, Frank, Goulette, & Travis, 2015). Racial differences in detention reflect disparities in the decision to deny bail as well as differences in bail amounts and ability to pay. Schlesinger (2005) reports that black and Hispanic defendants are about half as likely as white defendants to be released on bail. Many scholars view pretrial detention as a punishment in itself (Feeley, 1979) because it stigmatizes the defendant, disrupts family life and employment, and makes it harder to prepare a defense. Importantly, pretrial detention also exerts strong pressure on a defendant to plead guilty (Patterson & Lynch, 1991; Sutton, 2013). This suggests that racial patterns of detention shape subsequent disparities in plea bargaining in consequential ways. If the goal is to understand disparity in plea bargaining, then it is necessary to consider the broader context of earlier criminal justice decisions that shape the contours of subsequent plea negotiations.

Relative to research on initial charging and case acceptance decisions, considerably less scholarship focuses on racial disparity in plea bargaining processes. Much early work on the topic originated in political science, examining negotiated pleas in select jurisdictions as part of a more holistic attempt to understand the determinants of case resolution (Eisenstein & Jacob, 1977; Eisenstein, Flemming, & Nardulli, 1988; Nardulli, Eisenstein, & Flemming, 1988). Collectively, this scholarship provides little evidence of systematic racial disparity in plea bargaining. Nardulli, Flemming, and Eisenstein (1986), for instance, concluded that "widespread manipulation and disparities . . . are not inherent attributes of the guilty plea process" (p. 1128). The work also found that negotiated pleas result from group-based consensus rather than adversarial concessions, or in the words of Malcolm Feeley (1979), pleas represent "a type of normative endeavor—a joint assessment of the incident and the accused's actions and character" (p. 463).

Most recent work concentrates more narrowly on specific plea-related decisions, such as the defendant's decision to enter a guilty plea or go to trial. Some studies find no significant racial differences in the likelihood of a guilty plea (Kingsnorth, Lopez, Wentworth, & Cummings, 1998; Miethe, 1987; Wooldredge & Griffin, 2005). Wooldredge and Griffin (2005), for instance, report no differences for white, black, or Mexican American defendants in the receipt of negotiated guilty pleas before or after the passage of sentencing guidelines in Ohio. Most research, however, finds some evidence of racial differences, with minority defendants typically being less likely to plead guilty and more likely to go to trial (Albonetti, 1990; Metcalfe & Chiricos, 2018).

Albonetti (1990) found that the probability of pleading guilty was .11 lower for black defendants than for white defendants. Similarly, Meyer and Gray (1997) examined plea decisions for driving under the influence (DUI) offenders in a California county and reported that white offenders were twice as likely as minorities to enter a guilty plea. Similar work by Frenzel and Ball (2008) in Pennsylvania showed that black defendants were less likely to enter into both negotiated and non-negotiated guilty pleas, with no differences for Latino defendants. Most recently, Metcalfe and Chiricos (2018) analyzed data from one Florida county and concluded that blacks, especially black males, were less likely to enter plea agreements, though the researchers lacked the ability to separately examine Latino defendants. Finally, Sutton (2013) analyzed State Court Processing Statistics (SCPS) data (i.e., data from the 75 largest U.S. counties) and found that Latino defendants were less likely to plead guilty than white defendants, though he found no differences between black and white offenders.

In addition to research that examines racial differences in the likelihood of pleading guilty, there is also a smaller literature on prosecutorial discretion to reduce charge severity during plea bargaining. In general, scholars observe that a wide array of considerations influence plea negotiations, including legal factors, case strength, organizational caseloads, courtroom workgroup dynamics, and individual attorney and defendant preferences (Bibas, 2004; Johnson et al., 2016; Nardulli et al., 1988). This work suggests that prosecutors offer more favorable deals when cases involve weaker evidence and less serious offenses (Edkins, 2011; Holmes, Daudistel, & Farrell, 1987). Evidence for racial disparity in negotiated pleas, on the other hand, remains decidedly mixed. Most extant work focuses on charge reductions and reports little substantiation of systematic disparity by race or ethnicity (Albonetti & Hepburn, 1996; Kingsnorth et al., 1998; Wooldredge & Griffin, 2005). Shermer and Johnson (2010), for instance, found that female defendants were more likely than male defendants to have their charges reduced in federal court, but they reported no evidence of racial or ethnic disparity. Moreover, some studies find that minority defendants are actually more likely to receive charge reductions, though some scholars suggest this may reflect overcharging in these cases (Holmes et al., 1987).

Other recent work also offers preliminary evidence for the importance of race and ethnicity. Kutateladze et al. (2014) found that blacks were more likely than whites to receive custodial plea offers that included jail or prison time. Metcalfe and Chiricos (2018) similarly reported that black defendants who pleaded guilty received lesser plea discounts relative to white defendants. Although relatively little work examines defense attorneys, there is evidence that race may also be salient for them. Edkins (2011) showed that defense attorneys recommended significantly higher sentences and were more likely to invoke a custodial sentence for black defendants. Similarly, Eisenberg and Johnson (2003) found evidence of implicit bias favoring white defendants in death penalty cases, and recent work by Hester (2017) argues that higher-quality attorneys may be more successful at "judge shopping," which could further disadvantage indigent defendants. As Kutateladze et al. (2012) summarize, "overall research finds that the effect of race and ethnicity on prosecutorial decision-making is inconsistent, and it is not always blacks or Latinos/as who are treated more punitively" (p. 1).

Plea Discounts and Trial Penalties

One reason that it is important to examine racial disparity in negotiated guilty pleas is that there is a robust literature that finds stark differences in punishments for plea and trial convictions (Bushway et al., 2014; King, Soule, Steen, & Weidner, 2005; Ulmer, Eisenstein, & Johnson, 2010). The concept of a plea discount, or trial penalty, is rooted in the idea that court actors institutionalize longer sentences for trial defendants in order to encourage guilty pleas and dispose of cases on crowded court dockets. Scholars have long debated plea discounts, with critics arguing that the trial penalty has grown so large that "rational offenders, however factually or legally innocent," will no longer "subject their cases to jury scrutiny" (McCoy, 2005, p. 69).

Empirically, the presence of a trial tax is one of the most robust findings in the literature. Early work by Smith (1986) showed that defendants were almost 30% less likely to be incarcerated if they were convicted by a guilty plea instead of at trial, though he also demonstrated that much of this disparity was offset by the potential for acquittal at trial (cf. Abrams, 2011). In their comparison of five guidelines systems, King et al. (2005) found a significant plea discount for most offenses in all five states. Ulmer et al. (2010) similarly reported a stark trial penalty in federal sentencing, with average sentences roughly one-third longer for defendants convicted at trial. Taken together, recent research on the trial penalty concurs with the early observations of Blumstein, Cohen, Martin, and Tonry (1983), who noted that the "strongest and most consistently found effect of case-processing variables is the role of guilty pleas in producing less severe sentences" (p. 18).

However, only a handful of studies attempt to quantify the magnitude of plea bargaining discounts. Piehl and Bushway (2007) outlined a valuable approach in which they compared individual sentences to the counterfactual punishments that would have occurred in the absence of a plea bargain. Their results indicated that plea bargaining has a substantial effect on punishment, though its exact magnitude varied across sentencing regimes. Shermer and Johnson (2010) evaluated the average sentencing discount associated with charge bargaining in federal court and found that, on average, a plea bargain reduced federal sentences by nearly 20%. Finally, Wright and Engen (2006) concluded that plea bargaining determinations can actually have larger effects on punishment than final sentencing decisions.

The broader implication of these findings is that racial disparities in who pleads guilty, and in the size of average plea discounts, may contribute directly to patterns of racial inequality in punishment. If minority defendants are more likely to go to trial, because they have less trust in the system or because they receive less favorable plea deals, they may receive harsher sentences. Moreover, organizational perspectives on sentencing suggest the decision to plead guilty is an important indicator of a defendant's culpability that can have a significant impact on punishment decisions (Kramer & Ulmer, 2002). To the extent that minority defendants are less likely to plead guilty, judges may view them as less cooperative, less remorseful, and less deserving of leniency. Overall, though, few studies examine the underlying reasons for racial differences in pleading guilty, or their potential to contribute to systemic disparity in punishment.

Plea Bargaining and Cumulative Disadvantage

Given the central role that plea negotiations play in punishment, it is crucial for researchers to consider how guilty pleas fit into the broader flow of criminal cases and how they contribute to patterns of cumulative disadvantage for minority defendants (Baumer, 2013; Kutateladze et al., 2014; Spohn, 2013). Conducting this type of research is challenging; it requires information on a broad array of case-processing outcomes, along with methodological approaches that capture the cascading nature of racial disadvantage. Few studies have adequately addressed the issue, but findings from the available literature generally support the idea that disadvantages accumulate for minority defendants as cases progress through the system (Kutateladze et al., 2014; Stolzenberg, D'Alessio, & Eitle, 2013; Sutton, 2013; Wooldredge et al., 2015).

One recent study of cumulative disadvantage examined criminal cases in New York City and found significant disparities for black and Latino defendants in pretrial detention, custodial plea offers, and sentencing (Kutateladze et al., 2014). Operating under the assumption that a greater number of negative outcomes indicates greater disadvantage, these authors found that black and Latino defendants received constellations of case outcomes that were more punitive than those for white defendants. Similarly, Sutton's (2013) assessment of cumulative disadvantage in pretrial detention, guilty pleas, and sentencing also provided evidence of cumulative race effects. He reported sizeable disparities for both black and Latino defendants and found that the specific pathways to disadvantage differed for the two groups. Lastly, Stolzenberg et al.'s (2013) evaluation of eight courtroom decisions demonstrated that race and ethnicity had little effect on individual case-processing outcomes, but when the researchers considered the multiple decisions together, meaningful disparities for black and white defendants were revealed.

The scope of research on cumulative disadvantage also includes case outcomes that are often examined in isolation, such as wrongful convictions, false guilty pleas, and exonerations. A growing literature has investigated these topics (Gross, 2008; Redlich & Shteynberg, 2016), but little work has yet to focus specifically on racial disparities (Gross, Possley, & Stephens, 2017; Smith & Hattery, 2011; Norris & Bonventre, 2015). Gross et al. (2017) note that the majority of innocent defendants wrongfully convicted and later exonerated are African American, while Smith and Hattery (2011) demonstrate that the ratio of exonerations to incarcerations is higher for African Americans than for whites, and that it is especially high for cases involving black offenders and white victims.

Future work that integrates plea bargaining research, wrongful convictions, and other approaches to racial disparity could be quite valuable for advancing our understanding of racial inequalities in punishment. Overall, the limited work on race, plea bargaining, and cumulative disadvantage suggests that it is crucial to take a holistic approach that explicitly considers how disparities multiply across sequential case-processing decisions. Undoubtedly, research of this ilk will be essential for better situating plea bargaining within the broader context of criminal case flows, and for clarifying both the quality and magnitude of racial disparities in punishment.

Current Limitations and Future Directions for Research

Existing scholarship has undeniably improved our understanding of race and guilty pleas, but overarching conclusions from this body of work must be taken cautiously. Extant work remains underdeveloped in a number of ways. First, guilty plea research operationalizes plea bargaining in myriad ways that often make it difficult to draw reliable generalizations. Plea bargaining is a complex process that involves multiple actors (Nardulli et al., 1988) in repeated discursive exchanges (Emmelman, 1996) across multiple stages of the pretrial process (Feeley, 1979). Most studies focus on a reduction in the most serious charge (Shermer & Johnson, 2010), others examine changes in the number of counts (Wilmot & Spohn, 2004), and only a few consider sentencing negotiations (Miethe, 1987). Because studies define plea bargains in different ways, it is not surprising that evidence for racial and ethnic disparity is mixed and inconsistent, so one priority for future work is the development of clearer definitions of what constitutes a plea bargain in criminal courts.

Existing research rarely draws meaningful distinctions among different types of guilty pleas (Frenzel & Ball, 2008; Johnson, 2003), and it also seldom captures the full range of concessions that are available during the negotiation process (Johnson et al., 2016). Most plea bargaining research relies on simplistic outcome measures, such as whether or not any charge reduction occurs, without delving into finer distinctions that often distinguish the overall quality of a plea deal. In addition to alterations in the number, type, and relative severity of charges, prosecutors have a wealth of other bargaining chips at their disposal, ranging from pretrial diversion (Albonetti & Hepburn, 1996) to the application of mandatory minimums (Ulmer, Kurlychek, & Kramer, 2007). Seldom do studies fully consider these various levers, and when they do, it is typically in isolation of other negotiated outcomes.

Second, contemporary plea bargaining research remains significantly limited by a lack of high-quality, publically available data on negotiated guilty plea processes. Much early plea research relied on data from the Prosecutor Management Information System (PROMIS), which was abandoned in the early 1980s (e.g., Albonetti, 1991). Other work commonly relies on SCPS data (e.g., Bushway & Piehl, 2007), which have not been collected since 2009 and may now be discontinued altogether. Much guilty plea research is also considerably dated, which means that findings may not accurately represent plea negotiations in contemporary courtrooms. Available data on guilty pleas typically lack important information on key aspects of the negotiation process and are often restricted in their ability to answer essential questions, such as why some defendants plead guilty and others do not. The research community will likely need to implement additional methodological approaches to investigate these issues properly, such as large-scale surveys with court actors, qualitative interviews with defendants, or multi-method approaches that combine these types of innovations.

Some of the most promising research draws from data independently collected by researchers that provide more detailed information on plea agreements. These types of studies are time and resource intensive, so they are rare in the literature. Moreover, they typically are restricted to small samples of specific types of offenses from few jurisdictions, limiting their generalizability (e.g., Albonetti, 1992; Kingsnorth et al., 1998). Even when researchers collect data sets for a broad range of offenses, they commonly suffer from omitted variables like high-quality measures of the strength of evidence (Bushway et al., 2014; Kutateladze et al., 2016). Moreover, few studies examine racial groups other than blacks and whites, and studies that include Latinos often report conflicting results (Frenzel & Ball, 2008; Sutton, 2013; Wooldredge & Griffin, 2005). In addition to developing larger and more diverse samples, future work needs to focus on the growing Latino population and on other underrepresented groups such as Asian and Native American defendants (Alvarez & Bachman, 1996; Johnson & Betsinger, 2009).

Third, extant research has yet to investigate the various ways that contextual factors influence the guilty plea process. Prior work indicates that trials are more common for some offenses like crimes of serious violence (Reaves, 2013) and suggests there may be significant jurisdictional variations in how guilty pleas operate (Nardulli et al., 1988; Ulmer et al., 2010). Wright and Engen (2006) note that idiosyncratic features of the criminal code shape the range of possibilities in plea negotiations, making some crimes more amenable to bargains than others. Although Albonetti (1990) showed that the effects of certain case factors, such as type of counsel and use of a weapon, differ for whites and blacks, little research has since replicated these findings. Similarly, Bibas (2004) has argued, "Lawyers . . . differ greatly in their abilities, skills and resources, and in their incentives to secure discovery, counteract biases, navigate intricate sentencing laws, and bargain with repeat players" (p. 2545). To date, though, few contemporary studies incorporate attorney characteristics or consider broad organizational forces that shape plea negotiations, despite theoretical arguments for their importance (Eisenstein & Jacob, 1977; Johnson, 2003; Nardulli et al., 1988). Studies that address these issues have significant potential to advance our understanding of the subtleties that shape guilty pleas.

Finally, new efforts need to be made to align current empirical investigations of race and plea bargaining with existing theoretical paradigms. Sociolegal approaches to racial disparity argue that court actors are prone to view minority defendants as more blameworthy, dangerous, and likely to reoffend (Edkins, 2011; Shermer & Johnson, 2010; Smith & Levinson, 2011). Psychological theories suggest that racial disparities may reflect implicit biases among prosecutors and defense attorneys, whereas economic perspectives advocate for rational choice perspectives to explain negotiated plea outcomes. Although scholars routinely employ all of these theoretical arguments, they seldom test them explicitly in empirical work.

Capturing these types of theoretical influences is difficult, but a number of promising approaches are available. Recent sentencing work, for example, uses booking photos to investigate attributions of dangerousness associated with facial appearance (Johnson & King, 2017; King & Johnson, 2016). Researchers could extend this type of work to plea bargaining. Similarly, work in psychology utilizes implicit association tests (IATs) as an indirect measure of implicit bias in judicial decision-making (Rachlinski et al., 2009), but to our knowledge, this approach has yet to be used with prosecutors or defense attorneys. Finally, scholarship testing the shadow-of-the-trial model employs innovative survey designs with court actors that allow for the experimental manipulation of key case characteristics, such as strength of evidence (Bushway et al., 2014; Bushway & Redlich, 2012). This work offers valuable insights into the factors that shape plea outcomes, but it has yet to be adapted to the study of racial and ethnic disparity. Future work that builds on these approaches holds potential to substantially improve our understanding of the underlying sources of racial disparity in the guilty plea process.

Future work also needs to identify and test alternative theoretical pathways. In particular, few studies of guilty pleas include measures of racial attitudes toward the criminal justice system. If minority defendants are less trusting of the justice system, or if they have less bargaining power, they may be less likely to enter into plea negotiations and less able to secure favorable plea deals. Although scholars have speculated about these influences (Albonetti, 1990), we are aware of no empirical work that explicitly tests the links between race, quality of plea offers, justice system attitudes, and plea bargaining outcomes.

The next wave of guilty plea scholarship will need to be creative in expanding on existing research. One promising direction is for researchers to work more closely with practitioners in cooperative research collaborations. Nir (2018) provides an overview of strategies for cultivating successful relationships with court practitioners, and several recent studies offer invaluable examples of this type of work (Frederick & Stemen, 2012; Kutateladze & Andiloro, 2014; Spohn & Tellis, 2014). Although collecting primary data is time consuming, we would argue that the research rewards far outweigh the costs. This approach is also useful for expanding the types of research questions examined. For instance, most work focuses only on felony cases, even though misdemeanors comprise the lion's share of court caseloads (Feeley, 1979). Collaborative partnerships offer an opportunity to not only collect original data but also broaden the scope of prior investigations by expanding the breadth of inquiry to new and understudied issues.

Utilizing recent technological advances also holds promise for advancing research on race and plea bargaining. Many jurisdictions now have automated case management systems that can provide detailed information on guilty plea processes, and new statistical techniques improve the ability to link data sets across agencies (e.g., Kutateladze et al., 2014; Rehavi & Starr, 2014; Shermer & Johnson, 2010). All of these advances are significant because improved policy and fair and effective prosecution will require new and innovative data to advance our understanding of racial and ethnic inequality in plea bargaining.

Conclusion

Overall, extant research provides a number of valuable insights into racial and ethnic disparity in guilty pleas. Most studies report that black and Latino defendants are significantly less likely than white defendants to plead guilty. A number of studies identify disparities in different stages of criminal case processing, but few find convincing evidence of systematic disadvantage across all stages of prosecution. However, research rarely captures nuances in plea bargaining, such as variations in quality and types of plea offers. One of the most robust findings is that there is a significant plea discount, or trial penalty, at sentencing, so racial differences in guilty pleas have important consequences for final punishment. As such, it is vital to situate the guilty plea in the context of upstream and downstream case-processing decisions that shape, and are shaped by, guilty plea negotiations. Despite widespread recognition of the importance of plea bargaining in American courts (Bibas, 2004; Johnson et al., 2016; Nardulli et al., 1988), empirical research that focuses on racial and ethnic inequality in plea bargains remains scarce.

Because of this scarcity, the evidence base is not robust enough to support strong conclusions regarding wholesale changes in policy, but some intriguing propositions are worthy of discussion. First, a number of legal scholars argue for increased oversight in plea bargaining (Alschuler, 1968; Bibas, 2004; McCoy, 2005). The biggest roadblock for assessing unwarranted disparities is a lack of public, transparent, reliable record-keeping. Racial inequality in guilty pleas may be related to covert negotiation processes that are not part of the public record, subject to formal review, or reversible through established legal channels. We advocate for the systematic collection and reporting of data on negotiated plea offers, as well as for judicial participation and oversight in the negotiated plea process. Internal review boards could conduct periodic reviews of plea offers to ensure fairness and equality in prosecution, and judges could act as neutral arbiters over disputes arising from the guilty plea process.

An additional step that might be taken is the implementation of formal charging and plea bargaining guidelines, similar to those that have been established in many states for judicial sentencing decisions (Pfaff, 2018). Many prosecutors' offices have internal charging policies, but the promulgation of formal plea guidelines would help to systematize the process, and it would also provide for easier examination and review of charging decisions. This could also offer a foundation for establishing formal mechanisms of appeal, and it would provide defendants with greater legal recourse in case of guilty plea disputes. Finally, the courts might also implement additional safeguards to address disparities in guilty pleas, such as racial sensitivity and implicit bias training. Such training can be effective by making individuals aware of biases that could otherwise affect their decision-making. In general, we agree with Bibas (2004), who argued for enhanced "safeguards, such as discovery mechanisms, debiasing interventions, use of mediators or other structured dispute resolution, and judicial involvement" (p. 2545) in guilty pleas.

Despite the promise of these types of policy recommendations, stronger empirical evidence will be needed to support wholesale reforms in plea bargaining. The next generation of plea research needs to begin to disentangle how, where, and why race and ethnicity shape plea decisions. Understanding the underlying sources of racial inequality in the justice system is paramount because unwarranted disparities foster public mistrust, impede our ability to promote public safety, and fuel perceptions of inequality that can strain race relations in the United States (Ruth & Reitz, 2003; Western, 2006). Disparities that arise from plea bargaining are especially pernicious, because they often serve as a pathway to differential imprisonment. By working to build more comprehensive data sets on race and guilty pleas, by expanding the scope of theoretical questions asked and the methodological approaches utilized, and by striving to develop new and innovative ways to better test the underlying theoretical constructs that link defendant race to plea outcomes, future endeavors can significantly improve our understanding of racial inequality in one of the most important and least studies arenas of the criminal justice system—the negotiated guilty plea.

References

Abrams, D. S. (2011). Is pleading really a bargain? *Journal of Empirical Legal Studies*, *8*(1), 200–221. doi: 10.1111/j.1740-1461.2011.01234.x

Albonetti, C. (1987). Prosecutorial discretion: The effects of uncertainty. *Law & Society Review*, *21*(2), 291–313. doi: 10.2307/3053523

Albonetti, C. A. (1990). Race and the probability of pleading guilty. *Journal of Quantitative Criminology*, *6*(3), 315–334. doi: 10.1007/BF01065413

Albonetti, C. A. (1991). An integration of theories to explain judicial discretion. *Social Problems*, *38*(2), 247–266. doi: 10.2307/800532

Albonetti, C. A. (1992). Charge reduction: An analysis of prosecutorial discretion in burglary and robbery cases. *Journal of Quantitative Criminology*, *8*(3), 317–333. doi: 10.1007/BF01064551

Albonetti, C. A., & Hepburn, J. (1996). Prosecutorial discretion to defer criminalization: The effects of defendant's ascribed and achieved status characteristics. *Journal of Quantitative Criminology*, *12*(1), 63–81. doi: 10.1007/BF02354471

Alschuler, A. W. (1968). The prosecutor's role in plea bargaining. *University of Chicago Law Review*, *36*(1), 50–112. doi: 10.2307/1598832

Alschuler, A. W. (1981). The changing plea bargaining debate. *California Law Review*, *69*(3), 652–730. doi: 10.2307/3480237

Alschuler, A. W. (1983). Implementing the criminal defendant's right to trial: Alternatives to the plea bargaining system. *University of Chicago Law Review, 50*(3), 931–1050. doi: 10.2307/1599531

Alvarez, A., & Bachman, R. D. (1996). American Indians and sentencing disparity: An Arizona test. *Journal of Criminal Justice, 24*(6), 549–561. doi: 10.1016/S0047-2352(96)00039-6

Ayres, I., & Siegelman, P. (1995). Race and gender discrimination in bargaining for a new car. *American Economic Review, 85*(3), 304–321. doi: 10.2307/1341506

Banaji, M. R., & Greenwald, A. G. (2016). *Blindspot: Hidden biases of good people.* New York: Delacorte Press.

Baumer, E. P. (2013). Reassessing and redirecting research on race and sentencing. *Justice Quarterly, 30*(2), 231–261. doi: 10.1080/07418825.2012.682602

Bibas, S. (2004). Plea bargaining outside the shadow of trial. *Harvard Law Review, 117*(8), 2463–2547. doi: 10.2307/4093404

Blumstein, A., Cohen, J., Martin, S. E., & Tonry, M. H. (Eds.). (1983). *Research on sentencing: The search for reform* (Vol. 1). Washington, DC: National Academy Press.

Bobo, L. D., & Thompson, V. (2006). Unfair by design: The war on drugs, race, and the legitimacy of the criminal justice system. *Social Research: An International Quarterly, 73*(2), 445–472.

Bureau of Justice Statistics. (2003). *Prevalence of imprisonment in the U.S. population, 1974–2001*. Washington DC: Bureau of Justice Statistics, U.S. Department of Justice.

Bureau of Justice Statistics. (2016). *Correctional populations in the United States, 2015*. Washington DC: Bureau of Justice Statistics, U.S. Department of Justice.

Bushway, S. D., & Piehl, A. M. (2007). Social science research and the legal threat to presumptive sentencing guidelines. *Criminology & Public Policy, 6*(3), 461–482. doi: 10.1111/j.1745-9133.2007.00447.x

Bushway S. D., & Redlich A. D. (2012). Is plea bargaining in the "shadow of the trial" a mirage? *Journal of Quantitative Criminology, 28*(3), 437–454. doi: 10.1007/s10940-011-9147-5

Bushway S. D., Redlich A. D., & Norris R. J. (2014). An explicit test of plea bargaining in the "shadow of the trial." *Criminology, 52*, 723–754. doi: 10.1111/1745-9125.12054

Chambliss, W. J., & Seidman, R. B. (1971). *Law, order, and power*. Reading, MA: Addison-Wesley.

Correll, J., Park, B., Judd, C.M., & Wittenbrink, B. (2002). The police officer's dilemma: Using ethnicity to disambiguate potentially threatening individuals. *Journal of Personality and Social Psychology, 83*(6), 1314–1329. doi: 10.1037/0022-3514.83.6.1314

Demuth, S. (2003). Racial and ethnic differences in pretrial release decisions and outcomes: A comparison of Hispanic, black, and white felony arrestees. *Criminology, 41*(3), 873–908. doi: 10.1111/j.1745-9125.2003.tb01007.x

Dixon, J. (1995). The organizational context of criminal sentencing. *American Journal of Sociology, 100*(5), 1157–1198. doi: 10.1086/230635

Dyer, G. M., & Judge, B. (1989–1990). Criminal defendants' waiver of the right to appeal—An unacceptable condition of a negotiated sentence or plea bargain. *Notre Dame Law Review, 65*, 649–670.

Edkins, V. A. (2011). Defense attorney plea recommendations and client race: Does zealous representation apply equally to all? *Law and Human Behavior, 35*(5), 413–425. doi: 10.1007/s10979-010-9254-0
Eisenberg, T., & Johnson, S. L. (2003). Implicit racial attitudes of death penalty lawyers. *DePaul Law Review, 53*, 1539–1777.
Eisenstein J., Flemming, R., & Nardulli, P. (1988). *The contours of justice: Communities and their courts.* Boston: Little Brown.
Eisenstein, J., & Jacob, H. (1977). *Felony justice: An organizational analysis of criminal courts.* Boston: Little Brown.
Emmelman, D. S. (1996). Trial by plea bargain: Case settlement as a product of recursive decisionmaking. *Law and Society Review, 30*(2), 335–360. doi: 10.2307/3053962
Feeley, M. M. (1979). *The process is the punishment: Handling cases in a lower criminal court.* New York: Russell Sage Foundation.
Frederick, B., & Stemen. D. (2012). *The anatomy of discretion: An analysis of prosecutorial decision making—technical report.* New York: Vera Institute of Justice.
Frenzel, E. D., & Ball, J. D. (2008). Effects of individual characteristics on plea negotiations under sentencing guidelines. *Journal of Ethnicity in Criminal Justice, 5*(4), 59–82. doi: 10.1300/J222v05n04_03
Frohmann, L. (1997). Convictability and discordant locales: Reproducing race, class, and gender ideologies in prosecutorial decisionmaking. *Law and Society Review, 31*(3), 531–556. doi: 10.2307/3054045
Gillis, J., & Alexander, B. (2004). *Report finds discrimination in Honda auto loan markups.* Consumer Federation of America. Retrieved from http://www.consumerfed.org/pdfs/072704_Honda_Loan_Discrimination_Release.pdf
Gross, S. R. (2008). Convicting the innocent. *Annual Review of Law and Social Science, 4*, 173–192. doi: 10.1146/annurev.lawsocsci.4.110707.172300
Gross, S. R., Possley, M., & Stephens, K. (2017). *Race and wrongful convictions in the United States.* National Registry of Exonerations, Newkirk Center for Science and Society, University of California-Irvine.
Gurin, P., Gurin, G., & Morrison, B. M. (1978). Personal and ideological aspects of internal and external control. *Social Psychology, 41*(4), 275–296. doi: 10.2307/3033581
Guthrie, C., Rachlinski, J. J., & Wistrich, A. J. (2009). The "hidden judiciary": An empirical examination of executive branch justice. *Duke Law Journal, 58*(7), 1477–1530. doi: 10.2139/ssrn.1374346
Hagan, J. (1989). Why is there so little criminal justice theory? Neglected macro- and micro-level links between organization and power. *Journal of Research in Crime and Delinquency 26*(2), 116–135. doi: 10.1177/0022427889026002002
Hagan, J., & Albonetti, C. (1982). Race, class, and the perception of criminal injustice in America. *American Journal of Sociology, 88*(2), 329–355. doi: 10.1086/227674
Harris, R. A., & Springer, J. F. (1984). Plea bargaining as a game: An empirical analysis of negotiated sentencing decisions. *Review of Policy Research, 4*(2), 245–258. doi: 10.1111/j.1541-1338.1984.tb00210.x
Hartley R., Maddan S., & Spohn C. (2007). Concerning conceptualization and operationalization: sentencing data and the focal concerns perspective—A research note. *Southwest Journal of Criminal Justice 4*(1), 58–78.

Hester, R. (2017). Judicial rotation as centripetal force: Sentencing in the court communities of South Carolina. *Criminology, 55*(1), 205–235. doi: 10.1111/1745-9125.12132

Hindelang, M. J. (1978). Race and involvement in common law personal crimes. *American Sociological Review, 43*(1), 93–109. doi: 10.2307/2094764

Holmes M. D., Daudistel H. C., & Farrell R. A. (1987). Determinants of charge reductions and final dispositions in cases of burglary and robbery. *Journal of Research in Crime and Delinquency, 24*(3), 233–254. doi: 10.1177/0022427887024003004

Irwin, J. F., & Real, D. L. (2010). Unconscious influences on judicial decision-making: The illusion of objectivity. *McGeorge Law Review, 43*, 1–18.

Johnson, B. D. (2003). Racial and ethnic disparities in sentencing departures across modes of conviction. *Criminology, 41*(2), 449–490. doi: 10.1111/j.1745-9125.2003.tb00994.x

Johnson, B. D., & Betsinger, S. (2009). Punishing the "model minority": Asian-American criminal sentencing outcomes in federal district courts. *Criminology, 47*(4), 1045–1090. doi: 10.1111/j.1745-9125.2009.00169.x

Johnson, B. D., & King, R. D. (2017) Facial profiling: Race, physical appearance, and punishment. *Criminology, 55*(3), 520–547. doi: 10.1111/1745-9125.12143

Johnson, B. D., King, R. D., & Spohn, C. (2016). Sociolegal approaches to the study of guilty pleas and prosecution. *Annual Review of Law and Social Science, 12*, 479–495. doi: 10.1146/annurev-lawsocsci-110615-084755

Johnson, B. D., & Lee, J. G. (2013). Racial disparity under sentencing guidelines: A survey of recent research and emerging perspectives. *Sociology Compass, 7*(7), 503–514. doi: 10.1111/soc4.12046

Kang, J., Bennett, M., Carbado, D., Casey, P., Dasgupta, N., Faigman, D., . . . Mnookin, J. (2012). Implicit bias in the courtroom. *UCLA Law Review, 59*(5), 1124–1186.

King, R. D., & Johnson, B. D. (2016). A punishing look: Skin tone and Afrocentric features in the halls of justice. *American Journal of Sociology, 122*(1), 90–124. doi: 10.1086/686941

King, N. J., Soule, D. A., Steen, S., & Weidner, R. R. (2005). When process affects punishment: Differences in sentences after guilty plea, bench trial, and jury trial in five guidelines states. *Columbia Law Review, 105*(4), 959–1009.

Kingsnorth, R., Lopez, J., Wentworth, J., & Cummings, D. (1998). Adult sexual assault: The role of racial/ethnic composition in prosecution and sentencing. *Journal of Criminal Justice, 26*(5), 359–371. doi: 10.1016/S0047-2352(98)00012-9

Kochel, T. R., Wilson, D. B., & Mastrofski, S. D. (2011). Effect of suspect race on officers' arrest decisions. *Criminology, 49*(2), 473–512. doi: 10.1111/j.1745-9125.2011.00230.x

Kramer, J., & Steffensmeier, D. (1993). Race and imprisonment decisions. *Sociological Quarterly, 34*(2), 357–376. https://doi.org/10.1111/j.1533-8525.1993.tb00395.x

Kramer, J. H., & Ulmer, J. T. (2002). Downward departures for serious violent offenders: Local court "corrections" to Pennsylvania's sentencing guidelines. *Criminology, 40*(4), 897–932. doi: 10.1111/j.1745-9125.2002.tb00977.x

Kutateladze, B. L., & Andiloro, N. R. (2014). *Prosecution and racial justice in New York County—technical report*. National Institute of Justice. Award Number: 2011-DJ-BX-0038.
Kutateladze, B. L., Andiloro, N. R., & Johnson, B. D. (2016). Opening Pandora's box: How does defendant race influence plea bargaining? *Justice Quarterly, 33*(3), 398–426. doi: 10.1080/07418825.2014.915340
Kutateladze, B. L., Andiloro, N. R., Johnson, B. D., & Spohn, C. (2014). Cumulative disadvantage: Examining racial and ethnic disparity in prosecution and sentencing. *Criminology, 52*(3), 514–551. doi: 10.1111/1745-9125.12047
Kutateladze, B. L., Lawson, V. Z., & Andiloro, N. R. (2015). Does evidence really matter? An exploratory analysis of the role of evidence in plea bargaining in felony drug cases. *Law and Human Behavior, 39*(5), 431–442. doi: 10.1037/lhb0000142
Kutateladze, B., Lynn, V., & Liang, E. (2012). *Do race and ethnicity matter in prosecution? A review of empirical studies*. New York: Vera Institute of Justice.
Landes, W. M. (1971). An economic analysis of the courts. *Journal of Law and Economics, 14*(1), 61–108. doi: 10.1086/466704
McCoy, C. (2005). Plea bargain as coercion: The trial penalty and plea bargaining reform. *Criminal Law Quarterly, 50*, 67–107.
Metcalfe, C., & Chiricos, T. (2018). Race, plea, and charge reduction: An assessment of racial disparities in the plea process. *Justice Quarterly, 35*(2), 223–253. doi: 10.1080/07418825.2017.1304564
Meyer, J. A., & Gray, T. (1997). Drunk drivers in the courts: Legal and extra-legal factors affecting pleas and sentences. *Journal of Criminal Justice, 25*(2), 155–163. doi: 10.1016/S0047-2352(96)00058-X
Miethe, T. D. (1987). Charging and plea bargaining practices under determinate sentencing: An investigation of the hydraulic displacement of discretion. *Journal of Criminal Law & Criminology, 78*(1), 155–176. doi: 10.2307/1143578
Missouri v. Frye, 566 U.S. No. 10–444. (2012).
Nardulli, P. F., Eisenstein, J., & Flemming, R. B. (1988). *The tenor of justice: Criminal courts and the guilty plea process*. Urbana and Chicago: University of Illinois Press.
Nardulli, P. F., Flemming, R. B., & Eisenstein, J. (1986). Criminal courts and bureaucratic justice: Concessions and consensus in the guilty plea process. *Journal of Criminology and Criminal Law, 76*(4): 1103–1131. doi: 10.2307/1143503
Nir, E. (2018). Approaching the bench: Accessing elites on the judiciary for qualitative interviews. *International Journal of Social Research Methodology, 21*, 77–89. doi: 10.1080/13645579.2017.1324669
Norris, R. J., & Bonventre, C. L. (2015). Advancing wrongful conviction scholarship: Toward new conceptual frameworks. *Justice Quarterly, 32*(6), 929–949. doi: 10.1080/07418825.2013.827232
Oore, D. G., Gagnon, A., & Bourgeois, D. (2013). When white feels right: The effects of in-group affect and race of partner on negotiation performance. *Negotiation and Conflict Management Research, 6*(2), 94–113. doi: 10.1111/ncmr.12005
Patterson, E. B., & Lynch, M. J. (1991). Bias in formalized bail procedures. In M. J. Lynch & E. B. Patterson (Eds.), *Race and criminal justice*. Albany, NY: Harrow and Heston.

Pfaff. J. (2018). The need for prosecutorial guidelines. In C. Surprenant (Ed.). *Rethinking punishment in the era of mass incarceration*. New York: Taylor and Francis.

Piehl, A. M., & Bushway, S. D. (2007). Measuring and explaining charge bargaining. *Journal of Quantitative Criminology*, *23*(2), 105–125. doi: 10.1007/s10940-006-9023-x

Quinney, R. (1970). *The social reality of crime*. Boston: Little Brown.

Rachlinski, J. J., Johnson, S. L., Wistrich, A. J., & Guthrie, C. (2009). Does unconscious racial bias affect trial judges? *Notre Dame Law Review*, *84*, 1195–1246.

Reaves, B. A. (2013). *Felony defendants in large urban counties, 2009 statistical tables*. Washington, DC: U.S. Department of Justice, Bureau of Justice Statistics.

Redlich, A. D., & Shteynberg, R. (2016). To plead or not to plead: A comparison of juvenile and adult true and false plea decisions. *Law and Human Behavior*, *40*(6), 611–625. doi: 10.1037/lhb0000205

Rehavi, M. M., & Starr, S. B. (2014). Racial disparity in federal criminal sentences. *Journal of Political Economy*, *122*(6), 1320–1354. doi: 10.1086/677255

Reinganum, J. (1988). Plea bargaining and prosecutorial discretion. *American Economic Review*, *78*(4), 713–728.

Ruth, H. S., & Reitz, K. R. (2003). *The challenge of crime: Rethinking our response*. Cambridge, MA: Harvard University Press.

Savitsky, D. (2012). Is plea bargaining a rational choice? Plea bargaining as an engine of racial stratification and overcrowding in the United States prison system. *Rationality and Society*, *24*(2), 131–167. doi: 10.1177/1043463112441351

Schlesinger, T. (2005). Racial and ethnic disparity in pretrial criminal processing. *Justice Quarterly*, *22*(2), 170–192. doi: 10.1080/07418820500088929

Seidel, M. D., Polzer, J. T., & Stewart, K. J. (2000). Friends in high places: The effects of social networks on discrimination in salary negotiations. *Administrative Science Quarterly*, *45*(1), 1–24. doi: 10.2307/2666977

Shermer, L. O., & Johnson, B. D. (2010). Criminal prosecutions: Examining prosecutorial discretion and charge reductions in U.S. federal district courts. *Justice Quarterly*, *27*(3), 394–430. doi: 10.1080/07418820902856972

Smith, D. A. (1986). The plea bargaining controversy. *Journal of Criminal Law and Criminology*, *77*(3), 949–968. doi: 10.237/1143445

Smith, E., & Hattery, A. J. (2011). Race, wrongful conviction & exoneration. *Journal of African American Studies*, *15*(1), 74–94. doi: 10.1007/s12111-010-9130-5

Smith, R. J., & Levinson, J. D. (2011). Impact of implicit racial bias on the exercise of prosecutorial discretion. *Seattle University Law Review*, *35*, 795–826.

Spohn, C. (2000). Thirty years of sentencing reform: The quest for a racially neutral sentencing process. In J. Horney (Ed.) *Criminal justice 2000: Vol. 3. Policies, processes, and decisions of the criminal justice system* (pp. 427–501). Washington, DC: U.S. Department of Justice, National Institute of Justice.

Spohn, C. (2013). Racial disparities in prosecution, sentencing, and punishment. In S. Bucerius & M. Tonry (Eds.), *The Oxford handbook of ethnicity, crime, and immigration* (pp. 166–193). New York: Oxford University Press.

Spohn, C., Beichner, D., & Davis-Frenzel, E. (2001). Prosecutorial justifications for sexual assault case rejection: Guarding the "gateway to justice." *Social Problems, 48*(2), 206–235. doi: 10.1525/sp.2001.48.2.206
Spohn, C., & Tellis, K. (2014). *Policing and prosecuting sexual assault: Inside the criminal justice system*. Boulder, CO: Lynne Rienner.
Staats, C. (2013). *State of the science: Implicit bias review, 2013*. Columbus, OH: Kirwan Institute.
Steffensmeier, D., Ulmer, J., & Kramer, J. (1998). Interaction of race, gender, and age in criminal sentencing: The punishment cost of being young, black, and male. *Criminology, 36*(4), 763–798. doi: 10.1111/j.1745-9125.1998.tb01265.x
Stolzenberg, L., D'Alessio, S. J., & Eitle, D. (2013). Race and cumulative discrimination in the prosecution of criminal defendants. *Race and Justice, 3*(4), 275–299. doi: 10.1177/2153368713500317
Sutton, J. R. (2013). Structural bias in the sentencing of felony defendants. *Social Science Research, 42*(5), 1207–1221. doi: 10.1016/j.ssresearch.2013.04.033
Tashakkori, A., & Thompson, V. D. (1991). Race differences in self-perception and locus of control during adolescence and early adulthood: Methodological implications. *Genetic, Social, and General Psychology Monographs, 117*(2), 133–152.
Tomic, A., & Hakes, J. K. (2008). Case dismissed: Police discretion and racial differences in dismissals of felony charges. *American Law and Economics Review, 10*(1): 110–141. doi: 10.1093/aler/ahn006
Uhlmann, E. L., & Cohen, G. L. (2007). "I think it, therefore it's true": Effects of self-perceived objectivity on hiring discrimination. *Organizational Behavior and Human Decision Processes, 104*(2), 207–223. doi: 10.1016/j.obhdp.2007.07.001
Ulmer, J. T. (2012). Recent developments and new directions in sentencing research. *Justice Quarterly, 29*(1), 1–40. doi: 10.1080/07418825.2011.624115
Ulmer J. T., Eisenstein J., & Johnson B. D. (2010). Trial penalties in federal sentencing: Extra-guidelines factors and district variation. *Justice Quarterly, 27*(4), 560–592. doi: 10.1080/07418820902998063
Ulmer, J. T., Kurlychek, M. C., & Kramer, J. H. (2007). Prosecutorial discretion and the imposition of mandatory minimum sentences. *Journal of Research in Crime and Delinquency, 44*(4), 427–458. doi: 10.1177/0022427807305853
Unnever, J. D., Gabbidon, S. L., & Higgins, G. E. (2011). The election of Barack Obama and perceptions of criminal injustice. *Justice Quarterly, 28*(1), 23–45. doi: 10.1080/07418825.2010.493525
Walker, S., Spohn, C., & DeLone, M. (2004). *The color of justice: Race, ethnicity and crime in America*. Belmont, CA: Wadsworth Publishing.
Ward, G., Farrell, A., & Rousseau, D. (2009). Does racial balance in workforce representation yield equal justice? Race relations of sentencing in federal court organizations. *Law & Society Review, 43*(4), 757–806. doi: 10.1111/j.1540-5893.2009.00388.x
Western, B. (2006). *Punishment and inequality in America*. New York: Russell Sage Foundation.
Wilmot, K., & Spohn, C. (2004). Prosecutorial discretion and real-offense sentencing: An analysis of relevant conduct under the federal sentencing guidelines. *Criminal Justice Policy Review, 15*(3): 324–343. doi: 10.1177/0887403403259434

Wooldredge, J., Frank, J., Goulette, N., & Travis, L. (2015). Is the impact of cumulative disadvantage on sentencing greater for black defendants? *Criminology & Public Policy*, *14*(2), 187–223. doi: 10.1111/1745-9133.12124

Wooldredge, J., & Griffin, T. (2005). Displaced discretion under Ohio sentencing guidelines. *Journal of Criminal Justice*, *33*(4), 301–316. doi; 10.1016/j.jcrimjus.2005.04.001

Wright, R., & Engen, R. (2006). The effects of depth and distance in a criminal code on charging, sentencing, and prosecutor power. *North Carolina Law Review*, *84*(6), 1935–1982.

Wu, J. (2016). Racial/ethnic discrimination and prosecution: A meta-analysis. *Criminal Justice and Behavior*, *43*(4): 437–458. doi: 10.1177/0093854815628026

Yinger, J. (1998). Evidence on discrimination in consumer markets. *Journal of Economic Perspectives*, *12*(2), 23–40. doi: 10.1257/jep.12.2.23

6

Juvenile Justice and Plea Bargaining

Allison D. Redlich, Tina Zottoli,

and Tarika Daftary-Kapur

At the end of the nineteenth century and into the twentieth century, states segregated their justice systems, creating separate courts for youth and adults. At that time, it had become evident to youth advocates, justices, and policymakers that children were not little adults, and that criminal courts were not appropriate settings for rehabilitating impressionable and wayward youth. At the beginning of the twenty-first century, the Supreme Court, in a series of decisions (e.g., *JDB v. North Carolina*, 2011; *Miller v. Alabama*, 2012; *Roper v. Simmons*, 2005), reaffirmed the inherent differences between youth (those aged 17 years and younger) and adults, particularly in relation to their culpability and blameworthiness, and in their abilities to make knowing, intelligent, and voluntary legal decisions.

Despite having separate justice systems, defendants in juvenile and criminal courts are convicted using the same mechanism—the guilty plea. That is, in both courts, almost all (95% or more) adjudicated defendants agree to accept responsibility for the crime and plead guilty (Redlich, Bibas, Edkins, & Madon, 2017). Pleading guilty in criminal court and pleading guilty in juvenile court may look quite different, however. These two systems are premised on different philosophies, implement different procedures, and disparately attend to due process rights (Feld, 2017). As a result, the validity of these guilty plea decisions, including the degree to which defendants understand and appreciate the decision (as legally required), the reasons behind them, and the circumstances surrounding them, may play out differently across criminal and juvenile courts. In addition, the possibility of innocent defendants pleading guilty to crimes not committed has been raised in both courts but not always for the same reasons (Dervan, 2012; Drizin & Luloff, 2007). Nonetheless, research on youth guilty pleas has not always clearly demarcated whether the research and its findings are relevant to juvenile or criminal court, or both. This is particularly important in light of the fact that youth may be charged in either system, depending on the jurisdiction.

In this chapter, we review the extant research on youth defendants and guilty pleas. Guided by this available research, we focus on three areas: (1) the circumstances surrounding guilty plea decisions (e.g., access to attorneys, time to make decisions); (2) youths' knowledge about guilty plea decisions and whether they were made voluntarily; and (3) the rationales underlying guilty plea decisions. In doing so, we review what is known specific to youth defendants, and to the extent possible, we note whether the research is relevant to pleas entered in juvenile or criminal court. Additionally, across these three areas we address plea decision-making by guilty and innocent defendants, highlighting the similarities and differences. We conclude with a call for future research and implications for juveniles involved in the juvenile or adult criminal justice systems.

Adolescents as Defendants

In both criminal and juvenile court, youth understanding and appreciation of legal procedures and policies is expected, even if not always present. As such, examining the capabilities, circumstances, and reasons underlying juvenile defendants' legal decision-making has long been an endeavor of psycho-legal scholars. It was perhaps Grisso's (1981) seminal study of youths' understanding and appreciation of *Miranda* rights that began the modern era of scholarship in youth legal comprehension. Over the past 40 years of study, social scientists have learned that juveniles are more likely than adults to have deficits in the capacities necessary to participate competently at trial (Cooper, 1997; Grisso et al., 2003; McKee, 1998; Savitsky & Karras, 1984; Viljoen, Odgers, Grisso, & Tillbrook, 2007), are less likely to understand their rights (Grisso, 1981; Redlich, Silverman, & Steiner, 2003; Viljoen, Klaver, & Roesch, 2005), are more likely to comply with police (Kassin et al., 2010), and are less likely to fully appreciate future consequences (Steinberg et al., 2009). These deficiencies have largely been ascribed to their immature cognitive, socioemotional, and neurological development. Both neurological and sociobehavioral research has established that pre- and post-adolescence are periods of tremendous growth and development. It is within this backdrop of developmental immaturity that juvenile defendants' decision-making in accepting or rejecting guilty pleas is often examined.

In Table 6.1, 12 published studies are listed that we believe to be a complete representation of the published literature pertaining to juvenile guilty pleas.[1] We did not include the series of focus groups and qualitative interviews conducted by the National Juvenile Defender Center (NJDC) (although we do

[1] We note here that the study by Schmidt, Reppucci, and Woolard (2003) was not included. The word *plea* was found three times in a 24-page article, and the study focused on youth–attorney relationships. However, the authors did find that, in comparison to youth (aged 12–17), adults (aged 19–35) were more likely to spontaneously mention guilty pleas in the context of a hypothetical vignette (all participants were pretrial detainees in Virginia).

Table 6.1 Summary of Guilty Plea Studies Pertaining to Youth

Cite	Method	Ages (Years)/Court	Location	Circumstances	Understanding	Rationales	Innocence
Daftary-Kapur & Zottoli (2014)	Interviews of youth charged as adults ($n = 40$)	13–18 (age at time of interview)/criminal court	New York City, NY	Yes	Yes	Yes	No
Grisso et al. (2003)	Hypothetical vignette with justice-involved and community youth and adults ($n = 1,393$)	G1: 11–17 G2: 18–24/juvenile and criminal court	Los Angeles, CA; Philadelphia, PA; northern FL; northern, central, and western VA	Yes	Yes	Yes	No
Kaban & Quinlan (2004)	Interviews and assessments of justice-involved youth ($n = 98$)	9–17/juvenile court	Massachusetts	Yes	Yes	No	No
Malloy, Shuman, & Cauffman (2014)	Interviews of incarcerated youth ($n = 193$)	14–17 (males only; age at time of incarceration)/court unclear	California	Yes	No	Yes	Yes
Peterson-Badali & Abramovitch (1993)	Hypothetical vignette/experiment ($n = 192$)	G1: 9–11; G2: 12–13; G3: 14–16; G4: 18–24/court NA	Toronto, Canada	Yes	Yes	Yes	No
Redlich & Bonventre (2015)	Archival analysis of tender-of-plea (ToP) forms ($n = 208$)	Juvenile and criminal courts	US–National	Yes	Yes	No	Yes

(continued)

Table 6.1 Continued

Cite	Method	Ages (Years)/Court	Location	Circumstances	Understanding	Rationales	Innocence
Redlich & Shteynberg (2016)	Hypothetical vignette/ experiment ($n = 189$)	G1: 13–17; G2: 18–24/court NA	Albany, NY	Yes	Yes	Yes	Yes
Sanborn (1992)	Observations ($n \geq 75$)* Interviews with court personnel ($n = 100$) State law analysis ($n = 51$)	Juvenile court	Law analysis: US–national; observations and interviews: northeastern state (urban, suburban, and rural juvenile courts)	Yes	Yes	No	Yes (fact-based pleas)
Schissel (1993)	Observation-coding of juvenile court ($n = 581$; for plea data)	12–15/juvenile court	Edmonton, Canada	Yes	No	No	No
Tepfer, Nirider, & Tricarico (2010)	Archival examination of youth exonerations ($n = 103$)	11–19 (age at time of arrest)/juvenile and criminal court	US–National	Yes (see App. D)	No	No	Yes
Viljoen, Klaver, & Roesch (2005)	Interviews and assessments with youth defendants ($n = 152$)	11–17/juvenile court	Washington	Yes	Yes	No	No
Zottoli, Daftary-Kapur, Winters, & Hogan (2016)	Interviews with justice-involved youth and adults ($n = 97$)	G1: 13–17; G2: 18–54 (age at time of arrest)/ criminal court	New York City	Yes	No	No	Yes

*The total number of observations in the Sanborn study is unclear. Sanborn reported that he observed at least five plea hearings with each of 15 judges.

cite these throughout the chapter). Their focus was on access to legal representation and they were not scientific studies per se. We also did not include overviews or non-empirical law review articles (e.g., Drizin & Luloff, 2007). We also looked for studies outside of the United States and Canada but did not turn up many examples.[2] Finally, we excluded several recent experimental studies conducted exclusively with college student samples (e.g., Henderson, 2016; Wilford & Wells, 2017). Although some entities define youth as being up to age 25 (e.g., the United Nations, see http://www.unesco.org/new/en/social-and-human-sciences/themes/youth/youth-definition/), the U.S. criminal justice system draws a bright line at younger than 18 years.

Table 6.1 provides the methods, sample size, court (juvenile and/or criminal), and location of data collection for all 12 studies listed. In addition, as our focus in this chapter is on circumstances surrounding the plea, youth understanding of the plea, plea rationales, and innocence, the table also notes whether the study examined these issues. Of the 12 studies we identified, 10 were conducted in the United States and 2 in Canada. Five studies interviewed adolescent defendants pre- or post-plea (one additional study surveyed juvenile court professionals about youth pleas); three studies examined plea decision-making via hypothetical vignettes; three analyzed existing information about the context of juvenile guilty pleas (state laws, plea forms, youth exonerations); and two conducted systematic observations of juvenile court pleas. Most (11 of 12) used one method only. Only two studies, both of which presented hypothetical vignettes and compared youth to adults, were experiments, in that random assignment and manipulated conditions were used.

Seven studies focused exclusively on juvenile defendants, and the remaining five compared juvenile and adult defendants or courts. Ages of participants ranged from 9 to 54 years, and sample sizes ranged from 40 to nearly 1,400, with most studies reporting samples of between 100 and 200 participants.

We coded all 12 studies as having examined circumstances related to youth plea decisions. However, we construed "circumstances" broadly to include aspects such as perceived evidence strength (e.g., Peterson-Badali & Abramovitch, 1993; Viljoen et al., 2005), an educational intervention (e.g., Kaban & Quinlan, 2004), and whether there were confessions (true or false) in evidence (e.g., Tepfer, Nirider, & Tricarico, 2009; Viljoen et al., 2005). Eight studies were relevant to youths' plea understanding and legal comprehension, and six investigated the reasons underlying plea decisions. Finally, 6 of the 12 studies looked at false guilty pleas among real or mock innocent defendants.

[2] We did find an ethnographic study of a children's court in Tasmania (Travers, 2007), but its focus was on sentencing after guilty pleas had taken place. We also found a qualitative description of a pilot youth court in Scotland (Piacentini & Walters, 2006), but it was largely an overview without data.

Only one study to date (Redlich & Shteynberg, 2016) has examined all four of these issues.

Guilty Plea Decisions: Circumstances

Courtroom hearings in juvenile and criminal courts are typically depicted as complex, intimidating events often unnavigable to those unfamiliar with the local culture (Bach, 2009; Bibas, 2004; Drizin & Luloff, 2007). Because of the immaturities in development described earlier, youth may not act in their best interest when deciding whether to accept or reject plea deals. These immaturities may be exacerbated when factors such as amount of attorney contact and communication, decisional time frames and exploding offers, and plea discounts are taken into account. Given the space constraints of this chapter, we will focus on these three circumstances, though there are many other circumstances (alone and in combination) that can also influence plea decision-making. In addition, because these circumstances can vary depending on whether the plea is processed in juvenile or criminal court, we note the relevant court examined in the research reviewed (see also Table 6.1).

Attorney Contact and Communication

Contact and communication with attorneys is likely to play a key role in what factors are given weight by both adults and youth when deciding whether to accept a plea deal. Attorneys are best positioned to identify whether their clients are competent decision-makers and what deficiencies exist in their legal knowledge and appreciation of consequences. Buss (2000) has suggested ways in which attorneys can promote the decision-making competency of their clients in juvenile court. For example, attorneys can enhance their client's participation in the trial process through instruction such as providing careful explanations, using appropriate language, and encouraging youth to ask questions. These strategies could lead to an increase in a youth's participation as a defendant, and as such improve decision-making.

Caseloads play a crucial role in the level of contact attorneys have with clients. It is well established that prosecutors and public defenders (who handle the majority of criminal and juvenile court cases; Wolf Harlow, 2003) often handle crushing caseloads that surpass recommended numbers (Work, 2014). Limited research has examined the relationship between prosecutor caseload pressures and plea bargains. In a study of Illinois state criminal courts, prosecutor caseloads were significantly and positively correlated with felony guilty-plea rates (Wooldredge, 1989). In a more recent study, Kutateladze, Andiliro, and Johnson (2014) found that pleas resulting in custodial sentences were more common for prosecutors with higher caseloads.

Public defenders face similar pressures to achieve justice through guilty pleas (Work, 2014), and the limited data that exist suggest that high caseloads may negatively impact plea decisions. For example, in two recent studies, it was found that youth who had accepted plea deals in criminal court met with their attorneys an average of two times—usually in conjunction with court appearances—before pleading guilty (Daftary-Kapur & Zottoli, 2014; Zottoli, Daftary-Kapur, Winters, & Hogan, 2016). In contrast, adults met with their attorneys more frequently (reporting an average of 4.7 meetings) before entering a plea (Zottoli et al., 2016). Authors of an assessment of juvenile courts in Illinois found that attorneys are usually appointed at the first appearance or at the conclusion of the first appearance. They also found that the majority of juvenile court cases ended in pleas that were entered at the first appearance (Crawford, Dohrn, Geraghty, Moss, & Puritz, 2007). Other juvenile court assessments revealed frequent waivers by youth to their right to counsel, high plea rates, insufficient advocacy (e.g., filing motions, investigating cases), high rates of turnover among juvenile court attorneys, and attorneys being generally ignorant of adolescent development (Miller-Wilson & Puritz, 2003). These findings are troubling, as youth likely require more time and more explanation and repetition of complex information than adults facing the same choices (Buss, 2000).

Several possibilities for this discrepancy in consultations exist, not least of which, and perhaps most relevant here, is that adults are more likely to reach out and initiate more contact with their attorneys. Limited contact with attorneys may explain why 40% of the transferred youth interviewed by Daftary-Kapur and Zottoli (2014) stated that their attorneys did not tell them what would happen if they did not accept their plea offers, and why more than 40% of the youth could not articulate the most basic of rights they had waived when accepting their plea deals. Of course, it may be that attorneys did inform the youth of these aspects, but given the infrequency and compressed time frames of their meetings, the youth simply did not comprehend or retain the information. Either way, these data emphasize the realities faced by overburdened attorneys in juvenile and criminal courts, especially if they are not attuned to the developmental needs of juvenile clients.

Decisional Time Frames

Anecdotally, we know that prosecutors, and occasionally judges, tend to make offers that are only valid for short periods of time (leaving defense attorneys little to no time to investigate cases), a phenomenon sometimes referred to as *exploding offers* (Caldwell, 2012; Dervan, 2012; Work, 2014). Time-limited offers may be a practical result of the caseload pressures faced by prosecutors (Work, 2014). Zottoli et al. (2016) recently reported on data from an ongoing study of youth and adults who pleaded guilty to felonies in New York City criminal courts. The amount of time between notification and acceptance of plea offers ranged from minutes to months, with significant differences by age group. Nearly half of the youth (49%) reported that they had less than an hour to make their decisions, while the majority of adults (60%) reported having more than a day to decide whether or not to accept the deal (Zottoli et al., 2016). Importantly, although youth reported these time pressures, the interview protocol used did not allow the researchers to differentiate between explicit time limits given by district attorneys or judges and pressures that were exerted by other factors, such as the knowledge that one would return to pretrial detention (discussed in the next section) if a deal was not accepted on a given date.

Regardless of the source, in time-pressured and emotionally charged situations, decision-making may be compromised by a tendency to rely on peripheral cues, a failure to consider the breadth of potential outcomes, and a focus on the most salient short-term consequences of an option. The decision-making of youth has been shown to be particularly susceptible to time pressure and emotion (Crone & van der Molen, 2004; Gardner & Steinberg, 2005; Miller & Byrnes, 2001; Prencipe et al., 2011). Courts should therefore consider whether youth have been given ample time to weigh the offer and its consequences before making a decision to accept or reject a plea.

Pretrial Detention

A common, proximate explanation given for the acceptance of plea deals is simply to get out of jail (Bach, 2009; Gross, Jacoby, Matheson, Montgomery, & Patil, 2005; Redlich, Summers, & Hoover, 2010). Pretrial detention as a potentially coercive factor for guilty pleas has been discussed by legal scholars (e.g., Bibas, 2004; Kellough & Wortley, 2002) but has received less attention from the scientific community. Daftary-Kapur and Zottoli (2014) found that pretrial detention impacted the decision to accept a plea deal for youth charged as adults in New York City—one-quarter of the youth specifically mentioned "getting out of jail" as a reason for taking their plea offers. And the threat of returning to pretrial detention may have resulted in the apparently high rate of "on-the-spot" decisions reported by the youth in that study, a theme we return to in the section on plea rationales. Given that youth decisions may be more strongly influenced by immediate, positive outcomes than decisions of adults (Cauffman & Steinberg, 2012), researchers should seek to investigate the relative impact of pretrial detention on the plea decisions of youth and adults, especially in contexts where the sentence offered in a plea is probation and/or time served (i.e., getting out of jail).

Innocence and the Role of Circumstances

Over the past 25 years increasing attention has been paid to wrongful convictions, particularly in criminal courts (Norris, 2017). Currently, there are 417 known false guilty pleas in the National Registry of Exonerations (see Chapter 7, this volume); approximately 10% of these individuals were under the age of 18 when the crimes for which they were convicted were reported. There are a number of factors that may make innocent juveniles prone to false guilty pleas, including the aforementioned factors of high attorney caseloads, large plea discounts, and pretrial detention. High attorney caseloads can result in fewer investigations and more pressure to plea, contributing to the problem of false guilty pleas. Malloy, Shulman, and Cauffman (2014) found that attorney pressure strongly predicted self-reported false admissions of guilt (i.e., confessions and guilty pleas) in a sample of youth incarcerated for serious crimes. Zottoli et al. (2016) found in their study that significant percentages of the youth (26.5%) and adults (19%) claimed they were not guilty of any of the charges, yet all had pleaded guilty. Other factors such as exploding offers, pressure from prosecutors, and other techniques designed to gain compliance can lead to false guilty pleas. False confessions to the police may also lead to false guilty pleas. Of the seven youth who falsely pleaded guilty in Tepfer et al.'s (2009) sample of exonerated youth, five of them had also falsely confessed to the police (see also Perillo, 2015; Redlich, 2010b).

Most of the studies on false guilty pleas in youth have examined youth who were convicted in criminal court. To this point, Tepfer and colleagues (2009) noted that their study included "few juvenile court cases simply because those cases are confidential and rarely publicized, often making it impossible to obtain information about them. Even if those cases were not confidential, moreover, juvenile court defendants typically do not make use of appeals and often have limited access to post-disposition procedures that enable the innocent to clear their names" (p. 898; citations omitted). Overall, little attention has been paid to the risk of wrongful convictions in juvenile court (Drizin & Luloff, 2007), and issues such as confidentiality and rare use of appeals are only two such factors that serve to distinguish the identification of false guilty pleas in juvenile versus criminal court.

In summary, the circumstances that often surround pleas, such as limited attorney contact, insufficient time, and other pressures, are likely to make for ill-informed decisions. When the developmental characteristics of juveniles are considered in concert with these circumstances, as well as the possibility of actual innocence, the risks of miscarriages of justice—of either not receiving due process or being wrongly convicted—increase.

Guilty Plea Decisions: Knowing and Voluntary

Another area of research that has received considerable attention by psycholegal scholars is the comparison of juveniles and adult defendants with respect to their legal comprehension (e.g., Grisso et al., 2003). For example, in their seminal study on competence to stand trial, Grisso and his colleagues (2003) determined that, regardless of juvenile justice involvement, youth aged 11–15 years had significantly more adjudicative competence deficits (e.g., understanding of key roles; reasoning relevant to attorney–client discussions) in comparison to those aged 16–24 years.

Researchers have also begun to examine juveniles' actual plea comprehension, either by itself or in comparison to adults' comprehension. As shown in Table 6.1, studies have been conducted using a variety of methods, including surveys or interviews of juvenile justice professionals and defendants, experimental lab studies and hypothetical vignette studies, and systematic court observations. On the whole, these studies tend to support two basic findings: (1) youth defendants are unlikely to make knowing and voluntary plea decisions (e.g., Daftary-Kapur & Zottoli, 2014; Kaban & Quinlan, 2004), and (2) court procedures and processes do not promote—and may even deter—knowing and voluntary decision-making (e.g., Redlich & Bonventre, 2015; Sanborn, 1992). A third possibility explored in this section is the degree to which legal comprehension and false guilty pleas are related.

Knowing and Voluntary Plea Decisions

Given the general landscape of psycho-legal research on juvenile defendants' capabilities in the legal system, it is not surprising that much of the research concludes that youth tend not to make knowing and voluntary plea decisions, particularly in contrast to adult defendants. Redlich and Shteynberg (2016) brought at-risk community youth and young adults into the laboratory for an experiment on hypothetical plea decision-making. Participants were asked to imagine that they were either guilty or innocent of an armed robbery, given other relevant details (e.g., 75% chance of conviction at trial), and asked to make a plea decision. To help with this decision, participants read a written tender-of-plea (ToP) form, which reviewed their rights and consequences, and heard an oral colloquy before a "judge" (confederate in a black robe with a gavel). After entering their written and oral plea decisions, participants were interviewed about their plea decision (e.g., rationales and perceived voluntariness) and assessed on adjudicative competence, plea comprehension, and knowledge of vocabulary terms related to guilty pleas. Plea comprehension measured understanding of basic (e.g., that guilty pleas must be voluntary) and more nuanced (e.g., that the prosecutor does not have to prove guilt beyond a reasonable doubt) concepts. Plea vocabulary included a list of words that were present in the ToP form/colloquy, which participants were asked to define.

In addition to youth scoring significantly lower than adults on the plea comprehension and vocabulary measures, youths' levels of knowledge and understanding were found to be quite low. For example, a perfect score on the plea vocabulary measure would be a 38. On average, youth scored 13.77 (SD = 8.99), indicating a mean score of 36% correct. Not reported in Redlich and Shteynberg (2016) were scores on the individual vocabulary words. We present them here to highlight the general lack of understanding of participants and to provide examples of incorrect definitions (see Kaban & Quinlan, 2004, for similar examples with justice-involved youth). As shown in Table 6.2, for all but 3 of the 19 words, the majority (half or more) of juveniles

Table 6.2 Percent Incorrect on Plea Vocabulary Words*

Word/Phrase	Juveniles	Adults	Example of Incorrect Definition
Liable	58%	18%	To trust; rely on
Impartial	85%	59%	Not the whole thing
Cross-examine	70%	40%	Observe reactions of witnesses at trial
Subpoena	85%	46%	How many charges
Self-incrimination	65%	31%	When you talk for yourself
Presumption of innocence	63%	41%	Being accused of something you did not do
Burden of proof	70%	58%	Evidence; an alibi
Reasonable doubt	69%	47%	Having second thoughts
Unanimous	69%	31%	Nobody finds out
Appeal	76%	30%	When you're good-looking
Waive	66%	32%	Saying "hi"
Restitution	84%	50%	I rest my case
Concession	98%	89%	Discussion in the back room
Unlawful influence	62%	45%	Under the influence of a drug
Motion	76%	61%	Movement; very upset
Plea	38%	27%	Asking people to reconsider
Sentence	15%	5%	Like you write a sentence
Right	28%	21%	Am I right or am I wrong?
Mandatory penalty	64%	40%	Sentence that must be paid whether you are guilty or innocent

*From Redlich and Shteynberg (2016).

incorrectly defined the word or did not know what the word meant. Table 6.2 shows that the young adults' accuracy was low as well; on five concepts ("burden of proof," "concession," "plea," "sentence," and "right"), adults and youth did not differ significantly, scoring similarly poorly. It is important to remember that these vocabulary words were used in the ToP/colloquy and that participants had multiple opportunities to ask questions or for clarification (which few did).

In an earlier study, Kaban and Quinlan (2004) examined the knowledge of actual juvenile defendants aged 9 to 17 years. Without instruction, on average, youth could define only 2 of 36 words correctly. After instruction, accuracy improved to five words, but overall, it was clear that the youth lacked understanding of the very words that would be used in the plea hearings. Similarly, Daftary-Kapur and Zottoli (2014) found that fewer than half of the youth in their sample who were convicted by guilty plea could identify more than two of the five basic, definitional elements of plea deals (i.e., admission of guilt, offered by prosecutor, reduced time/charges, waiver of trial, and waiver of appeal). Although the Kaban and Quinlan (2004), Daftary-Kapur and Zottoli (2014), and Redlich and Shteynberg (2016) studies were conducted in different locations, with different populations, more than a decade apart, and using distinct methods, their findings are strikingly similar.

Finally, there is also evidence suggesting that court professionals who deal with youth defendants believe that some juveniles do not understand the plea process. Sanborn (1992) interviewed 100 juvenile court judges, attorneys, and probation officers, asking them whether, in their opinion, youth understand most or all of the plea colloquy. Overall, only 46% of the sample answered "yes" to this question. However, at the same time, there are also indications that attorneys and judges are unaware of the difficulties youth often have in understanding the guilty plea process. In the next section, we turn to how existing juvenile court procedures and policies are likely to do little to promote understanding.

Juvenile Court Plea Procedures and Policies

Since 1999 the National Juvenile Defender Center (NJDC) has assessed more than 20 states' juvenile courts, primarily focusing on youths' access to and the quality of legal representation. Regarding pleas, the NJDC assessments noted common problems across sites, such as high rates of pleas; pleas occurring early in the process (leaving no time for investigation, trust building, or education); unknowledgeable pleas; developmentally inappropriate, incomplete, and even inaccurate plea colloquies; and systemic setting problems around culture and judge–attorney interactions. For example, in Illinois, Crawford et al. (2007) reported that "interviews with children and parents revealed that many did not understand what had occurred" (p. 43). Another assessment, conducted by the Center for Families, Children, and the Courts (2008), noted that "[youth and parent] participants recalled feeling that they were listening to a foreign language with terms, words, code numbers, and acronyms that they did not understand. The majority of . . . parents and youth reported leaving court with virtually no idea of what had happened and hoping that, once outside the courtroom, the youth's attorney or a probation officer would provide an explanation" (p. 87). Interestingly, however, defense attorneys interviewed in the same assessment felt that most information was conveyed to parents and youth in an easy-to-understand manner! Thus, it is clear that there was a disconnect between the givers and receivers of information.

These qualitative accounts, which demonstrate inadequate understanding of guilty pleas and legal processes, are in general agreement with the scientific research reviewed in the first part of this section (e.g., Kaban & Quinlan, 2004; Redlich & Shteynberg, 2016; Sanborn, 1992). Given these indications of low understanding among youth—and the requirement that pleas are knowing and intelligent—a relevant question to ask is what, if anything, is done to rectify this issue? In large part, it is the responsibility of the defense attorney to educate youth about general and specific legal information. The NJDC assessments, however, revealed numerous problems relevant to legal representation and resources which can be presumed to affect youth's understanding. For example, as noted earlier, most juvenile defenders have overburdened caseloads, which can lead to the absence of meaningful attorney–juvenile contact and, in turn, unknowing and unintelligent decision-making.

In a more formal sense, written ToP forms and oral plea colloquies are the mechanisms used by the courts to assess whether defendants have made knowing and voluntary plea decisions. Although now 25 years old, Sanborn's (1992) examination of states' juvenile court requirements for guilty pleas found that 39 states and the District of Columbia require judges to inform youth defendants of their rights before accepting pleas; however, the rights (if any specifically) mentioned were found to be highly variable. Thirty-three states require the judge to alert defendants of the possible sentences/dispositions and to explain the charges. Regarding voluntariness, 31 states require the judge to inquire about this, but as noted by Sanborn, "the directions [in re: voluntariness] are not explicit . . . only a few jurisdictions instruct judges to inquire into the presence of threats or promises" (p. 133). Finally, only 13 states (in 1992) directly or indirectly held *Boykin v. Alabama* (1969)—the Supreme Court case that made explicit the intelligent and voluntary requirements of a guilty plea and required that these be made part of the court record—as binding in juvenile court. When the sample of court professionals were asked if *Boykin* should apply in juvenile court, 95% believed it should.

Regarding ToP forms, a recent study analyzed the content and comprehensibility of these forms in juvenile and criminal courts (Redlich & Bonventre, 2015). Two primary findings emerged. First, ToP forms were found to exist significantly more often in criminal than in juvenile courts. Because oral plea colloquies are mandatory, this first finding indicates that juveniles, who are known to possess deficits in legal comprehension, are more likely to receive plea information in only one modality (oral), whereas adults are more likely to receive the information in two modalities (oral and written). Second, juvenile and criminal court ToP forms were found to be indistinguishable in content and in comprehensibility. For example, both courts' forms required an 11th- to 12th-grade reading level, on average, to fully understand the document. Most defendants (youth and adults), however, read at a sixth-grade level or lower; only 4% of the forms in the sample could be read at this level or below (Redlich & Bonventre, 2015).

Taken as a whole, the set of findings reported here do little to inspire confidence in the court's ability to recognize and deal with youths' deficiencies in plea comprehension in juvenile court, let alone criminal court, where consequences that youth face may be graver. Ensuring due process for those accused of crimes is intended not only to preserve the fundamental fairness and integrity of the system but also to protect the innocent from wrongful conviction. The problems identified here may increase the likelihood of innocent youth pleading guilty.

Innocence and Knowing/Voluntary Guilty Pleas

Although there is some evidence that youth may be at increased risk for false guilty pleas (Redlich, 2010a; Redlich & Shteynberg, 2016), little research has examined relationships between innocence and plea knowingness (for either youth or adults). Indeed, of the 12 studies listed in Table 6.1, only 3 examined both understanding and innocence, and of those, only one examined the relationship between them.

The one study (Redlich & Shteynberg, 2016) to examine relations between innocence, plea decisions, and legal understanding found different patterns of results by guilt status. Specifically, among those asked to assume guilt, there were significant and positive correlations between the decision to plead guilty and adjudicative competence understanding and reasoning scores and on plea vocabulary. In contrast, among those asked to assume innocence, the correlations between the plea decision and measures of general and specific legal understanding were negative and non-significant. However, Redlich and Shteynberg controlled for age in these analyses because of differential plea rates by age groups (and guilt/innocence). Here, instead of controlling for age, the correlations are computed separately by age group. Despite the reduction in sample size for each group, we can still see divergent patterns. In Figure 6.1, correlations by age group for the plea decision and measures of legal comprehension for those asked to assume *guilt* are shown. For juveniles, but not adults, increased legal comprehension was related to an increased willingness

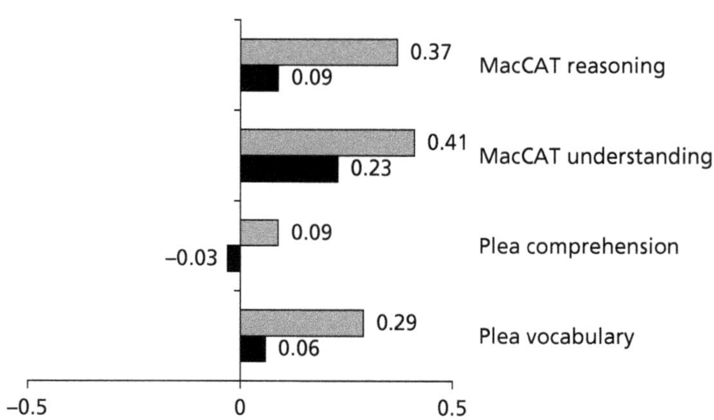

Figure 6.1 Correlations between plea knowledge measures and plea decision by age group when guilty.

Notes: 0 = not guilty plea; 1 = guilty plea; light bars = juveniles; dark bars = adults; MacCAT = MacArthur Competence Assessment Tool: Criminal Adjudication.

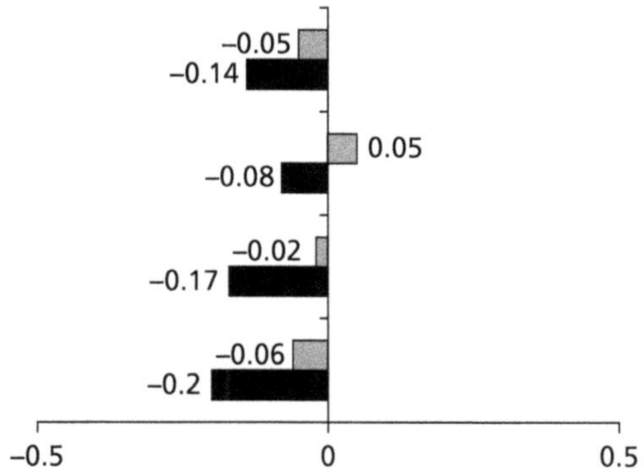

Figure 6.2 Correlations between plea knowledge measures and plea decision by age group when innocent.
Notes: 0 = not guilty plea; 1 = guilty plea; light bars = juveniles; dark bars = adults; MacCAT = MacArthur Competence Assessment Tool: Criminal Adjudication.

to plead guilty, indicating that the original results in Redlich and Shteynberg's (2016) study were largely driven by juveniles. In Figure 6.2, which displays the same relations for those asked to assume *innocence*, we see the opposite. Decreased legal comprehension was related to a willingness to plead guilty when innocent, but only for adults, not for juveniles. Drawing conclusions from this one study would, of course, be premature. Determining whether and how guilt/innocence status and legal comprehension are related is worthy of future study for both juvenile and adult defendants.

In summary, many studies have compared the capabilities and understanding of juveniles and adults in the legal system, and, with rare exception, youth are found to have less knowledge about and less of an appreciation for legal terminology, concepts, and outcomes than adults. Research on the knowledge relevant to plea decision-making supports these consistent conclusions. Nonetheless, courts and court professionals have seemingly done little to alter their procedures to ensure that youths pleading guilty are making knowing and voluntary decisions.

Guilty Plea Decisions: Rationales

There are many reasons why individuals will choose to waive their rights, even if innocent, and plead guilty. One important consideration may be that they and/or their attorneys perceive the evidence of guilt as damning and a jury likely to convict. As shown in Table 6.1, to date, six published studies have examined youth rationales for pleading guilty. Across these studies, which used several types of methods, a common theme has emerged. Specifically, the immaturity of judgement that often typifies youth decision-making—a focus on short-term benefits and consequences, a tendency to comply with authority, and susceptibility to peer influence—is apparent in the rationales that youth give for their plea decisions.

Immaturity of Judgement

Consistent with developmental data in other areas of youth decision-making, research has found that youth tend to focus more on the short-term than longer-term consequences or benefits of pleading guilty. As previously discussed, Daftary-Kapur and Zottoli (2014) interviewed 40 youth charged as adults in New York City who had pleaded guilty. Prior to asking youth about their own guilty plea decisions, youth were asked, generally, why someone might enter a guilty plea. The majority of these generic rationales (60%) reflected a short-term orientation, with the modal reason "to give up fighting the system" given by 35% of the youth. Another quarter of the sample said that people take plea deals to get out jail (i.e., pretrial detention) as soon as possible. One-third of the sample, however, did acknowledge that that people take plea deals to get lower sentences or avoid jail or prison sentences. In contrast, when the youth were asked about the factors that contributed to their own decisions, none of the youth mentioned reduced sentences. The most common individual rationales given were going home (70%), ending the legal process (60%), and getting out of jail (50%).[3]

In comparison, another interview study examining youths' plea rationales, conducted by Malloy and her colleagues (2014), reported a smaller percentage (18%) of youth who claimed to have pleaded guilty (when reportedly guilty) to get the process over with. Whereas none of the Daftary-Kapur and Zottoli (2014) sample cited pleading guilty to get reduced sentences, 36% of the Malloy et al. (2014) youth cited this reason. Further, whereas none of the youth in the Daftary-Kapur and Zottoli (2014) sample cited their actual guilt as a reason they pleaded guilty, 18% of the Malloy et al. (2014) self-reported guilty youth gave their actual guilt or desire to be truthful as a rationale for their pleas. In an earlier hypothetical plea-decision study that compared the reasons children and adults gave for guilty plea decisions, children and those in early adolescence were more likely than adults to justify a guilty plea by referring to a person's actual guilt (Peterson-Badali & Abramovitch, 1993). The authors concluded that youth were not distinguishing between legal and moral reasoning in the same way that adults were. That is, youth focused more on their actual wrongdoing, whereas adults recognized their legal right to force the state to prove guilt with evidence.

Differences in the rationales provided by the youth in the only two field studies to date may reflect that fact that the samples were drawn from two

[3] Youth could provide multiple responses, thus the percentages do not add up to 100%.

different populations. Malloy et al. (2014) drew their sample from a sample of post-conviction, incarcerated youth in California. In contrast, in New York City, from which the Daftary-Kapur and Zottoli (2014) sample was drawn, youth facing all but the most serious charges (e.g., murder) are most often offered probation in exchange for their guilty pleas. Regardless of these differences, across both studies, youth rarely spontaneously reported thinking about longer-term consequences, such as being able to get a job in the future or being able to finish school.

Although Daftary-Kapur and Zottoli (2014) and Malloy et al. (2014) did not examine the rationales that youth provided for pleading by youth of different ages, there is some evidence—again, consistent with developmental science—that consideration of long-term factors increases with age. For example, using identical vignettes, Grisso et al. (2003) compared youth and adult decision-making across three hypothetical legal scenarios (an interrogation, an attorney consult, and a plea deal) in justice-involved youth and adults and in matched community samples. Adults were more likely than youth to consider the odds of winning at trial in their plea decisions, and across all three scenarios recognition of long-term consequences increased with age. Similarly, Redlich and Shteynberg (2016), also within the context of a hypothetical vignette, asked juveniles and young adults to endorse their level of agreement with each of seven possible rationales for their plea decisions (e.g., "I was thinking about what would happen in the near future"; "I did not want to risk losing at trial"). Compared to young adults, youth who rejected plea deals were less likely to endorse that they were thinking about the long-term effects of their decisions than adults, and, though not reaching significance at $p < .05$, youth tended to be more likely to believe that a better deal would come along if they rejected the deal on the table (small-sized effect, $d = .29$). Finally, Viljoen and colleagues (2005) interviewed detained juvenile defendants about their pending plea decisions and found that older (age 15 to 17 years) but not younger (age 11 to 14 years) youth considered the evidence in the case. They also found that youth with higher IQs and those who received peer advice and had more prior arrests or had spent more time in custody were more likely than other defendants to say that they would accept a plea bargain if offered.

Overall, these field and vignette studies support the premise that age and development influence plea decision-making. Preliminary data from a series of interviews with adults and juveniles convicted by guilty plea lend further support that youth do, in fact, show clear developmental differences from adults in terms of their focus on the more immediate and short-term consequences for their decisions, the number of collateral consequences that they can identify, and in their appreciation of the impact of their conviction on their personal situations (Zottoli, Daftary-Kapur, & Tahan, 2017). However, to date, there are no published data comparing the rationales for plea decisions of youth and adults actually convicted by guilty plea.

Innocence and Youth Plea Rationales

Much of the research on guilty pleas has examined willingness to plead when guilty versus innocent, and, perhaps unsurprisingly, this research has generally found that innocent participants are significantly less likely to plead guilty than are guilty ones (Gazal-Ayal & Tor, 2012). In comparing youth and adults, innocent youth have been shown to be more likely than innocent adults to plead guilty in a vignette-based study (Redlich & Shteynberg, 2016). And among youth and adults who pleaded guilty in New York City, youth were more likely than adults to claim that they were innocent (Zottoli et al., 2016). Nonetheless, only 2 of the 12 studies listed in Table 6.1 examined plea rationales and innocence.

First, in the Malloy et al. (2014) sample of 14- to 17-year-old boys incarcerated in a secure juvenile facility in California, 25% of the sample (n = 49) claimed to have entered a false guilty plea. In some ways, the reasons provided by these self-reported innocent youths looked similar to the reasons reported by the self-reported guilty youth. For example, 51% of the self-reported innocent youth and 36% of the self-reported guilty youth claimed to have pleaded guilty to get reduced sentences, and 14% and 10%, respectively, claimed that they were under duress or felt pressured to plead guilty. However, compared to self-reported guilty youth, youth who claimed to have made false guilty pleas were much less likely to say their pleas were based on perception of the evidence against them (20% and 3%, respectively). Moreover, 31% of the self-reported innocent youth claimed to have pleaded guilty to protect someone else, which Malloy et al. (2014) speculated may have been due to California's "three strikes" law (i.e., to protect someone else from getting a more severe punishment for a third conviction; see also Redlich et al., 2010). In contrast, only 1% of the true guilty plea sample claimed to have pleaded guilty to protect someone else.

The second study that examined differences in rationales between innocent and guilty participants is the hypothetical vignette study with at-risk community youth and young adults, by Redlich and Shteynberg (2016). In general, and consistent with prior studies on plea deals with adults (e.g., Bordens, 1984), innocent participants were less likely to accept plea offers that included jail time. While there was no overall difference in plea deal acceptance rates between youth and adults in the guilty condition, innocent youth were approximately 2.5 times more likely to plead guilty than innocent adults (a small-sized effect, $\phi = .23$). Rationales were examined separately for those accepting plea offers and those rejecting plea offers. Although there were some differences found by age group overall (e.g., as reviewed earlier, endorsement of long-term consequences/benefits of pleading guilty), there was only one significant interaction effect of age group and guilt/innocence status. Specifically, among those who pleaded guilty and were assigned to assume they were actually guilty, young adults were more likely to endorse the rationale "I didn't think my public defender lawyer would do a good job at trial" than juveniles.

Among those assigned to the innocent scenarios who pleaded guilty, juveniles and adults did not differ in their endorsement of this rationale. Redlich and Shteynberg also found significant main effects of guilt/innocence, such that those who were asked to assume innocence (regardless of age) claimed not to have pleaded guilty because they thought the truth would come out at trial, but were less likely than the mock guilty participants to think that the prosecutor would offer a better plea deal. In addition, the "guilty" were more likely than the "innocent" to accept the plea offer because it was "the right thing to do."

As a group, innocent defendants may be more risk averse than guilty ones (see Bibas, 2004; Covey, 2007). In the Malloy et al. (2014) study, for example, it was the self-reported innocent youth, more so than the self-reported guilty youth, who were likely to say that they pleaded guilty for lesser punishment. Nonetheless, in a series of studies with young adults in hypothetical vignettes, participants acting in the role of innocent defendants were consistently found to be more risk-seeking than guilty defendants (as defined by their willingness to go to trial under the same odds), a phenomenon the authors partly attributed to resistance toward the substantive unfairness of the situations (Tor, Gazal-Ayal, & Garcia, 2010). Clearly, more research is needed on youth plea decision-making when participants are innocent and when they are guilty, and under a variety of circumstances.

Conclusions and Directions for Future Research

In this chapter we reviewed what social scientists have discovered, to date, on youth and guilty pleas. Although preliminary, the extant research points to the conclusions that (1) youth, like adults, often have little time to meet with their attorneys and to make plea decisions; (2) in part because of these time constraints, as well as immature development, youth are less likely than adults to make knowing (and perhaps voluntary) plea decisions, and (3) youths' reasoning underlying their plea decisions reflects an immaturity in judgement that so often characterizes adolescence. In addition, innocent youth may be particularly susceptible to these circumstances, placing them at greater risk for wrongful conviction (Drizin & Luloff, 2007).

These conclusions, however, are based on limited data from studies that used different methodologies, used samples from different populations, and are relevant to different court systems—although, as noted earlier, several consistencies have been found. On the one hand, the topic of juvenile guilty pleas is just beginning to garner attention. Of the studies reviewed here, all but two were conducted after the start of the twenty-first century. In contrast to the knowledge base on child victim/witnesses and juvenile defendant trial competency, the amount of research on juvenile guilty pleas can be considered meager. On the other hand, 12 published studies is an excellent beginning, and the fact that most have been conducted in the recent past bodes well for an increasing trajectory of research. Indeed, we know of at least six new (but to date unpublished) studies on juvenile pleas. For example, Fountain (2017) recently completed her dissertation in which she conducted a semi-structured interview study of juvenile defense attorneys and a vignette study with justice-involved youth and their parents about plea decision-making.

There are many directions for future research and theoretical development. Most models of plea decision-making (e.g., shadow of the trial; Mnookin & Kornhauser, 1979; Nagel & Neef, 1979) are based on theories of rational choice/expected utility and predict that any rational person will accept a plea deal if the penalty offered in exchange for the plea is less than the expected value of trial (Bushway, Redlich, & Norris, 2014; Redlich, Wilford, & Bushway, 2017). Of course, individual decision-making—and, in particular, that of adolescents—often deviates from the rational (De Martino, Kumaran, Seymour, & Dolan, 2006; Kahneman & Tversky, 2000), and criminal defendants rarely have access to all the information that they need to make an estimate of the odds of winning at trial (Douglass, 2001). Furthermore, although limited, research on plea decision-making suggests that various other factors, beyond the probability of conviction, are important to defendants (e.g., actual innocence, Gazal-Ayal & Tor, 2012); group and individual differences, including young age, may moderate the effects of these variables on defendant decision-making (Grisso et al., 2003; Smith, 2007).

In addition, many questions remain about the reasons youth give for their plea decisions, what these stated reasons tell us about youth decision-making in the context of pleas, and whether these decisions are voluntary. For example, experimental studies may be able to shed light on whether youth and adults differ in their capacities to estimate likelihood of conviction from evidence disclosures and how they subsequently use that information in their decision-making, or on how age moderates the impact of trial penalty or conviction probability on decision-making. Field interviews can provide further understanding of the context of the decisions youth and adults are faced with across different jurisdictions and whether youth and adults respond differently to various situational pressures, such as pretrial detainment, or plea offers that pit probation against incarceration. Finally, our understanding of how youth make decisions would benefit tremendously from testing targeted hypotheses derived from developmental decision-making models (e.g., fuzzy trace theory, Reyna, Adam, Poirier, LeCray, & Brainerd, 2005; the self-regulated model, Byrnes, 1998; dual-process models, Klaczynski, 2001).

To illustrate, Helm and Reyna (2017) examined the plea decision-making of adult participants from the perspective of fuzzy trace theory (FTT), a theory that proposes individuals tend to encode and remember information in verbatim (precise, specific) or gist (fuzzy, impressionistic) representations. They found that participants who relied on verbatim information processing were less likely to be influenced by their guilt or innocence than those who relied more on gist processing. This study has implications for our understanding of youth plea decisions in that FTT predicts and has found that children and adolescents are more likely than adults to approach decisions via verbatim processing.

In short, plea decision-making will naturally reflect the inherent dispositional traits of defendants and the exigencies of the situations that defendants find themselves in. It is therefore important for social scientists to continue to conduct research using a variety of methods, including field studies (across numerous jurisdictions) with different populations, experimental lab studies, systematic observations, and archival analyses of actual cases in juvenile and criminal courts. Because the prevalence of adjudication by guilty plea is unlikely to diminish anytime soon, it is imperative that our scientific understanding of the process of pleas and the youth and adults who enter into them continues to grow.

References

Bach, A. (2009). *Ordinary injustice: How America holds court*. New York: Henry Holt and Company.

Bibas, S. (2004). Plea bargaining outside the shadow of a trial. *Harvard Law Review, 117*(8), 2463–2547. doi: 10.2307/4093404

Bordens, K. S. (1984). The effects of likelihood of conviction, threatened punishment, and assumed role on mock plea bargaining decisions. *Basic and Applied Social Psychology, 5*, 59–74. doi: 10.1207/s15324834basp0501_4

Boykin v. Alabama, 89 U.S. S. Ct. 1709 (1969).

Bushway, S., Redlich, A. D., & Norris, R. (2014). An explicit test of plea bargaining in the "shadow of the trial." *Criminology, 52*, 723–754. doi: 10.1111/1745-9125.12054

Buss, E. (2000). The role of lawyers in promoting juveniles' competence as defendants. In T. Grisso & R. G. Schwartz (Eds.), *Youth on trial: A developmental perspective on juvenile justice* (pp. 243–265). Chicago, IL: University of Chicago Press.

Byrnes, J. P. (1998). *The nature and development of decision making: A self-regulation model*. Mahwah, NJ: Lawrence Erlbaum & Associates.

Caldwell, H. (2012). Coercive plea bargaining: The unrecognized scourge of the justice system. *Catholic University Law Review, 61*, 63–98.

Cauffman, E., & Steinberg, L. (2012). Emerging findings from research on adolescent development and juvenile justice. *Victims and Offenders, 7*, 428–449. https://doi.org/10.1080/15564886.2012.713901

Center for Families, Children, and the Courts. (2008). *Juvenile delinquency court assessment 2008, Volume 1*. Judicial Council of California/Administrative Office of the Courts.

Cooper, D. K. (1997). Juveniles' understanding of trial-related information: Are they competent defendants? *Behavioral Sciences & the Law, 15*(2), 167–180.

Covey, R. (2007). Reconsidering the relationship between cognitive psychology and plea bargaining. *Marquette Law Review, 91*, 213–247.

Crawford, C., Dohrn, B., Geraghty, T. F., Moss, M. B., & Puritz, P. (2007). *Illinois: An assessment of access to counsel and quality of representation in delinquency proceedings*. Retrieved from http://www.law.northwestern.edu/legalclinic/cfjc/documents/ILAssessmentReport.pdf

Crone, E. A., & van der Molen, M. W. (2004). Developmental changes in real life decision making: Performance on a gambling task previously shown to depend on the ventromedial prefrontal cortex. *Developmental Neuropsychology 25*(3), 251–279. https://doi.org/10.1207/s15326942dn2503_2

Daftary-Kapur, T., & Zottoli, T. M. (2014). A first look at the plea deal experiences of juveniles tried in adult court. *International Journal of Forensic Mental Health, 13*, 323–336. doi: 10.1080/14999013.2014.960983

De Martino, B., Kumaran, D., Seymour, B., & Dolan, R. J. (2006). Frames, biases, and rational decision-making in the human brain. *Science, 313*, 684–687. doi: 10.1126/science.1128356

Dervan, L. E. (2012). Bargained justice: Plea bargaining's innocence problem and the Brady safety-valve. *Utah Law Review, 51*, 51–97.

Douglass, J. G. (2001). Fatal attraction? The uneasy courtship of brady and plea bargaining. *Emory Law Review, 50*(2), 437–517.

Drizin, S. A., & Luloff, G. (2007). Are juvenile courts breeding grounds for wrongful convictions? *North Kentucky Law Review, 34*, 257–322.

Feld, B. (2017). *The evolution of the juvenile court: Race, politics, and the criminalizing of juvenile justice*. New York: New York University Press.

Fountain, E. (2017). *Adolescent plea bargains: Developmental and contextual influences of plea bargain decision making*. Unpublished doctoral dissertation.

Gardner, M., & Steinberg, L. (2005). Peer influence on risk taking, risk preference, and risky decision making in adolescence and adulthood: An experimental study. *Developmental Psychology, 41*(4), 625–635. doi: 10.1037/0012-1649.41.4.625

Gazal-Ayal, O., & Tor, A. (2012). The innocence effect. *Duke Law Journal, 62*, 339–401. doi: 10.2139/ssrn.1878498

Grisso, T. (1981). *Juveniles' waiver of rights: Legal and psychological competence*. New York: Plenum Press.

Grisso, T., Steinberg, L., Woolard, J., Cauffman, E., Scott, E., Graham, S., . . . Schwartz, R. (2003). Juveniles' competence to stand trial: A comparison of adolescents' and adults' capacities as trial defendants. *Law and Human Behavior, 27*, 333–364. http://dx.doi.org/10.1023/A:1024065015717

Gross, S. R., Jacoby, K., Matheson, D. J., Montgomery, N., & Patil, S. (2005). Exonerations in the United States 1989 through 2003. *Journal of Criminal Law and Criminology, 95*, 523–560. doi: 0091-4169/05/9502-0523

Helm, R. K., & Reyna, V. F. (2017). Logical but incompetent plea decisions: A new approach to plea bargaining grounded in cognitive theory. *Psychology, Public Policy, and Law, 23*(3), 367–380. http://dx.doi.org/10.1037/law0000125

Henderson, K. S. (2016). *Investigating true and false predictors of guilty pleas*. Unpublished doctoral dissertation.

JDB v. North Carolina, 564 U.S., 261 (2011).

Kaban, B., & Quinlan, J. C. (2004). Rethinking a "knowing, intelligent and voluntary waiver" in Massachusetts' juvenile courts. *Journal of the Center for Families, Children, and the Courts, 5*, 35–55.

Kahneman, D., & Tversky, A. (2000). *Choices, values, and frames*. New York: Cambridge University Press.

Kassin, S. M., Drizin, S., Grisso, T., Gudjonsson, G., Leo, R. A., & Redlich, A. D. (2010). Police-induced confessions: Risk factors and recommendations. *Law and Human Behavior, 34*, 3–38. doi: 10.1007/s10979-009-9188-6

Kellough, G., & Wortley, S. (2002). Remand for plea: Bail decisions and plea bargaining as commensurate decisions. *British Journal of Criminology, 42*(1), 186–211. doi: 10.1093/bjc/42.1.186

Klaczynski, P. A. (2001). Framing effects on adolescent task representations, analytic and heuristic processing and decision making. Implications for the normative/descriptive gap. *Journal of Applied Developmental Psychology, 22*(3), 289–309. doi: 10.1016/S01933973(01)00085-5

Kutateladze, B. L., Andiliro, N. R., & Johnson, B. (2014). Opening Pandora's box: How does defendant race influence plea bargaining? *Justice Quarterly, 33*(3), 1–29. doi: 10.1080/07418825.2014.915340

Malloy, L. C., Shulman, E. P., & Cauffman, E. (2014). Interrogations, confessions, and guilty pleas among serious adolescent offenders. *Law and Human Behavior, 38*, 181–193. http://dx.doi.org/10.1037/lhb0000065

McKee, G. R. (1998). Competency to stand trial in preadjudicatory juveniles and adults. *Journal of the American Academy of Psychiatry and the Law, 26*(1), 89–99. http://dx.doi.org/10.1016/S1353-1131(99)90180-3

Miller v. Alabama, 132 S. Ct. 2455 (2012).

Miller, D. C., & Byrnes, J. P. (2001). To achieve or not to achieve: A self-regulation perspective on adolescents' academic decision making. *Journal of Educational Psychology, 93*(4), 677–685. doi: 10.1037/0022-0663.93.4.677

Miller-Wilson, L. S., & Puritz, P. (2003, October). *Pennsylvania: An assessment of access to counsel and quality of representation in delinquency proceedings.* Retrieved from https://jlc.org/sites/default/files/publication_pdfs/PA%20Assesment%20of%20Access%20to%20Counsel.pdf

Mnookin, R. H., & Kornhauser, L. (1979). Bargaining in the shadow of the law: The case of divorce. *Yale Law Journal, 88*, 950–997. doi: 10.2307/795824

Nagel, S. S., & Neef, M. G. (1979). *Decision theory and the legal process.* Lexington, MA: Lexington Books.

Norris, R. J. (2017). *Exonerated: A history of the innocence movement.* New York: New York University Press.

Peterson-Badali, M., & Abramovitch, R. (1993). Grade related changes in young people's reasoning about plea decisions. *Law and Human Behavior, 17*, 537–552. doi: 10.1007/bf01045072

Perillo, J. T. (2015, March). Precursors to false guilty pleas: An examination of exonerations. Presentation at the American Psychology-Law Society conference, San Diego, CA.

Piacentini, L., & Walters, R. (2006). The politicalization of youth crime in Scotland and the rise of the 'Burberry' court. *Youth Justice, 6*, 43–59.

Prencipe, A., Kesek, A., Cohen, J., Lamm, C., Lewis, M. D., & Zelazo, P. D. (2011). Development of hot and cool executive function during the transition to adolescence. *Journal of Experimental Child Psychology, 108*, 621–637. doi: 10.1016/j.jecp.2010.09.008

Redlich, A. D. (2010a). The susceptibility of juveniles to false confessions and false guilty pleas. *Rutgers Law Review, 62*, 943–957. http://dx.doi.org/10.1037/12085-003

Redlich, A. D. (2010b). False confessions, false guilty pleas: Similarities and differences. In G. D. Lassiter & C. Meissner (Eds.), *Interrogations and confessions: Current research, practice, and policy*. Washington, DC: APA Books.

Redlich, A. D., Bibas, S., Edkins, V., & Madon, S. (2017). The psychology of defendant plea decision-making. *American Psychologist, 72*, 339–352. doi: 10.1037/a0040436

Redlich, A. D., & Bonventre, C. L. (2015). Content and comprehensibility of juvenile and adult tender-of-plea forms: Implications for knowing, intelligent, and voluntary guilty pleas. *Law and Human Behavior, 39*(2), 162–176. doi: 10.1037/lhb0000118

Redlich, A. D., & Shteynberg, R. V. (2016). To plead or not to plead: A comparison of juvenile and adult true and false plea decisions. *Law and Human Behavior, 40*(6), 611–625. doi: 10.1037/lhb0000205

Redlich, A. D., Silverman, M., & Steiner, H. (2003). Factors affecting preadjudicative and adjudicative competence in juveniles and young adults. *Behavioral Sciences and the Law, 21*, 1–17. doi: 10.1002/bsl.543

Redlich, A. D., Summers, A., & Hoover, S. (2010). Self-reported false confessions and false guilty pleas among offenders with mental illness. *Law and Human Behavior, 34*, 79–90. doi: 10.1007/s10979-009-9194-8

Redlich, A. D., Wilford, M., & Bushway, S. D. (2017). Understanding guilty pleas through the lens of social science. *Psychology, Public Policy, and Law, 23*(4), 458. doi: 10.1037/law0000142

Reyna, V. F., Adam, M. B., Poirier, K. M., LeCray, C. W., & Brainerd, C. J. (2005). Risky decision making in childhood and adolescence: A fuzzy-trace theory approach. In J. E. Jacobs, P. A. Klaczynski, J. E. Jacobs, & P. A. Klaczynski (Eds.), *The development of judgment and decision making in children and adolescents* (pp. 77–106). Mahwah, NJ: Lawrence Erlbaum & Associates.

Roper v. Simmons, 543 U.S. 551 (2005).

Sanborn, J. B. (1992). Pleading guilty in juvenile court: Much ado about something very important to young defendants. *Justice Quarterly, 9*, 127–150. doi: 10.1080/07418829200091281

Savitsky, J. C., & Karras, D. (1984). Competency to stand trial among adolescents. *Adolescence, 19*(74), 349–358.

Schissel, B. (1993). A sociolegal analysis of Canadian youth justice: The impact of offender's race on judicial decisions. *Journal of Criminal Justice, 21*, 533–552. doi: 10.1016/0047-2352(93)90042-L

Schmidt, M. G., Reppucci, N. D., & Woolard, J. (2003). Effectiveness of participation as a defendant: The attorney-juvenile client relationship. *Behavioral Sciences and the Law, 21*, 175–198. http://dx.doi.org/10.1002/bsl.532

Smith, A. (2007). "I ain't taking no plea: The challenge in counseling young people facing serious time. *Rutgers Law Review, 60*, 11–31.

Steinberg, L., Graham, S., O'Brien, L., Woolard, J., Cauffman, E., & Banich, M. (2009). Age differences in future orientation and delay discounting. *Child Development, 80*, 28–44.

Tepfer, J. A., Nirider, L. H., & Tricarico, L. M. (2009). Arresting development: Convictions of innocent youth. *Rutgers Law Review, 62*, 887. Retrieved from http://pegasus.rutgers.edu/~review/vol62n4/Tepfer.pdf

Tor, A., Gazal-Ayal, O., & Garcia, S. M. (2010). Fairness and the willingness to accept plea bargain offers. *Journal of Empirical Legal Studies*, *7*, 97–116. doi: 10.1111/j.1740-1461.2009.01171.x

Travers, M. (2007). Sentencing in the children's court: An ethnographic perspective. *Youth Justice*, *7*, 21–35. doi: 10.1177/1473225406074817

Viljoen, J. L., Klaver, J., & Roesch, R. (2005). Legal decisions of preadolescent and adolescent defendants: Predictors of confessions, pleas, communication with attorneys, and appeals. *Law and Human Behavior*, *29*(3), 253–277. doi: 10.1007/s10979-005-3613-2

Viljoen, J. L., Odgers, C., Grisso, T., & Tillbrook, C. (2007). Teaching adolescents and adults about adjudicative proceedings: A comparison of pre- and post-teaching scores on the MacCAT-CA. *Law and Human Behavior*, *31*(5), 419–432. http://dx.doi.org/10.1007/s10979-006-9069-1

Wilford, M. M., & Wells, G. L. (2017). Plea-bargaining law: The impact of innocence, trial penalty, and conviction probability on plea outcomes. Unpublished manuscript.

Wolf Harlow, C. (2003). *Education and correctional populations*. Washington, DC: Bureau of Justice Statistics Special Report, U.S. Department of Justice, Office of Justice Programs.

Wooldredge, J. D. (1989). An aggregate-level examination of the caseload pressure hypothesis. *Journal of Quantitative Criminology*, *5*, 259–283. http://dx.doi.org/10.1007/BF01062740

Work, M. (2014). Creating constitutional procedure: Frye, Lafler, and plea bargaining reform. *Journal of Criminal Law and Criminology*, *104*, 457–487.

Zottoli, T. M., Daftary-Kapur, T., & Tahan, E. (2017, March). Differences in the decision making of youth and adults who pleaded guilty to felonies in New York City. Paper presented at the annual conference of the American Psychology and Law Society, Seattle, WA.

Zottoli, T. M., Daftary-Kapur, T., Winters, G. M., & Hogan. C. (2016). Plea discounts, time-pressures and false guilty pleas in youth and adults who pleaded guilty to felonies in New York City. *Psychology, Public Policy, and Law*, *22*, 250–259. doi: 10.1037/law0000095

7

Innocence and Plea Bargaining

Miko M. Wilford and Annmarie Khairalla

On August 5, 1977, Kerry Max Cook was arrested for the rape and murder of Linda Jo Edwards (Cook, 2007). Almost 1 year after Cook's initial arrest, his trial finally began. During the trial, Cook was presented with evidence the State had collected against him, and his attorneys were provided the opportunity to cross-examine all adversarial witnesses. He was also allowed to call his own witnesses, build his own evidence, and present his own theory of the facts. After the State and his defense rested their cases, he was granted the right to a verdict from a jury of his peers. After a verdict of guilty was returned, a separate sentencing judgment was rendered, and Kerry Max Cook was sentenced to death by lethal injection.

Cook spent 19 years on death row (Cook, 2007). During that time, he attempted suicide twice—the second time he left a note stating, "I really was an innocent man. . . ." In November of 1996, Cook's conviction was overturned by the Texas Court of Criminal Appeals, who cited repeated episodes of prosecutorial misconduct. This decision effectively nullified all legal procedures involving Cook's case that occurred after his arrest in 1977. While awaiting his fourth trial, the State approached him with several offers involving a guilty plea—he rejected all of them. Finally, on the first day of jury selection, the State offered Cook a plea deal for a sentence of time served, which would require no admission of guilt. The deal would release Cook from incarceration immediately. Cook reluctantly agreed to the deal, but only after altering the evidentiary form to reflect his innocence—a stipulation that his defense team assumed would be a deal-breaker.

In a 10-minute session, the court upheld and approved the final plea—the only plea deal accepted without an admission of guilt in a capital murder case in Texas history (Cook, 2007). This plea effectively replaced several of the rights that Cook had been afforded when he was first charged: he could not confront his accusers, cross-examine adversarial witnesses, receive a verdict from a jury of his peers, etc. The steps taken Cook's second time through the justice system represent the process for most criminal defendants. The *Federal Rules of Criminal Procedure* (Committee on the Judiciary, 2016), which describes the procedural process for individuals accused of a crime in the United States, details a number of processes that, in actuality, elude most defendants. Instead, for most suspects, the procedural process ends at the examination or bond hearing—both provide an opportunity for the accused to enter a guilty plea. Once that happens, the process (sans appeal) is over and most constitutional rights afforded to defendants are waived. Plea bargaining is not an exception to the rules of criminal procedure; plea bargaining is the new rule (Fisher, 2000). Under this new rule, there are many tools available to prosecutors to help them secure convictions—whether the convicted be guilty or innocent.

Types of Pleas

A true guilty plea occurs when a factually guilty defendant pleads guilty; a false guilty plea, by contrast, occurs when a factually innocent defendant pleads guilty (Zottoli, Daftary-Kapur, Winters, & Hogan, 2016). Given the frequency with which defendants face multiple charges, the difference between a true guilty plea and a false guilty plea is not always clear. A plea deal could require defendants to plead guilty to multiple counts of the same crime or to several different crimes. Thus, a plea deal could involve the defendant truly pleading guilty to crimes they did commit, as well as falsely pleading guilty to crimes they did not commit (Piehl & Bushway, 2007). It could also involve guilty defendants pleading guilty to crimes that differ from those they actually committed. Further, a false guilty plea conviction can occur without a guilty plea: An innocent defendant could enter a traditional guilty plea, which includes a guilt admission, or they could enter a *nolo contendere* plea or Alford plea.

Guilty Pleas without Admissions of Guilt

A *nolo contendere* (no contest) plea does not require a defendant to admit guilt; instead, the defendant neither admits guilt nor asserts innocence (Redlich & Özdoğru, 2009). An Alford plea allows defendants to maintain their innocence but still accept the terms of a plea deal. Generally, defendants enter into Alford pleas because they believe the prosecution has enough evidence to convict them at trial (Blume & Helm, 2014). When a defendant enters any type of plea, a judge is required to review the evidence to ensure that there is a "sufficient factual basis of guilt" before the defendant accepts the plea (Redlich & Özdoğru, 2009). For standard plea deals, the guilt admission can contribute greatly to establishing this sufficient factual basis of guilt. However, defendants who enter a *nolo contendere* plea are not admitting guilt, and defendants entering an Alford plea are asserting their innocence. Thus, judges must theoretically use evidence other than a guilt admission to accept plea deals involving these types of pleas. Guidelines for determining sufficient evidence have yet to be created, and, as a result, judges use different standards to decide whether to accept *nolo contendere* and Alford pleas.

Notably, both *nolo contendere* and Alford pleas could increase the number of factually innocent defendants pleading guilty, because they allow a defendant the benefits of a plea deal (e.g., immediate release from pretrial detention) without having to falsely admit guilt (Blume & Helm, 2014; Nhan, Polzer, & Polzer, 2013). The effects of these pleas, particularly Alford pleas, and how they can be potentially abused by the State are clearly seen in the case of Kerry Max Cook, as well as in the later case of the West Memphis Three. The West Memphis Three were teenagers from West Memphis, Arkansas: Damien Echols, Jason Baldwin, and Jessie Miskelley, who were arrested for the murder of three 8-year old boys in 1993 (Blume & Helm, 2014). Given the brutality of the murders, as well as the age of the victims, the pressure on the small town's police to solve the crime was extremely high (Berlinger & Sinofsky, 1996). Unfortunately, the boys' bodies were found in a creek, which substantially reduced the amount of evidence police were able to collect. An offhand comment made by an officer at the crime scene led all the investigators to conclude that the murders were part of a satanic ritual—this became the assumed motivation behind the murders. To corroborate this motive, the State secured a trial expert to confirm that elements of the crime and possessions found in the boys' homes were characteristic of satanic beliefs and rituals. The expert was discredited at trial when the defense demonstrated his degree was fraudulent.

A three-part HBO documentary presented the dubious case and trial "expert" to a national audience, adding pressure on local law enforcement to investigate the case further (Berlinger & Sinofsky, 1996). In 2007, a forensic test revealed that DNA found at the crime scene did not match either the victims or the defendants (Blume & Helm, 2014). Meanwhile, national coverage of the case continued, and another documentary was announced (and released in 2012, entitled *West of Memphis*). After multiple appeals, the Arkansas Supreme Court ordered a state trial judge to reconsider the impact of the DNA evidence on the potential convictions of the West Memphis Three. The judge never got the chance to make a decision; instead, before the hearing, the prosecution offered the West Memphis Three an Alford plea: they could accept a plea for time served, and still maintain their innocence publicly. The offer came with a stipulation that the deal was only valid if all three defendants accepted. Although the DNA was compelling, they all chose to accept the plea. By offering an Alford plea, the State was able to maintain the case as solved,[1] avoid paying any compensation to the West Memphis Three (for the time they

---

1 The State could maintain the case as solved despite widespread belief that the real murderer or murderers were still at-large and despite results of the 2007 DNA test, which implicated one of the victim's step-fathers as the potential culprit (Blume & Helm, 2014).

spent in prison), quiet public outcries to "release the West Memphis Three," and save themselves the resources required for another trial.

Capturing the Magnitude of the False Guilty Plea (Innocence) Problem

Documenting false guilty pleas is difficult. Although the National Registry of Exonerations (2017) reported a record number of cases involving false guilty pleas, the overall number remains relatively low (~18%), considering the number of cases adjudicated by plea (~95%). Unfortunately, issues related to Alford and *nolo contendere* pleas, as well as a number of other factors, make overturning plea convictions and discovering false guilty pleas particularly difficult.

First, the Innocence Project and similar organizations serve as the primary source for identifying wrongful convictions. Given the volume of cases that the Innocence Project receives, stringent criteria must be applied to determine those they choose to pursue. This often means that cases in which the defendant accepted a plea deal are excluded from consideration (Redlich, 2010). Second, exonerating evidence, like DNA, tends to only exist for severe crimes (e.g., rape, murder), and plea deals are less common (though, admittedly, still numerous) for severe crimes. For instance, in 2009, roughly 73% of state-felony murder convictions were resolved by guilty plea versus 97.1% of state-felony driving-related crimes (Bureau of Justice Statistics, 2015).

Third, plea convictions are extremely difficult to overturn. By accepting a plea deal, defendants waive their right to several types of appeal (e.g., challenges of coerced confession, claims of improper grand jury selection, prosecutorial defects, claims of illegal search and seizure, denial of due process rights to a speedy trial, and challenges based on an entrapment defense; Eisen & Rooney, 2002). In fact, prosecutors can require defendants to waive their right from having pre-plea discussions used against them before the prosecutor will even begin negotiating (Leonard, 2008).

To further illustrate the difficulty in overturning a plea conviction, let us return to the case of Kerry Max Cook. Two months after Cook was released (after accepting a plea), his defense attorney filed a request for results from a DNA test of semen found on the murder victim's underwear (Cook, 2007). The test matched a man with whom the victim had been having a locally notorious affair—a man who denied having had any sexual contact with her for weeks prior to the murder. Although this evidence might normally be considered exonerating, Smith County continues to assert that Cook is guilty and that his decision to accept a plea supports his guilt. Today, over 15 years after these DNA results were released, Cook is still the convicted murderer of record for Linda Jo Edwards. Notably, the plea offered to Kerry Max Cook was a *nolo contendere* plea, and some have argued that the changes he made to the evidentiary form transformed it to an Alford plea. Unfortunately, as was true of the West Memphis Three, the type of plea Cook accepted is irrelevant when considering his conviction status—despite no admission of guilt and the results of multiple DNA tests, Cook's case is not "officially" considered one of a false guilty plea (Grissom, 2012; Hall, 2012).

Documented False Guilty Pleas

Despite these hurdles, recent numbers indicate that we are getting better at documenting false guilty pleas, with the number of recorded exonerations involving pleas rising steadily (National Registry of Exonerations, 2017). Many false guilty pleas have arisen from high-profile scandals that, when revealed, resulted in multiple exonerations. In one of the largest of these scandals—the Rampart scandal, in Los Angeles—over 100 criminal convictions were overturned (Williams, 2001). In at least 32 of these cases police fabricated evidence, and in 25 of those cases defendants pleaded guilty (Covey, 2013). Defendants who knew they were innocent and that the evidence against them had to be fraudulent were still compelled to accept plea deals. This is no surprise, given that defendants who rejected plea offers suffered punishments five times greater if they were convicted at trial. Tulia, Texas was home to a similar police misconduct scandal. Defendants who refused plea deals in those cases suffered sentences 13 times harsher than those of people who pled guilty (Covey, 2013). These scandals have produced numerous overturned convictions—both from guilty pleas and juries.

Shortly after the Tulia scandal, on November 2, 2001, 27 people were arrested in a drug sweep in Hearne, Texas. The arrests were predicated primarily on testimony provided by a confidential informant (Bikel, 2004). Many of the suspects could not afford bail and were forced to await trial in jail, some for over 5 months. Seven of these suspects pleaded guilty and were then released but put on probation. After a single day of trial, the critical testimony of the confidential informant was discredited, prompting all charges against the suspects to be dropped, except for the seven suspects who accepted plea deals. Those seven people remain convicted (Bikel, 2004). Thus, although the evidence was discredited, because the convictions were not overturned, these cases are also excluded from counts of false guilty pleas. Regardless, these incidents in California and Texas show that the innocent do plead guilty. They also illuminate some of the factors that can drive them to do so (e.g., pretrial detention, distrust of the system, large plea discounts, etc.), which will be addressed in more detail later in this chapter.

Self-Reported False Guilty Pleas

Although there are few verified cases in which people have pled guilty falsely (e.g., Rampart and Tulia scandals), field reports have recorded additional self-reported false guilty pleas (Bordens & Bassett, 1985; Redlich, Summers, & Hoover, 2010; Viljoen, Klaver, & Roesch, 2005; Zottoli et al., 2016). In a sample of 1,249 mentally ill criminal justice participants, false guilty plea rates ranged from 27% to 41% (Redlich et al., 2010). In a field study in Washington state, 9 out of 152 (~6%) juvenile defendants reported that they had falsely pled guilty (Viljoen et al., 2005). A similar study in New York found that 20% of the interviewed juveniles and 40% of the interviewed adults reported that the crime for which they pleaded guilty more closely resembled the crime that they had actually committed than the crime for which they were originally charged (Zottoli et al., 2016). But, another 26% of juveniles and 19% of adults reported being completely innocent.

Lab-Recorded False Guilty Pleas

Unfortunately, there is no way to determine whether self-reported false guilty pleas were, in fact, false. However, experimental research has indicated that false guilty pleas do occur (Bordens, 1984; Dervan & Edkins, 2013; McAllister & Bregman, 1986; Redlich & Shteynberg, 2016; Tor, Gazal-Ayal, & Garcia, 2010; Wilford & Wells, 2018; Wilford, Wells, & Shestak, 2018). Investigations of false guilty pleas have relied primarily on two different research methodologies: vignettes and high-stakes simulations. The vignette method typically involves giving participants text that describes a crime, and asking if they would accept or reject a plea offer within the context of the narrative. High-stakes simulations rely on deception to put participants in situations in which they believe they are being accused of actual wrongdoing (in an academic setting) and could either accept a deal or face a worse but uncertain punishment.

Overall, vignette studies have recorded false guilty plea rates of around 20% (although a number of variable manipulations can cause this number to fluctuate; Bordens, 1984; Gregory, Mowen, & Linder, 1978, Exp. 1; McAllister & Bregman, 1986; Redlich & Shteynberg, 2016; Tor et al., 2010). Guilty participants, in these same studies, accept plea offers at rates of 70–80% on average. Interestingly, high-stakes simulations generally yield higher false guilty plea rates than vignette studies, with an average of around 50% (Dervan & Edkins 2013; Wilford & Wells, 2018; Wilford et al., 2018).[2] In these same studies, the plea acceptance rate among the guilty has ranged from 75% to 90%. Taken together, these studies highlight the potential prevalence of false guilty pleas, while also demonstrating that the innocent are generally more resistant to plea offers than the guilty.

---

[2] Gregory et al. (1978, Exp. 2) also employed a unique high-stakes simulation in which they recorded no false guilty pleas; however, their study included only eight participants.

The Psychology of False Guilty Pleas

Reasons to Plead Guilty

In a number of field studies researchers have interviewed actual offenders and defendants to determine why people plead guilty (Bordens & Bassett, 1985; Viljoen et al., 2005; Zottoli et al., 2016). Bordens and Bassett (1985) created a taxonomy of seven broad factors that encapsulated all the reasons the people they surveyed (regardless of actual guilt or innocence) provided for accepting plea offers: prosecutorial pressure, indirect pressure (e.g., avoiding more severe punishment, reduce family-related issues), remorse, sentence-related motivations (i.e., plea discount), expediency, acquiescence (e.g., following advice from an attorney), and likelihood of conviction. Ultimately, they concluded that most of the reasons defendants gave for accepting pleas boiled down to some type of pressure—pressure from the prosecutor, their own attorney, peers, co-defendants, family members, and conscience, among others.

Viljoen et al. (2005) interviewed 152 youth defendants and found that the majority were planning on pleading guilty. Consistent with Bordens and Bassett's (1985) findings, defendants who were planning on pleading guilty (whether guilty or innocent) were more likely to be advised to do so by attorneys, parents, and/or peers than those planning on pleading not guilty. Redlich et al. (2010) also found that a significant proportion of mentally ill offenders who claimed to have pled guilty falsely said they did so because of pressure from others (18%). This group also said they admitted guilt to protect someone else, or because they perceived the situation as futile.

Defendants also frequently face time pressures—plea offers are provided with an expiration attached, and sometimes the best offer is the one presented first. For instance, the New York County District Attorney's Office has adopted a best-first policy, with the best plea deals presented at initial arraignment; any subsequent plea offers become less favorable (Kutateladze, Andiloro, & Johnson, 2016). Relatedly, Zottoli et al. (2016) found that multiple defendants reported accepting offers after being given less than an hour to deliberate. Thus, not only do prosecutors typically wish to avoid trial by securing plea convictions, they also often wish to secure them as early in the process as possible. Redlich et al. (2010) also found evidence of time pressure among those who reported making a false guilty plea. Specifically, 9% of offenders stated that they accepted a plea when they were under the influence of a substance or because they did not know better, which suggests that if time had not been a factor, offenders could have waited until they sobered up or until their comprehension of the situation had improved.

While plea deals by definition involve some leniency, these sentencing discounts can be so large that even innocent defendants would rather plead guilty than risk the longer sentence that would result if convicted at trial (McCoy, 2005). Prosecutors can offer large sentencing discounts, or even decrease the number of charges a defendant faces, to secure more pleas

(Bordens & Bassett, 1985; Zottoli et al., 2016). Defense attorneys, who also have large caseloads, may pressure defendants to plead guilty, believing it is in the defendant's best interest or because it is the easiest solution (Bordens & Bassett, 1985; Viljoen et al., 2005; Zottoli et al., 2016). While the average plea discount has been recorded at around 20–30% (Ulmer, Eisenstein, & Johnson, 2010), extreme discounts have also been documented, especially in cases involving crimes that carry mandatory minimum penalties (Horwitz, 2015). For instance, Weldon Angelos was sentenced to 55 years in prison, the minimum sentence the judge could enforce given the three counts of gun possession during a drug-trafficking crime for which Angelos was found guilty. Prior to his trial, prosecutors had offered to reduce Angelos' charges to one count of gun possession during a drug-trafficking crime, which had a prescribed sentence of 15 years. In other words, Angelos' decision to go to trial resulted in a penalty that was 40 years longer than the one he could have received if he had agreed to plead guilty. Further, in interviews of New York City defendants, Zottoli et al. (2016) reported sentencing discounts of up to 80% for adults and 95% for youth. In situations like these, the deal is often too good to pass up, even if one is facing a low-probability conviction.

Research studies have also examined the reasons people give for accepting pleas. Studies examining the impact of the plea discount have produced somewhat mixed results, with vignette studies finding a consistent effect (Bordens, 1984; Gregory et al., 1978), and high-stakes simulations failing to find a significant effect (Dervan & Edkins, 2013; Wilford et al., 2018). For average adults, evidence or probability of conviction has also been shown to affect plea outcomes (Bordens, 1984; Gregory et al., 1978; Tor et al., 2010; Wilford et al., 2018). Tor et al. (2010) found an effect of perceived fairness of the plea offer, with study participants who were told their offer was relatively worse than offers made to others being more likely to reject than those told their offers were comparable to others' offers.

Redlich and Shteynberg (2016) asked a sample of juveniles and adults in a vignette study to indicate the degree to which seven different rationales corresponded to their reasoning for accepting plea offers. The most endorsed responses related to the risk of losing at trial and believing the plea offered was a good deal. Guilty individuals also considered their guilt by stating that accepting the plea was the right thing to do. Similarly, in a simulation study, Wilford et al. (2018) found that both innocent and guilty participants (in response to an open-ended question) claimed to have accepted the plea deal because they perceived it as the easiest alternative or because they wanted to avoid potentially worse consequences. However, a significant proportion of guilty participants accepted the plea, simply because of their actual guilt.

Individual Differences and False Guilty Pleas

Research examining individual differences (e.g., demographics) or cognitive biases that could lead an innocent person to plead guilty is limited. Analyses of actual case dispositions have demonstrated an impact of minority status on plea outcomes (Albonetti, 1990; Frenzel & Ball, 2007; Kellough & Wortley, 2002; Kutateladze et al., 2016; Sommers, Goldstein, & Baskin, 2014; also see Chapter 5, this volume). Redlich et al. (2010) noted that minority offenders were more likely to report entering false guilty pleas than the non-minority offenders surveyed. Further, a laboratory study using actual defense attorneys as participants showed that attorneys tended to recommend harsher plea bargains to their African American clients than they did to their Caucasian clients (Edkins, 2011).

Juvenile status has produced mixed effects in plea research, with surveys of actual defendants producing no effect of age on self-reported plea outcomes (Malloy, Shulman, & Cauffman, 2014; Redlich et al., 2010; Viljoen et al., 2005). Within non-adult samples, however, research has indicated that adolescents, as compared to young adults, could be more likely to accept plea offers (Grisso et al., 2003) and more likely to acquiesce to authority figures, such as attorneys, who may have their own motives for wanting someone to plead guilty (Redlich, Wilford, & Bushway, 2017; Wilson, 2016). Research has also shown that adolescents are more likely to focus too much on short-term consequences (e.g., current suffering) and can fail to take important considerations (e.g., conviction probability) into account when making a plea decision (Bordens & Bassett, 1985; Daftary-Kapur & Zottoli, 2014; Viljoen et al., 2005). Juveniles may also lack the legal knowledge required for making plea-related decisions (Redlich & Shteynberg, 2016). These factors are made more problematic considering the often limited contact juveniles have with their defense attorneys (Zottoli et al., 2016). See Chapter 6 of this volume for a lengthier discussion of juvenile plea decisions.

A few studies have documented the effect of cognitive abilities on the decision to plead. Results have been mixed, with Redlich et al. (2010) finding no impact of years of education on reported false guilty pleas, and Wilford et al. (2018) finding an inconsistent impact of intelligence on plea outcomes. In contrast, Viljoen et al. (2005) found that defendants who planned on pleading not guilty scored lower on measures of cognitive ability than defendants who planned on pleading guilty. Further research regarding the impact of intelligence on plea outcomes is important when we consider that, on average, defendants read at or below the sixth-grade level (Redlich & Bonventre, 2015). This is problematic given that forms used to describe pleas and plea offers (i.e., tender-of-plea forms) are frequently written at an eighth-grade level or higher. Further, in a study testing the plea-related knowledge of defendants who pleaded guilty, two-thirds of the participants scored below 60% (Redlich & Summers, 2012). Thus, it is possible that cognitive ability could have some bearing on the decision to plea, but the prevalence of higher-order vocabulary and legalese could be masking this effect by making it difficult for almost anyone to understand the situation.

Modeling Plea Decision-Making

The dominant model of plea decision-making is currently the shadow-of-the-trial model (see Chapter 2 this volume). This model posits that sentencing discounts offered during plea deals reflect the perceived probability of conviction multiplied by the expected punishment the defendant would receive if convicted at trial (Bibas, 2004; Bushway & Redlich, 2012; Bushway, Redlich, & Norris, 2014). This model could be used to determine the magnitude of the discount a prosecutor should offer a defendant during plea deals. It could also be used to predict whether a defendant would accept a particular plea offer. For example, if a prosecutor thought a defendant would be sentenced to 20 years in prison if convicted at trial, and that the chances he would be convicted were around 75%, he should be willing to offer the defendant a sentence discount of at least 5 years. At 5 years, the expected value of the plea (100% × 15 years = 15 years) is equal to the expected value of trial (75% × 20 years = 15 years). Thus, given the advantages of accepting a plea offer (e.g., certainty, expediency, etc.), the shadow-of-the-trial model would lead us to predict that most defendants would accept this offer. If the prosecutor was particularly motivated to secure a plea conviction, he or she could theoretically offer an even larger discount (e.g., 10 years) so that the expected value of the plea (100% × 10 years = 10 years) outweighs the expected value of the trial. In this scenario, the shadow model would more definitively predict that defendants will accept the plea offer.

Interestingly, this model does not provide for a predictive effect of guilt status (Bibas, 2004), though justifiably, many scholars have argued that guilty individuals are also more likely to face stronger cases (i.e., higher probabilities of conviction; Easterbrook, 1992). While this is often true, history has shown that evidence strength is not always correlated to the likelihood of guilt or innocence. Many guilty individuals have faced weak cases and many innocent defendants have faced seemingly strong cases. Yet, the current shadow-of-the-trial model provides no predictive effect of guilt status beyond its potential relationship to the probability of conviction. This is particularly surprising given the robust effect of guilt status in research. A number of experimental studies (using both vignettes and high-stakes simulations) have repeatedly shown that guilt status has an impact on plea outcomes, even when probability of conviction and plea discount are kept constant (Bordens, 1984; Dervan & Edkins, 2013, Gregory et al., 1978; Redlich & Shteynberg, 2016; Tor et al., 2010; Wilford et al., 2018). Clearly, the omission of guilt status in the current shadow model reflects an incompatibility between this model and the findings of experimental research.

To illustrate the importance of this omission, consider the following hypothetical cases: Defendants X and Y are each accused of armed robbery, which carries a possible sentence of 10 years in prison. They were both arrested at the scene, and a search of their cars produced a gun (with a license to carry), a dark baseball cap, and large sunglasses that matched eyewitness descriptions of what the robbers possessed. With this evidence, the prosecutor believes she has a 70% chance of convicting each defendant at trial. Unfortunately, while Defendant X is guilty as charged, Defendant Y's only crime is having a cluttered car. According to the shadow-of-the-trial model, *both* defendants should be willing to accept a plea offer that provides a sentence discount of at least 3 years. Unfortunately, this neglects the effect that innocence will have on Defendant Y's decision. Defendant Y's innocence will likely make him more resistant to accepting plea offers despite his conviction probability; thus, he will increase his criterion for accepting a plea and reject any offer that provides less than 5 years off his potential sentence. Importantly, from a policy perspective, both sentence offers (7 years or 5 years) are equally legal. Thus, the prosecutor, particularly motivated to close these cases, decides to offer a sentencing discount of 5 years, which leads both defendants to accept. If the prosecutor had, instead, only offered a discount of 3 years, Defendant X would have accepted, but Defendant Y would have rejected and proceeded to trial. Proceeding to trial would increase Defendant Y's chances of discovering (or of the State discovering) potentially exonerating evidence that could lead the prosecutor to drop the charges or, at least, lower his chances of conviction at trial. Instead, the prosecutor, neglecting any potential impact of innocence, offered an equivalent discount to both defendants—a discount that maximized her probability of securing plea convictions.

Further, a couple of analyses that have compared sentences of those who pleaded guilty with those of people who went to trial actually found no sentencing-related advantage of pleading guilty when including cases that were dismissed by the prosecution (i.e., after an extended period of time, prosecutors drop the charges before a trial is scheduled to occur; Abrams, 2011; Shestak, Shockley, Keenan, Wilford, & Gonzales, in press). In other words, prosecutors can pursue plea deals in cases that they would, ultimately, not take to trial. Therefore, rejecting plea offers and continuing the process can sometimes be advantageous, both because it can result in acquittal at trial and because it can result in a prosecutorial dismissal. Thus, reining in the discounts prosecutors are allowed to offer could help protect innocent defendants who might then be able to maintain their resistance to pleading guilty—leaving time to be acquitted at trial or to have their charges dismissed.

If the shadow-of-the-trial model was completely accurate, prosecutors (including the one in the previous example) would possess little power to protect the innocent from accepting plea offers. If the probability of conviction is equivalent, innocent and guilty defendants will behave identically. However, research has indicated that guilt status does exert influence on plea outcomes, even when the probability of conviction is held constant. The omission of the role of guilt status on plea outcomes stems from the fact that the shadow-of-the-trial model is a normative model of decision-making—it assumes that actors behave in a consistently rational way. If defendants were perfectly rational, actual guilt status would not matter, only conviction probability would. Similarly, in economics, normative models have been subject to some criticism based on systematic errors demonstrating that people do not always act consistently (Kahneman, 2011). Some researchers, primarily in psychology, have argued that while normative models, like the expected utility model, clearly have prescriptive value, their descriptive or predictive value is limited. One of the factors that has been shown to produce preference reversals (inconsistencies) in economic decision-making is reference points. Whether individuals characterize an outcome as a gain or loss can affect how likely they are to roll the dice (seek risk) or seek certainty (avoid risk).

Perhaps this factor is also what is missed by the shadow-of-the-trial model. It is plausible that the omission of guilt status in this model is comparable to the omission of reference points in economic-normative models. It is well documented that the knowledge of one's innocence or guilt affects a number of perceptions (Kassin, 2005). Thus, it could also have an impact on one's perceptions of punishment such that the innocent perceive any punishment (discounted or not) as more of a loss than would a guilty individual (Wilford et al., 2018), making them potentially more willing to accept some risk in order to avoid loss. Guilty individuals, by contrast, could be more likely to see any potential discount in their sentence as a gain, causing them to be more risk avoidant. Thus, to some extent, plea bargaining could correspond to people's natural risk preferences—the innocent are more motivated to avoid any punishment they see as loss (i.e., reject pleas), and the guilty are more motivated to secure sentence discounts they see as gains (i.e., accept pleas). The prevalence of false guilty pleas could, therefore, be driven by factors that increase the attractiveness of pleas despite the innocent person's preference to accept risk as a way of avoiding loss. For instance, the magnitude of plea discounts could cause even a risk-seeking, innocent individual to decide that the difference between a 5-year sentence and a 10-year sentence is too great to gamble (just like Defendant X; McCoy, 2005).

Others have criticized the shadow-of-the-trial model for providing a clear formula by which prosecutors can always secure convictions, even in weak cases, by simply offering large sentencing discounts (Covey, 2007). If we take the previous example but adapt it such that the prosecutor believes her realistic chance of convicting the defendants at trial is only 10%, she could offer a sentence discount of 9 years to still entice both defendants to accept a plea conviction. Note that this extreme discount is legal in the real world, and recall that Zottoli et al. (2016) recorded plea discounts of 80% for adults and 95% for youth in New York City. Thus, without some changes in plea practice, both the shadow-of-the-trial model and research will continue to illuminate scenarios in which an innocent person will falsely plead guilty.

Preventing False Guilty Pleas

In an attempt to limit the number of false guilty pleas, at least two reforms have been suggested: plea-based ceilings and a partial ban on plea-bargaining. Both methods attempt to address the innocence problem by trying to reduce the magnitude of the sentencing discount offered during plea negotiations. The idea is that innocent defendants who are offered plea deals, particularly those with weak cases, should not have to worry about a significant increase in their potential punishment if they reject the plea. If that concern is no longer an issue, they might be more willing to go to trial instead of accepting automatic conviction via a plea deal (Covey, 2007; Gazal-Ayal, 2006).

Plea-based ceilings put a limit on the maximum sentence that can be recommended at trial if a plea offer is made and rejected (Covey, 2007). The maximum sentence that could be administered to a defendant would be determined by the original plea deal such that the trial sentence could only exceed the plea sentence by a set percentage (or ceiling). Covey gives an example of a defendant charged with bank robbery who would normally receive a 10-year sentence if convicted in a jurisdiction with a fixed discount of 33%. The prosecutor offers a plea deal of 5 years. If the defendant rejects the deal and goes to trial, the maximum sentence that could then be imposed is 7.5 years (i.e., a 5-year sentence is two-thirds a 7.5-year sentence, which means it provides a 33% sentencing discount compared to the one faced at trial). A defendant offered a plea deal would know exactly what is at stake if they were convicted at trial with a plea-based ceiling enforced. Plea-based ceilings limit the power of prosecutors to win even weak cases by offering substantial plea discounts. They would also make it easier for innocent defendants to reject plea deals and proceed to trials that are more likely to have favorable outcomes.

A partial ban on plea-bargaining, as proposed by Gazal-Ayal (2006), targets weaker cases. Gazal-Ayal (2006) suggests banning plea deals that have large sentencing discounts, because they are indicative of weak cases that should go to trial. Prosecutors generally give lenient plea deals when they know they do not have a strong case (Easterbrook, 1992). Weak cases are not always indicative of innocence, but innocence will often produce relatively weaker cases. A partial ban is a compromise between the current plea bargaining system, which allows most types of plea bargains, and an outright ban on all plea bargaining. Gazal-Ayal (2006) argues that the current plea bargaining system allows for too many innocent defendants to plead guilty. A prosecutor has the ability, regardless of the amount of evidence, to throw anything and everything at the wall in the hope that something "sticks"—that is, leads to a conviction. If pleas were no longer allowed in these cases, weaker cases would be dismissed because prosecutors would not be confident that they could secure convictions at trial. Yet, banning all plea bargaining would create a massive backlog on cases and limit the efficiency of the criminal justice system. A partial ban, like plea-based ceilings, also reduces the power of prosecutors. Prosecutors would no longer be able to offer increasingly more attractive concessions until a defendant agrees to a plea deal.

Future Directions

We still know relatively little about the decision to plead guilty; we know even less about the decision to plead guilty falsely. Yet, the Supreme Court has acknowledged that the U.S. justice system is now a system of pleas, and the late Antonin Scalia further noted in a dissent that the Court created "a whole new field of constitutionalized criminal procedure: plea-bargaining law," in 2012 (*Lafler v. Cooper*, p. 21). Clearly, now is the time for researchers to inform the development of plea bargaining law and commence reform of this system of pleas (Redlich et al., 2017).

Estimator versus System Variables

Whenever researchers are attempting to influence public policy, it is important to acknowledge what policy can affect and what it cannot. *Estimator variables* is the common term for those factors over which the legal system cannot exert direct control (e.g., guilt status), and *system variables* refers to those factors over which the legal system does have direct control (e.g., plea offers; Wilford & Wells, 2013). Any plea bargaining reform will be necessarily complex and will involve a number of legal actors and a number of potential procedures. But many of the reforms that have already been proposed focus on what is quickly becoming (as identified by models of plea decision-making as well as research on plea decisions) the most important system variable: the plea discount. Clearly, policy could prescribe an acceptable range for the plea discount through a partial ban or plea-based ceilings. We do not endorse either of these reforms specifically, nor do we close the door to any other reforms that have yet to be introduced. We believe further research should explore the impact of reforms that rein in the plea discount on the prevalence of false guilty pleas.

Another system variable that has been incorporated into both the confession and eyewitness literatures involves the requirement that legal procedures be video recorded (Kassin et al., 2010; National Research Council, 2014). In addition to recommending that interrogations and witness identification procedures be recorded, we would add that plea procedures should be recorded. More specifically, any meetings the prosecutor has with a defendant or a defendant's attorney should be recorded. While video recordings would be optimal, any form of recording (e.g., tape, transcripts, etc.) would be preferable to the current state of affairs in which plea meetings are usually held in private and are kept off the record. Recordings of plea procedures would not only make both sides more accountable, and possibly rein in the substantial discretionary powers afforded to the prosecution, but also provide a wealth of new information to researchers: types of offers (e.g., sentence bargaining, charge bargaining, etc.), timing of offers, number of offers, and time allotted to consider each offer. In addition to producing a rich database for researchers to examine, the information gleaned from these recordings could direct future research questions.

We should also consider variables that are more akin to estimator variables. Conviction probability, for instance, is primarily an estimator variable. To a large extent, the system cannot control what evidence is available to convict a defendant. However, the system could enforce increased investigation into cases that end in pleas, and it could limit the ability of prosecutors to pressure defendants into accepting pleas by citing their conviction records or their perceived probability of convicting the defendant. Currently, prosecutors can use their perceived probability of conviction, citing recent wins at trial or particularly memorable wins, when attempting to secure pleas (Bibas, 2004). Preliminary research has indicated that innocent individuals perceive their probability of conviction differently than guilty individuals (Wilford et al., 2018). Thus, it is possible that any strategy to increase perceptions regarding conviction probability could have an undue influence on the innocent. Again, further research is needed to clarify the effect that presenting estimates of conviction might have on the innocent versus the guilty.

The available research addressing how individual differences may influence the decision to plea is also greatly limited. While there have been some examinations of the influence that ethnicity and age can have on plea proceedings, a number of important questions still remain ambiguous or unanswered. We still do not know whether certain factors influence adolescents' and young adults' decision to plead differently than their older counterparts (see Chapter 6, this volume). Additionally, it is unclear whether age or other demographics impact the likelihood of one's adherence to the shadow-of-the-trial model when making plea decisions. Results examining the impact of ethnicity have also been mixed, and we do not know whether minority status makes one more or less likely to plead, let alone to falsely plead. Nor do we know enough about the influence ethnicity has on other actors during the plea process (e.g., defense counsel). Further, there are very few, if any, examinations of demographic variables aside from age and ethnicity (e.g., intelligence/cognitive ability, mental illness). Clearly, more research is needed to estimate the impact individual differences might have on both the decision to plead and the decision to plead falsely.

We conclude by mentioning the limited research on another very important estimator variable: guilt status. While the system cannot entirely control whether suspects are guilty or innocent, it can control a number of other procedures that could help to protect the innocent from impugning themselves. Current research has already revealed the impact that guilt status can have on the likelihood that one will plead guilty; future research should continue to investigate how this effect can be preserved. This is the only way we can maintain a system that is both efficient and fair.

References

Abrams, D. S. (2011). Is Pleading Really a Bargain? *Journal of Empirical Legal Studies, 8*(s1), 200–221. doi: 10.1111/j.1740-1461.2011.01234.x

Albonetti, C. A. (1990). Race and the probability of pleading guilty. *Journal of Quantitative Criminology, 6*, 315–334. doi: 10.1007/BF01065413

Berlinger, J., & Sinofsky, B. (1996). *Paradise lost: The child murders at Robin Hood Hills* [Documentary]. United States: Home Box Office (HBO).

Bibas, S. (2004). Plea bargaining outside the shadow of a trial. *Harvard Law Review, 117*(8), 2463–2547. doi: 10.2307/4093404

Bikel, O. (Writer & Director). (2004, June 17). *The Plea* [Television series episode]. In D. Fanning (Executive Producer), *Frontline*. Boston, MA: WGBH Educational Foundation.

Blume, J. H., & Helm, R. K. (2014). The unexonerated: Factually innocent defendants who plead guilty. *Cornell Law Review, 100*(1), 157–191.

Bordens, K. S. (1984). The effects of likelihood of conviction, threatened punishment, and assumed role on mock plea bargaining decisions. *Basic & Applied Social Psychology, 5*(1), 59–74.

Bordens, K. S., & Bassett, J. (1985). The plea bargaining process from the defendant's perspective: A field investigation. *Basic and Applied Social Psychology, 6*, 93–110. doi: 10.1207/s15324834basp_0602_1

Bureau of Justice Statistics. (2015). *Federal justice statistics, 2012—Statistical tables* (NCJ Report No. 248470). Washington DC: U.S. Department of Justice.

Bushway, S. D., & Redlich, A. D. (2012). Is plea bargaining in the 'shadow of the trial' a mirage? *Journal of Quantitative Criminology, 28*(3), 437–454. doi: 10.1007/s10940-011- 9147-5

Bushway, S. D., Redlich, A. D., & Norris, R. J. (2014). An explicit test of plea bargaining in the "shadow of the trial." *Criminology, 52*(4), 723–754. doi: 10.1111/1745-9125.12054

Committee on the Judiciary. (2016). *Federal Rules of Criminal Procedure*. Washington, DC: U.S. House of Representatives. Retrieved from http://www.uscourts.gov/file/18073/download

Cook, K. M. (2007). *Chasing justice: My story of freeing myself after two decades on death row for a crime I didn't commit*. New York: HarperCollins Publishers.

Covey, R. D. (2007). Fixed justice: Reforming plea bargaining with plea-based ceilings. *Tulane Law Review, 82*, 1237–1290.

Covey, R. D. (2013). Police misconduct as a cause of wrongful conviction. *Washington University Law Review, 90*, 1133–1189.

Daftary-Kapur, T., & Zottoli, T. M. (2014). A first look at the plea deal experiences of juveniles tried in adult court. *International Journal of Forensic Mental Health, 13*, 323–336. doi: 10.1080/14999013.2014.960983

Dervan, L. E., & Edkins, V. A. (2013). The innocent defendant's dilemma: An innovative empirical study of plea bargaining's innocence problem. *Journal of Criminal Law & Criminology, 103*(1), 1–48.

Easterbrook, F. H. (1992). Plea bargaining as compromise. *Yale Law Journal, 101*(8), 1969–1978.

Edkins, V. A. (2011). Defense attorney plea recommendations and client race: Does zealous representation apply equally to all? *Law and Human Behavior, 35*, 413–425. doi: 10.1007/s10979-010-9254-0

Eisen, L. B., & Rooney, I. R. (2002). Thirty-first annual review of criminal procedure: II. Preliminary proceedings: Guilty pleas. *Georgetown Law Journal, 90*, 1477–2599.

Fisher, G. (2000). Plea bargaining's triumph. *Yale Law Review, 109*(5), 857–1086. doi: 10.2307/797483

Frenzel, E. D., & Ball, J. (2007). Effects of individual characteristics on plea negotiations under sentencing guidelines. *Journal of Ethnicity in Criminal Justice, 5*(4), 59–82. doi: 10.1300/J222v05n04-03

Gazal-Ayal, O. (2006). Partial ban on plea bargains. *Cardozo Law Review, 27*, 2295–2349.

Gregory, W. L., Mowen, J. C., & Linder, D. E. (1978). Social psychology and plea bargaining: Applications, methodology, and theory. *Journal of Personality and Social Psychology, 36*(12), 1521–1530. doi: 10.1037/0022-3514.36.12.1521

Grisso, T., Steinberg, L., Woolard, J., Cauffman, E., Scott, E., Graham, S., . . . Schwartz, R. (2003). Juveniles' competence to stand trial: A comparison of adolescents' and adults' capacities as trial defendants. *Law and Human Behavior, 27*, 333–363. http://psycnet.apa.org/doi/10.1023/A:1024065015717

Grissom, B. (2012, July 5). As former death row inmate tries to clear his name, his life is on hold. *New York Times.*

Hall, M. (2012, March 31). Released but never exonerated, a man fights for freedom. *New York Times.*

Horwitz, S. (2015, August 15). Unlikely allies. *Washington Post.* Retrieved from http://www.washingtonpost.com/sf/national/2015/08/15/clemency-the-issue-that-obama-and-the-koch-brothers-actually-agree-on/

Kahneman, D. (2011). *Thinking fast and slow.* New York: Farrar, Straus, and Giroux.

Kassin, S. M. (2005). On the psychology of confessions: Does innocence put innocents at risk? *American Psychologist, 60*, 215–228. doi: 10.1037/0003-066X.60.3.215

Kassin, S. M., Drizin, S. A., Grisso, T., Gudjonsson, G. H., Leo, R. A., & Redlich, A. D. (2010). Police-induced confessions: Risk factors and recommendations. *Law and Human Behavior, 34*, 3–38. doi: 10.1007/s10979-009-9188-6

Kellough, G., & Wortley, S. (2002). Remand for plea: Bail decisions and plea bargaining as commensurate decisions. *British Journal of Criminology, 42*(1), 186–211.

Kutateladze, B. L., Andiloro, N. R., & Johnson, B. (2016). Opening Pandora's box: How does defendant race influence plea bargaining? *Justice Quarterly, 33*(3), 1–29. doi: 10.1080/07418825.2014.915340

Lafler v. Cooper, 132 U.S. 1376 (2012).

Leonard, D. P. (2008). Let's negotiate a deal. *Criminal Justice, 23*, 8–14.

Malloy, L. C., Shulman, E. P., & Cauffman, E. (2014). Interrogations, confessions, and guilty pleas among serious adolescent offenders. *Law and Human Behavior, 38*, 181–193. http://dx.doi.org/10.1037/lhb0000065

McAllister, H. A., & Bregman, N. J. (1986). Plea bargaining by defendants: A decision theory approach. *Journal of Social Psychology*, *126*, 105–110. doi: 10.1080/00224545.1986.9713576

McCoy, C. (2005). Plea bargaining as coercion: The trial penalty and plea bargaining reform. *Criminal Law Quarterly*, *50*, 67.

National Registry of Exonerations. (2017). *Exonerations by State map*. [Interactive data display]. Ann Arbor: University of Michigan Law School. Retrieved from http://www.law.umich.edu/special/exoneration/Pages/Exonerations-in-the-United-States-Map.aspx

National Research Council. (2014). *Identifying the culprit: Assessing eyewitness identification*. Washington, DC: National Academies Press. doi: 10.17226/18891

Nhan, J., Polzer, K., & Polzer, J. (2013). Discounted justice: The potential misuse of Alford pleas for future exonorees. *Social Science Journal*, *50*(3), 374–380. doi: 10.1016/j.soscij.2013.03.004

Piehl, A., & Bushway, S. (2007). Measuring and explaining charge bargaining. *Journal of Quantitative Criminology*, *23*(2), 105–125. doi: 10.1007/s10940-006-9023-x

Redlich, A. D. (2010). The susceptibility of juveniles to false confessions and false guilty pleas. *Rutgers Law Review*, 62, 943–957.

Redlich, A. D., & Bonventre, C. L. (2015). Content and comprehensibility of juvenile and adult tender-of-plea forms: Implications for knowing, intelligent, and voluntary guilty pleas. *Law & Human Behavior*, *39*, 162–176. doi: 10.1037/lhb0000118

Redlich, A. D., & Özdoğru, A. A. (2009). Alford pleas in the age of innocence. *Behavioral Sciences & the Law*, *27*, 467–488. doi: 10.1002/bsl.876

Redlich, A. D., & Shteynberg, R. V. (2016). To plead or not to plead: A comparison of juvenile and adult true and false plea decisions. *Law and Human Behavior*, *40*, 611–625. doi: 10.1037/lhb0000205

Redlich, A. D., & Summers, A. (2012). Voluntary, knowing, and intelligent pleas: Understanding the plea inquiry. *Psychology, Public Policy & Law*, *18*(4), 626–643. http://dx.doi.org/10.1037/a0026066

Redlich, A. D., Summers, A., & Hoover, S. (2010). Self-reported false confessions and false guilty pleas among offenders with mental illness. *Law and Human Behavior*, *34*, 79–90. doi: 10.1007/s10979-009-9194-8

Redlich, A. D., Wilford, M. M., & Bushway, S. (2017). Understanding guilty pleas through the lens of social science. *Psychology, Public Policy & Law*, *23*(4), 458. http://dx.doi.org/10.1037/law0000142

Shestak, A., Shockley, K., Keenan, J. M., Wilford, M. M., & Gonzales, J. E. (in press). When a plea is no bargain at all: Comparing sentencing outcomes for Massachusetts defendants in non-sexual and sexual crimes [Miscarriages of Justice Special Issue]. *Albany Law Review*.

Sommers, I., Goldstein, J., & Baskin, D. (2014). The intersection of victims' and offenders' sex and race/ethnicity on prosecutorial decisions for violent crimes. *Justice System Journal*, *35*(2), 178–204. doi: 10.1080/009826X.2013.869153

Tor, A., Gazal-Ayal, O., & Garcia, S. M. (2010). Fairness and the willingness to accept plea bargain offers. *Journal of Empirical Legal Studies*, *7*(1), 97–116.

Ulmer J., Eisenstein, J., & Johnson, B. (2010). Trial penalties in federal sentencing: Extra-guidelines factors and district variation. *Justice Quarterly, 27*, 560–592.

Viljoen, J. L., Klaver, J., & Roesch, R. (2005). Legal decisions of preadolescent and adolescent defendants: Predictors of confessions, pleas, communication with attorneys, and appeals. *Law and Human Behavior, 29*, 253–277. doi: 10.1007/s10979-005-3613-2

Wilford, M. M., & Wells, G. L. (2013). Eyewitness system variables: Revisiting the system-variable concept and the transfer of system variables to the legal system. In B. L. Cutler (Ed.), *Reform of eyewitness identification procedures* (pp. 1–29). Washington, DC: American Psychological Association.

Wilford, M. M., & Wells, G. L. (2018). Bluffed by the delaer: Distinguishing false pleas from false confessions [Special section on Guilty Pleas]. *Psychology, Public Policy, and Law, 24*(2), 158–170. doi: 10.1037/law0000165

Wilford, M. M., Wells, G. L., & Shestak, A. (2018). Plea-bargaining law: The impact of innocence, trial penalty, and conviction probability on plea outcomes. Unpublished manuscript.

Williams, G. C. (2001). Incubating monsters: Prosecutorial responsibility for the Rampart scandal. *Loyola Law Review, 34*, 829–842.

Wilson, M. J. (2016). Defense attorney bias and the rush to the plea. *Kansas Law Review, 65*(2), 271–325.

Zottoli, T. M., Daftary-Kapur, T., Winters, G. M., & Hogan, C. (2016). Plea discounts, time pressures, and false-guilty pleas in youth and adults who pleaded guilty to felonies in New York City. *Psychology, Public Policy, And Law, 22*(3), 250–259. doi: 10.1037/law0000095

Section 3

RESULTS OF A SYSTEM OF PLEAS

8

Sentencing Disparity and Mass Incarceration

Rhys Hester

This chapter looks at how the system of pleas impacts two areas that receive special attention in criminal justice: (1) disparities in sentencing outcomes and (2) mass incarceration. The first section discusses ways plea bargaining leads to different punishment for individuals whose criminal conduct is otherwise similar. Throughout this chapter I use the term *disparities* to refer broadly to differences in punishment outcomes (not just race-based disparities, which are addressed more specifically in Chapter 5). These differences include reduced punishment due to count or charge severity reductions, or favorable sentence recommendations or agreements, in exchange for a willingness to plead guilty or provide assistance to prosecution and law enforcement. In addition, I discuss two areas where indirect punishment disparities emerge—pretrial detention and criminal history.

In second section of the chapter, I discuss how the system of pleas enables mass incarceration. By many measures the United States is the most punitive country in the world, incarcerating individuals at many times the rate of its Western peer nations (see Tonry, 2016; Useem & Piehl, 2008). This was not always the case; prior to the 1970s, U.S. incarceration rates were similar to those in other nations and had been stable for decades (Blumstein & Cohen, 1973; Tonry, 1996). Over time, more punitive sentiments took hold in America; policymakers began passing tough-on-crime laws and expanding the reach of the criminal justice system, including, among other things, through the so-called war on drugs. The system of pleas, which had been well established by this time, created the infrastructure that made mass incarceration possible. This last section of the chapter explores the relationship between our system of pervasive plea bargaining and mass incarceration.

Sentencing Disparity in a System of Pleas

Treating like cases alike has been a hallmark concern of sentencing reform for the past half-century (Frankel, 1972; Tonry, 1996). Yet, in numerous ways, the decision to waive one's constitutional right to a jury trial leads to differential treatment. Defendants willing to plead guilty benefit from deals that reduce the severity of their punishment. Evidence suggests these plea benefits, or trial penalties, vary by location and local practice (Johnson, Ulmer, & Kramer, 2008; Spohn & Fornango, 2009). Defendants may choose to forego their jury trial right for a variety of reasons: they may be presented with a plea offer to a less serious charge than the one they are initially accused of or to a reduced number of charges. Or they may be offered a more lenient sentence in exchange for providing substantial assistance to the government in the prosecution of some other defendant. Whatever the case, both empirical and normative questions arise.

Trial Penalties, Plea Discounts

A consistent finding of sentencing research is that offenders who are found guilty after trial get substantially longer sentences than similarly situated individuals who plead guilty (e.g., King, Soule, Steen, & Weidner, 2005; Ulmer & Bradley, 2006). Whether one refers to this as a trial penalty or a plea discount is probably largely a matter of semantics. More important than the label is the recognition that how a case is disposed of (via trial or plea) can have drastic impacts on punishment disparity.

Magnitude of the Disparities

A number of analyses of in/out and sentence-length decisions reveal the substantial punitive impact of guilt after trial rather than pleading guilty. These studies control for potentially countervailing influences, such as the severity and type of the offense committed, the individual's prior record, and demographic characteristics, among others. In other words, they ensure, to the extent possible, that similar cases are treated similarly for the comparison effects of trial versus plea. Ulmer and Bradley (2006), examining Pennsylvania sentencing data, found that guilt after jury trial was associated with a 2.7 times increase in the odds of incarceration, and among those incarcerated, sentence lengths were around 57% longer for those who chose a trial over a plea (see also Kramer and Ulmer [2009], who extended the Ulmer and Bradley analysis and reported similar results). Nancy King and colleagues (2005) examined trial/plea process effects in five sentencing guidelines jurisdictions (Kansas, Maryland, Minnesota, Pennsylvania, and Washington) on select offense types. The odds of incarceration were frequently two to three times greater for those sentenced after a jury trial compared to similarly situated defendants who pleaded guilty. Notably, there was substantial variation, with effect sizes in Maryland, for example, as high as five to six times for some offenses, and effect sizes much smaller or nonexistent in Washington (King et al., 2005). Hester and Hartman (2017), reporting average marginal effects of the in/out decision on sentencing in South Carolina, found that defendants convicted after a jury trial were, on average, 41% more likely to be incarcerated than defendants pleading guilty. Of those incarcerated, those not pleading guilty received prison sentences that were, on average, 57 months longer than similarly situated defendants who pleaded guilty. (For an overview of additional studies, see Kramer and Ulmer [2009, pp. 140–141].) In sum, the plea–trial divide appears to exert considerable influence, creating substantial differences in punishment.[1]

Explaining the Punishment Gap

Since U.S. defendants are assured a presumption of innocence and a constitutional right to trial, one might question why these gaps in punishment exist. Several explanations have been put forth. First, trial penalties may reflect the organizational efficiency concerns of prosecutors, judges, and defense attorneys (Kramer & Ulmer, 2009; see also Dixon, 1995). Trials consume much more time and resources than pleas. If courtroom actors are overburdened with a 5% trial rate, imagine the strain if even just 10% or 20% of cases went to trial with current caseloads. Perhaps, then, the system of pleas is maintained because courtroom actors can envision no other way of continuing to process the same number of cases. Consequently, when a defendant insists on a trial, severe sentences may be doled out to reinforce the message to defendants and defense attorneys that the alternative to plea bargaining carries substantial punishment risks.

Second, judges may credit defendants for showing remorse and accepting responsibility. Under this view, the punishment gap may be better thought of as a plea discount. Kramer and Ulmer (2009) present evidence from qualitative interviews of Pennsylvania trial judges, such as one who gave the following perspective: "People who plead guilty always argue that remorse is a

---

1 An alternative position is put forth by Abrams (2011, 2013), who suggests that there are, in fact, no trial penalties. Analyzing data from Cook County, Illinois, Abrams argues that when one factors in the probability of acquittal, those who plead guilty receive longer sentences than those who go to trial. But my interest is on differences in sentencing; individuals found not guilty at trial are not sentenced. As Kim (2015) observes, Abrams's is a different fashioning of the notion of a trial penalty, which has more traditionally been defined by the repercussions guilt-after-plea versus guilt-after-trial. From a behavioral economics perspective, how an offender perceives his or her likelihood of acquittal is certainly important to explore, but for current purposes it seems more appropriate to focus on sentences imposed by courtroom actors on defendants who are similarly situated, with mode of case disposition being the one distinguishing factor.

mitigating factor, and one cannot deny that. They are saying, 'I'm sorry, I did it'. I consider that a mitigating factor. . . . You could look at it as a penalty but there is no other way of doing it. You have to give people credit for pleading guilty and expressing remorse" (p. 100; see also Eisenstein, Flemming, & Nardulli, 1988).

Third, Kramer and Ulmer (2009) put forth the "bad facts" thesis—the idea that trials bring out details about the nature of the offense and the harm committed that would otherwise remain obscure in quickly administered guilty plea hearings (see also Brereton & Casper, 1982). Under this view, hearing eyewitness accounts, testimony about victimization, and perhaps even narratives from the victims themselves may leave a strong emotional impression that leads actors to pursue the upper ends of punishment. Intuitively, it may be one thing to hear a prosecutor's cold recitation of the facts that the defendant did commit a burglary on or around such-and-such a date, having broken and entered a given residence at nighttime, and did steal personal property of the homeowner valued at *x* dollars. It may be quite another to hear the homeowner's tearful account of fear and distress upon finding her home burglarized, her things rifled through, valued items taken and never recovered, and her persistent fear of having her home intruded into again.

Later I will discuss whether these explanations for the punishment gap are justifiable on normative grounds, but first I examine a similar source of sentencing disparity: substantial assistance discounts.

Substantial Assistance

Substantial assistance discounts are a related source of punishment disparity with plea bargaining. These are particularly salient in the federal system, where they are formalized into the guidelines (though similar discounts may apply, whether formally or informally, in other jurisdictions). According to Spohn and Fornango (2009), "Of all the decisions made by the AUSA [Assistant United States Attorney], none is more important than the decision to file a motion for a substantial assistance downward departure . . ."[2] (p. 814). Stith and Cabranes (1998) have called substantial assistance reductions a wellspring of disparity. Not only do these motions free judges to depart from guidelines recommendations (an outcome with muted significance following *United States v. Booker* (2005), the U.S. Supreme Court decision that rendered the federal guidelines advisory rather than mandatory), substantial assistance departures also allow judges to sentence without regard to mandatory minimum sentences (Hartley, Maddan, & Spohn, 2007). As Alschuler (2005) notes, "When a prosecutor seeks a substantial assistance departure, the bottom is the limit" (p. 114). On average, these departures cut recommended

---

[2] The AUSA, or Assistant United States Attorney, is the prosecutor representing the federal government in a given criminal case.

sentences in half, though there is considerable range within types of offenses and variation in who gets what, and how (Hartley et al., 2007).

Hartley and colleagues (2007) indicate that as many as one in five federal defendants receive a substantial assistance departure, with tremendous variation by district ranging from 5% to over 45% of cases receiving these departures. Others, like Johnson and colleagues (2008), have documented geographic variation in the use of these departure motions. And the filing of these motions also varies tremendously by prosecutor. Spohn and Fornango (2009), in a study of prosecutorial variation in substantial assistance motions in three federal jurisdictions, found that prosecutorial use of these motions ranged from around 10% to 50% of their caseloads, confirming earlier suggestions that prosecutorial discretion is a driving force of this disparity (e.g., Nagel & Schulhofer, 1992).

Thus, like plea bargaining more generally, substantial assistance departures appear to not only generate large disparities but also undercut uniformity across offense types, districts, and prosecutors. All of this for offenders who, all else being equal, do not differ in their culpability for their current offense or their need for deterrence, rehabilitation, or incapacitation from offenders who do not provide substantial assistance. How, if at all, these punishment gaps can be justified is addressed further later in the chapter. But next, I introduce one final category of mechanisms by which the system of pleas leads to sentencing disparities: indirect effects.

Indirect Effects

In addition to the more direct impacts of plea deals discussed here, punishment disparities can arise through case, offender, or processing factors that affect the type and dose of punishment. This may be problematic, such as when offenders (all else being equal) get longer sentences following their inability to post bail or because of the type of attorney they had. In other instances, whether a characteristic justifies increased punishment is unclear—for example, increased punishment on the basis of an offender's prior record (explored further later). Critical for the current discussion is that the indirect effect must operate differently under plea practices than it would in a system of trials. I focus on two of these areas here: pretrial status and criminal history.

Consider first pretrial detention. Prior research has found pretrial detention status to be a strong predictor of less favorable sentencing outcomes (e.g., Demuth, 2003; Spohn, 2008). Several recent studies have expanded our understanding of how and why pretrial detention exerts such a strong influence, and the answer appears to have a lot to do with plea bargaining (see Dobbie, Goldin, & Yang, 2016; Gupta, Hansman, & Frenchman, 2016; Heaton, Mayson, & Stevenson, 2017). The majority of criminal cases are ultimately resolved with probation or other non-incarceration sanctions. For accused persons likely to receive a non-prison sentence but who are currently jailed prior to adjudication, a get-out-of-jail card is a strong enticement to plead guilty.

This enticement to freedom may cause individuals to make concessions they would not otherwise make—perhaps they agree to more serious charges, a greater number of charges, more fines and fees, or longer terms of probation than they would have absent the choice of freedom factoring into the calculus. And, since pleading guilty disposes of the case, these accused persons lose the opportunity to assist in their own defense, potentially gathering evidence, or finding witnesses that might have otherwise led to the prosecutor reducing charges or dismissing the case. To the extent this is true, individuals detained prior to trial receive worse plea deals than similarly situated individuals not detained.

Gupta and colleagues (2016) found that being detained led to a 12% increase in the likelihood of conviction, and this effect appeared almost entirely driven by the fact that those detained pleaded guilty in order to get out of jail. As Heaton and colleagues (2017) observe, "For defendants with a job or apartment on the line, the chance to get out of jail may be impossible to pass up" (p. 716). If these accused individuals were instead released on bail (or their own recognizance), they would be in better positions to assist in their defenses, and they might be less inclined to take an unfavorable or unfair plea deal. Thus, owing to the system of pleas, bail release decisions appear likely to generate disparities in the sorts of offenses an individual pleads guilty to and in the possibility that a person will be found guilty of an offense. (These processes also likely generate racial disparities, as minorities experience pretrial detention at higher rates than those of white individuals; see, e.g., Demuth, 2003; Spohn, 2008.)

Another use of plea incentives that can lead to disparities is through charging practices aimed at maximizing the offender's prior record. Although more research is needed in this area, there is evidence from at least one jurisdiction that prosecutors have changed their bargaining practices to strategically maximize the future impact of prior record (see Frase, 2005; discussed further later in this chapter). Bargaining and disparity interact similar to the way pretrial detention can create differences in outcomes. Assuming an accused person's primary concern is the disposition (incarceration or non-incarceration) and not the other terms that lead to that outcome, prosecutors may be able to maximize unfavorable aspects of the plea—such as the severity of the offense, the number of offenses, the downstream impact of the offense, and the length of community supervision. Defendants will acquiesce because, for the short term at least, they are presented with a non-prison outcome.

Agreeing to a plea offer with these leveraged terms but a non-prison outcome can exacerbate disparities, for example, when the levered terms are aimed at maximizing the criminal history score. Frase's (2005) analysis of the Minnesota guidelines is instructive. He explains various changes in charging practices following the implementation of the Minnesota guidelines. While sentence bargaining decreased and some offenders received greater "vertical" charge reductions, there were also significant changes in the number of charges retained to conviction, what Frase (2005) calls "horizontal' charging" (p. 178). After a court decision allowed prosecutors to stack multiple charges and build an offender's criminal history in a single sentencing hearing, prosecutors engaged in "targeting to the disposition line," a practice by which they would bring multiple charges so that offenders could still receive a non-prison sentence for their current offense but so that in any future case they would be placed in the presumptive prison area of the grid (Frase, 2005, p. 178). In other words, prosecutors in this jurisdiction can sequentially build a defendant's criminal history score in a single sentencing hearing, moving that individual along the grid right up to the point where, at a future proceeding, the defendant will be faced with a presumptive prison sentence even for a low-severity offense.

Although this practice of stacking charges to increase criminal history may not be an option in some jurisdictions, there are other ways that prosecutors might strategically tailor bargains to maximize criminal history using similar tactics. The assumption here is that a defendant will agree to almost anything if he or she views the immediate outcome as advantageous. Thus, an individual might agree to plead guilty to a more serious crime than he or she thinks is appropriate if the prosecutor is nevertheless offering probation. Prosecutors could charge more serious crimes that will be assigned higher criminal history points in any future case, thereby inflating the downstream impact of prior record. And, as with pretrial detention effects, the general disparities in punishment that arise on the basis of prior record also manifest as racial disparities, since black offenders have, on average, more extensive criminal histories than those of white offenders (see, e.g., Frase, Roberts, Hester, & Mitchell, 2015; Ulmer, Painter-Davis, & Tinik, 2016).

Normative Considerations

Future research should carefully consider whether the plea–trial punishment gap is justifiable. If the plea penalties are viewed in retributive terms as fair and deserved, and if the much more severe trial penalties impose disproportionately severe penalties, then from the retributive perspective the punishment gap is problematic. Conversely, while constituting at most 5% of disposed cases, criminal trials are still a frequent occurrence, so we might presume that courtroom actors think carefully about the penalties they impose in these cases—and that they do not view them as undeserved. In that case, again from the retributive standpoint, we might ask whether retributive justice is being done in the 95% of cases in which much more lenient sentences are being assigned. This is particularly provocative as the three explanations just discussed do not appear to have retributive significance—neither making the system more efficient, nor presumably showing current remorse, nor failing to fully explore the details of the harm involved has any bearing on the moral blameworthiness that can be attributed to the individual at the time he or she committed the crime. Since plea penalties reflect the overwhelming supermajority of case dispositions under current U.S. practices, it seems a difficult task to support the punishment gap on the basis of just deserts.

If instead one of the utilitarian theories is used (or a hybrid theory like limiting retributivism, in which utilitarianism plays a prominent role—see Frase, 2013), the questions shift. Are current plea sentences sufficient for utilitarian outcomes like deterrence and incapacitation? If so, then it would seem difficult to justify more substantial trial penalties, since the increase in punishment would be gratuitous. If plea penalties are not sufficient for deterrence and incapacitation, but trial penalties are, then utilitarian theory would counsel for increased punishment in plea cases so that individuals are adequately deterred or incapacitated.

More likely, the dynamic of the system of pleas calls for a broader system-level account of punishment justification that goes beyond the traditional offender-focused theories of punishment. In this broader sense it might be argued that, collectively, it is better for general deterrent effects to hold more individuals accountable but for less severe punishment (than, conversely, to prosecute fewer individuals but punish the select few more severely). Such a position invites an empirical test of two of the fundamental aspects of deterrence theory: the certainty of punishment and the severity of punishment (see, e.g., Nagin, 1998), and the optimal trade-off between the two to maximize deterrence in the current U.S. criminal justice system.

Similarly, the steep discounts afforded for substantial assistance departures deserve some attention. Aside from issues that emerge from the disparate use across prosecutors, locations, and offense types, it is clear that these substantial assistance departures generate considerable disparities in the federal system (Hartley et al., 2007), raising the question of how they are supported under the traditional purposes of punishment. If we assume that offenders not receiving substantial assistance discounts are receiving their just deserts or are being punished so as to adequately satisfy other utilitarian goals like deterrence or incapacitation, the question likely again becomes a broader utilitarian one. Assistance discounts could advance the more general utilitarian greatest-good-for-the-greatest-number principle. Police and prosecutors are able to go after and secure evidence against offenders they might not otherwise be able to go after. It may well be that the public and policymakers embrace this utilitarian notion that informing offenders be given substantial leniency in order to secure convictions against individuals who presumably have committed more harmful offenses or pose greater threats to public safety. Even so, it is at least worth questioning whether this sort of exchange is being properly implemented.

For example, Safer and Crowl (1999) explain how, without stiff federal penalties and lenient substantial assistance departures, law enforcement would have never been able to bring down the ruthless Gangster Disciple street gang. But even if justifiable in some cases—and a tight-knit criminal organization allegedly responsible for considerable violence and murders is likely one of those cases—lingering questions remain. Are there, for example, certain types of offenders or certain types of higher-level targets that these discounts should be tailored toward? Should there be more guidance, and less prosecutorial discretion, in applying substantial assistance discounts? And should the discounts be limited so as not to exacerbate the disparities?

Future research might examine, for example, whether the nearly one in five defendants who receive a substantial assistance departure are providing information that eventually leads to securing a guilty conviction against a violent offender (or whether, as might also be possible, some of these lead instead to convictions for a drug trafficker who will spend a substantial amount of time in federal prison but who will also be replaced by other drug traffickers with no net benefit to the public). These are important questions to examine, since, as Safer and Crowl (1999) recognize, the off-setting concerns over uniformity must also be taken into account. They suggest that standard percentage reductions (e.g., 33% or 50% reductions) could be set and that other internal guidance could be established by the U.S. Department of Justice to minimize jurisdictional and prosecutorial variation.

In conclusion, the system of pleas currently employed in the United States leads to considerable punishment differentials through several different mechanisms. As scholars continue to document and explore these empirically, future research is needed to examine the disparities normatively, as treating like cases alike continues to be one of the hallmark goals of the system and holds a prominent place in most policy discussions related to sentencing and punishment. The next section turns to a different topic, but one that also occupies a prominent place in punishment policy discussions: mass incarceration.

Mass Incarceration in a System of Pleas

The system of pleas is mass incarceration's enabler. Plea bargaining came to dominate the American criminal justice well before the incarceration boom. While the courtroom actors who began to embrace plea bargaining in the nineteenth and early twentieth centuries would never have anticipated the drastic shift in use of imprisonment that would follow, the system of pleas they helped build did, in fact, provide the institutional infrastructure that made mass incarceration possible. And not only did the system of pleas establish a means of most efficiently processing multitudes of more criminal cases, but mass incarceration and the system of pleas are now intertwined in a symbiotic knot. Given enormous caseloads, prosecutors secure pleas through offers of suspended sentences and probation which, in turn, ultimately lead to more and longer incarceration terms.

Recall from Chapter 1 that plea bargaining has not always existed in the United States. In fact, a fair historical reading of Article III of the U.S. Constitution's jury trial provision ("The Trial of all Crimes, except in Cases of Impeachment; shall be by Jury[.]") would forbid waiving trial and pleading guilty (Amar, 2005; Bibas, 2011); having citizen jurors serve as guilt decision-makers was a check against potential corruption of government actors who might otherwise be able to circumvent the rule of law. Nevertheless, the practice of plea bargaining began to take root in the 1800s, expanded in the post–Civil War era, and proliferated in the first half of the 1900s (Alschuler, 1979). By the beginning of the era of mass incarceration in the 1970s, plea bargaining was well established as the primary way of resolving cases. The movement we now call mass incarceration hit the criminal justice system like a freight train. And while the impending impact of this freight train was unforeseen (see Blumstein & Cohen, 1973), plea bargaining had been laying the track for over a century.

There are several theories advanced to explain how American criminal justice made a nearly complete reversal from a system of exclusively trials to a system of almost exclusively pleas. These theories include the following: (1) pleas took hold owing to case pressures; (2) the increasing complexity of trials led to more pleas; (3) changes in the professionalization of police caused the shift; and (4) the reasons were really social and political causes external to the courtroom (Smith, 2005). George Fisher (2003) draws on several of these theories in his account of plea bargaining's path to dominance. Fisher discusses how plea bargaining offered something enticing to prosecutors, judges, and defendants and their counsel. For prosecutors, the benefits of certainty of conviction created an inexorable draw, "an almost primordial instinct of the prosecutorial soul" (p. 23). For judges, the benefits included efficiently disposing of cases and the assurance of not being reversed on appeal. For defendants guilty of crimes, plea bargaining offered reductions in punishment—either through favorable recommendations to more lenient sentences or through charge bargaining that put the defendant in a lower punishment category (sometimes even for a crime other than the one they actually committed). Another key component of Fisher's account is the connection between plea bargaining and the introduction of probation as a sentencing option. Fisher attributes the advent of probation to prosecutors seeking an option to attract defendant guilty pleas. He recounts how probation and plea bargaining emerged at about the same time and argues that probation sentences offered security of conviction for the prosecutor and a lenient outcome for the defendant.

This probable nexus between plea bargaining and probation is important to the connection to mass incarceration, for two reasons. First, the growth of individuals under community supervision, while given little scholarly attention until recently, is a problem that parallels mass incarceration—indeed, mass probation and mass incarceration are really part and parcel of a grander mass punishment phenomenon (e.g., Phelps, 2017). Probation, even in lieu of incarceration, is often a burdensome and disruptive intervention for many (see Feeley, 1979), and while it is surely an appropriate criminal justice response in some cases, it merits consideration as a potentially problematic policy outcome all on its own.

But there is a second important connection between probation and mass incarceration that has both direct and indirect impacts on prison populations.

There are currently around five million individuals under community supervision, and every year, hundreds of thousands of persons are given suspended sentences or direct probation as part of plea bargained case dispositions (Clear & Frost, 2014; Kaeble & Glaze, 2016). Many of these probationary sentences will end up transitioning to prison beds in the near future. Individuals who violate their probation, either through committing a new offense (however serious or minor) or through violating other terms of their parole, frequently end up in prison as a result. Generally, probation can be given as a pure form of punishment or as a suspended sentence. Details vary by jurisdiction, but with a suspended (or stayed) sentence, a judge can formally impose a term of incarceration and then suspend that jail or prison sentence, contingent upon successful completion of a term of probation. Thus, for instance, a judge might impose a sentence of "5 years in prison suspended upon 5 years probation." In these instances, offenders are "on the hook" for the incarceration sentence if they commit a new crime or violate their probation conditions. The offender could dutifully carry out 4 years on probation, but if he violates it before completion of the term, he could be forced to serve the entire 5-year incarceration term as a consequence. We know a substantial percentage of probationers will violate (Kaeble, Maruschak, & Bonczar, 2015; Phelps, 2017); consequently, these non-incarceration sentences, while enticing for those presented with a plea deal, will lead to prison time for many.

This form of "back-end sentencing" (see Travis, 2007) was discussed by several of the court professionals I interviewed as part of a larger project aimed at exploring the sentencing decisions of South Carolina trial judges (Hester, 2017a). During the course of the interviews, several judges mentioned the sentencing practices of a well-known judge I referred to with the pseudonym Judge Nash (Hester, 2017b). Whether Judge Nash was a harsh or lenient judge was somewhat of an enigma, owing to his practice of imposing the statutory maximum sentence and then suspending it on 5 years' probation (generally the maximum allowed under South Carolina law). While in some respects Judge Nash had the reputation of leniency and a willingness to give second chances, one judge estimated that Judge Nash actually had more offenders serving active time than any other judge in the state because of the number of offenders who were unable to "live out" the terms of their probationary sentences and the exceedingly long maximum sentences they were required to serve under Judge Nash's paradigm. The other judges I interviewed generally did not embrace this statutory maximum practice, but all of them gave suspended sentences where appropriate. And several discussed this tension between apparent leniency and potential punishment. For example, one judge routinely stressed this to defendants at the plea colloquy:

> I always tell them, if you are getting an eight-year prison sentence suspended on five years' probation, you are really getting a thirteen-year sentence. And you are getting the most due process you are ever going to get. You can go and live out all but one day of those five years'

> probation, but if you mess up on that last day, you'll go away and serve that eight-year sentence. And there won't be a trial or a bunch of due process or this long recitation of your rights—next time you'll just get sent away. (Hester, 2017b)

The effects of this back-end sentencing can be even more pronounced in other jurisdictions; in South Carolina, the site of my interviews, probation terms generally could not exceed 5 years in length. In many jurisdictions, probation terms can extend as long as the statutory maximum for the offense, meaning an individual can be under probation—and therefore subject to revocation and commitment to prison—for decades (see, e.g., Frase et al., 2015).

To summarize: When offenders who are initially placed on probation (a seemingly favorable disposition that likely induces many to plead guilty) have their probation subsequently revoked and are placed in prison, the plea-driven probation sentences end up having a significant impact on mass incarceration. All told, prosecutors are able to secure guaranteed guilty dispositions and defendants often receive favorable outcomes compared to what they might receive at trial, though many of these defendants will ultimately violate their probation terms and end up in prison. The system of pleas has allowed policymakers to quintuple the prison rate in a way that would have been impossible if every case were considered by a jury.

Conclusion

Sentencing disparities and mass incarceration are topics of universal concern in American criminal justice. This chapter has explored how the system of pleas creates disparities, how plea bargaining played an important enabling role in mass incarceration, and how plea-inducing suspended sentences continue to add up to more and more prison beds following revocations.

The intersection between these abiding concerns of equal treatment and mass incarceration merits a mention. Although this chapter has considered sentencing disparities more broadly, I turn here to racial disparities in particular. By most accounts, mass incarceration has had an especially devastating impact on minority communities. The imprisonment of young, black males, for example, has been so extensive that mass incarceration has fundamentally damaged communities of color, ultimately leading to more social disorganization, disadvantage, and a self-perpetuating cycle of crime in those communities (see, e.g., Clear, 2009).

Given the gravity of issues like racial bias and mass incarceration, future research should continue to explore these connections. What is particularly needed is research pointing to ways that criminal justice policies could offset these deleterious effects that have been fueled by the systemic practice of plea bargaining. For example, a number of jurisdictions are reforming bail practices, and research continues to expand in this area (see Stevenson

& Mayson, 2018). Frase and Roberts (2018) offer suggestions on how the negative impacts of prior record can be reduced in sentencing guidelines jurisdictions without affecting countervailing concerns like public safety (see also Hester, Frase, Roberts, & Mitchell, 2018).

These efforts would seem to be empowered by the consideration that some of the problems in American sentencing are made worse by the system of pleas. As our collective exultation of the American jury system is tempered by the reality of the system of pleas, research and policy efforts should strive to mitigate ways that plea bargaining contributes to undesirable outcomes in the American justice system.

References

Abrams, D. S. (2011). Is pleading really a bargain? *Journal of Empirical Legal Studies, 8*(1), 200–221. doi: 10.1111/j.1740-1461.2011.01234.x

Abrams, D. S. (2013). Putting the trial penalty on trial. *Duquesne Law Review, 51*, 777–833.

Alschuler, A. W. (1979). Plea bargaining and its history. *Columbia Law Review, 79*(1), 1–43. doi: 10.2307/1122051

Alschuler, A. W. (2005). Disparity: The normative and empirical failure of the federal guidelines. *Stanford Law Review, 58*(1), 85–117.

Amar, A. R. (2005). *America's Constitution: A biography*. New York: Random House.

Bibas, S. (2011). Regulating the plea-bargaining market: From caveat emptor to consumer protection. *California Law Review, 99*(4), 1117–1162. doi: 10.15779/Z38811K

Blumstein, A., & Cohen, J. (1973). A theory of the stability of punishment. *Journal of Criminal Law & Criminology, 64*(2), 198–207. doi: 10.2307/1142990

Brereton, D., & Casper, J. D. (1982). Does it pay to plead guilty? Differential sentencing and the functioning of criminal courts. *Law and Society Review, 16*, 45–70. doi: 10.2307/3053549

Clear, T. R. (2009). *Imprisoning communities: How mass incarceration makes disadvantaged neighborhoods worse*. New York: Oxford University Press.

Clear, T. R., & Frost, N. A. (2014). *The punishment imperative: The rise and failure of mass incarceration in America*. New York: New York University Press.

Demuth, S. (2003). Racial and ethnic differences in pretrial release decisions and outcomes: A comparison of Hispanic, black, and white felony arrestees. *Criminology, 41*(3), 873–908. doi: 10.1111/j.1745-9125.2003.tb01007.x

Dixon, J. (1995). The organizational context of criminal sentencing. *American Journal of Sociology, 100*(5), 1157–1198. doi: 10.1086/230635

Dobbie, W., Goldin, J., & Yang, C. (2016). *The effects of pre-trial detention on conviction, future crime, and employment: Evidence from randomly assigned judges* (No. w22511). National Bureau of Economic Research. doi: 10.3386/w22511

Eisenstein, J., Flemming, R., & Nardulli, P. (1988). *The contours of justice: Communities and their courts*. Boston: Little, Brown.

Feeley, M. M. (1979). *The process is the punishment: Handling cases in a lower criminal court*. New York: Russell Sage Foundation.
Fisher, G. (2003). *Plea bargaining's triumph: A history of plea bargaining in America*. Palo Alto, CA: Stanford University Press.
Frankel, M. (1972). *Criminal sentencing: Law without order*. New York: Hill and Wang.
Frase, R. S. (2005). Sentencing guidelines in Minnesota, 1978–2003. *Crime and Justice, 32*, 131–219. doi: 10.1086/655354
Frase, R. S. (2013). *Just sentencing: Principles and procedures for a workable system*. Oxford, UK: Oxford University Press.
Frase, R., & Roberts, J. V. (2018). *Criminal history enhancements*. Oxford, UK: Oxford University Press.
Frase, R. S., Roberts, J. V., Hester, R., & Mitchell, K. L. (2015). *Criminal history enhancements sourcebook*. Minneapolis: Robina Institute of Criminal Law and Criminal Justice, University of Minnesota.
Gupta, A., Hansman, C., & Frenchman, E. (2016). The heavy costs of high bail: Evidence from judge randomization. *Journal of Legal Studies, 45*(2), 471–505. doi: 10.1086/688907
Hartley, R. D., Maddan, S., & Spohn, C. C. (2007). Prosecutorial discretion: An examination of substantial assistance departures in federal crack-cocaine and powder-cocaine cases. *Justice Quarterly, 24*(3), 382–407. doi: 10.1080/07418820701485379
Heaton, P., Mayson, S., & Stevenson, M. (2017). The downstream consequences of misdemeanor pretrial detention. *Stanford Law Review, 69*, 711–794. doi: 10.2139/ssrn.2809840
Hester, R. (2017a). Judicial rotation as centripetal force: Sentencing in the court communities of South Carolina. *Criminology, 55*(1), 205–235. doi: 10.1111/1745-9125.12132
Hester, R. (2017b). Punishing for the past (sometimes): Perspectives on criminal history enhancements from non-guidelines judges. Unpublished manuscript.
Hester, R., Frase, R., Roberts, J. V., & Mitchell, K. (2018). Prior record enhancements at sentencing: Unsettled justifications and unsettling consequences. *Crime and Justice, 47*, 209–254.
Hester, R., & Hartman, T. K. (2017). Conditional race disparities in criminal sentencing: A test of the liberation hypothesis from a non-guidelines state. *Journal of Quantitative Criminology, 33*(1), 77–100. doi: 10.1007/s10940-016-9283-z
Johnson, B. D., Ulmer, J. T., & Kramer, J. H. (2008). The social context of guidelines circumvention: The case of federal district courts. *Criminology, 43*(3), 737–783. doi: 10.1111/j.1745-9125.2008.00125.x
Kaeble, D., & Glaze, L. (2016). *Correctional populations in the United States, 2015*. Washington, DC: Bureau of Justice Statistics, U.S. Department of Justice and Office of Justice Programs.
Kaeble, D., Maruschak, L. M., & Bonczar, T. P. (2015). *Probation and parole in the United States*. Washington, DC: Bureau of Justice Statistics, U.S. Department of Justice and Office of Justice Programs.
Kim, A. C. (2015). Understanding the trial penalty: An empirical analysis of the federal trial penalty and critique of the Abrams study. *Mississippi Law Journal, 84*(5), 1195–1256.

King, N. J., Soule, D. A., Steen, S., & Weidner, R. R. (2005). When process affects punishment: Differences in sentences after guilty plea, bench trial, and jury trial in five guidelines states. *Columbia Law Review, 105*(4), 959–1009.

Kramer, J. H., & Ulmer, J. T. (2009). *Sentencing guidelines: Lessons from Pennsylvania*. Boulder, CO: Lynne Rienner Publishers.

Nagel, I. H., & Schulhofer, S. J. (1992). A tale of three cities: An empirical study of charging and bargaining practices under the federal sentencing guidelines. *Southern California Law Review, 66*, 501–566.

Nagin, D. S. (1998). Criminal deterrence research at the outset of the twenty-first century. *Crime and Justice: A Review of Research, 23*, 1–42. doi: 10.1086/449268

Phelps, M. S. (2017). Mass probation: Toward a more robust theory of state variation in punishment. *Punishment & Society, 19*(1), 53–73. doi: 10.1177/1462474516649174

Safer, R. S., & Crowl, M. C. (1999). Substantial assistance departures: Valuable tool or dangerous weapon. *Federal Sentencing Reporter, 12*(1), 41–44. doi: 10.2307/20640216

Smith, B. P. (2005). Plea bargaining and the eclipse of the jury. *Annual Review of Law and Social Science, 1*, 131–149. https://doi.org/10.1146/annurev.lawsocsci.1.041604.115948

Spohn, C. C. (2008). Race, sex, and pretrial detention in federal court: Indirect effects and cumulative disadvantage. *University of Kansas Law Review, 57*, 879–901. doi: 10.17161/1808.20099

Spohn, C. C., & Fornango, R. (2009). US attorneys and substantial assistance departures: Testing for interprosecutor disparity. *Criminology, 47*(3), 813–846. doi:10.1111/j.1745-9125.2009.00163.x

Stevenson, M., & Mayson, S. G. (2018). Bail reform: New directions for pretrial detention and release. Unpublished manuscript.

Stith, K., & Cabranes, J. A. (1998). *Fear of judging: Sentencing guidelines in the federal courts*. Chicago: University of Chicago Press.

Tonry, M. (1996). *Sentencing matters*. New York: Oxford University Press.

Tonry, M. (2016). *Sentencing fragments: Penal reform in America, 1975–2025*. New York: Oxford University Press.

Travis, J. (2007). Back-end sentencing: A practice in search of a rationale. *Social Research, 74*(2), 631–644.

Ulmer, J. T., & Bradley, M. S. (2006). Variation in trial penalties among serious violent offenses. *Criminology, 44*(3), 631–670. doi: 10.1111/j.1745-9125.2006.00059.x

Ulmer, J., Painter-Davis, N., & Tinik, L. (2016). Disproportional imprisonment of black and Hispanic males: Sentencing discretion, processing outcomes, and policy structures. *Justice Quarterly, 33*(4), 642–681. doi: 10.1080/07418825.2014.958186

United States v. Booker, 543 U.S. 220 (2005).

Useem, B., & Piehl, A. M. (2008). *Prison state: The challenge of mass incarceration*. New York: Cambridge University Press.

9

Collateral Consequences and Disenfranchisement

Vanessa A. Edkins

Chevelle Nesbeth, a 20-year old, U.S. citizen originally from Kingston, Jamaica, was working part-time as a nail technician to pay her way through college (*U.S. v. Nesbeth*, 2016). While back in Jamaica visiting her boyfriend, two "friends" of Nesbeth's purchased her a return ticket to the United States and asked that she take with her suitcases to hand off to another individual upon arrival in the United States. Nesbeth agreed and was arrested at the airport with 602 grams of cocaine. She was convicted of importation with intent to distribute. She had no prior record or trouble with the law. In Nesbeth's sentencing hearing, Judge Frederic Block starkly departed from the federal sentencing guidelines and gave Nesbeth a relatively light sanction: 1 year of probation and 100 hours of community service, compared to the 33–41 months of incarceration recommended by the federal sentencing guidelines (Neyfakh, 2016). His reasoning? Nesbeth's real punishment was going to result from the automatic collateral consequences that the State would impose, consequences that Block referred to as potentially "devastating" (p. 2).

Collateral consequences refer to the local, state, and federal limitations and restrictions on employment, licensing, and government assistance that are imposed after a conviction, separate from any sentence handed down. While courts require defendants be made aware of any direct consequences of conviction (e.g., specific sentence imposed), the same is not true of collateral consequences (Chin, 2002; Lang, 2012), yet these "invisible" restrictions affect many of the common rights and privileges afforded to typical citizens. In a 42-page decision, Judge Block discussed how he had required the State to include the relevant collateral consequences in the presentence report, and he then proceeded to carefully outline how these were going to affect Nesbeth (*U.S. v. Nesbeth*, 2016). A student with lifelong aspirations to go into early-years education or social work, Nesbeth would be ineligible for government grants, loans, or work assistance for her remaining 2 years of college. She would be unable to attain access to federally assisted housing or other state assistance, such as food stamps. Travel back to Jamaica to see her extended family would be out of the question for the near future and, in fact, even local travel would be difficult since her driver's license would be revoked for at least 6 months. The presentence report also acknowledged that Nesbeth would need to adjust her future aspirations: Teaching and social work require criminal background checks and generally bar anyone with convictions from employment at facilities with children. In the presentence report, the State acknowledged that she would likely also be barred from working in the pharmaceutical industry, working for a transportation company or at an airport or airline, hospice work, work at financial institutions and labor organizations, enlisting in the army, collecting disaster relief assistance in the case of a natural disaster, possessing a firearm, adopting or fostering a child, serving as juror, and voting. Judge Block wrote,

> ". . . the collateral consequences Ms. Nesbeth will suffer, and is likely to suffer—principally her likely inability to pursue a teaching career and her goal of becoming a principal . . . —has compelled me to conclude that she has been sufficiently punished, and that jail is not necessary. . . " (p. 33)

The restrictions imposed on Chevelle Nesbeth are all too common. The large numbers of criminal convictions secured through guilty pleas have led to an unprecedented level of felon disenfranchisement (i.e., the loss of the right to vote) and imposition of collateral consequences.

Felon disenfranchisement is nothing new. In fact, denying civil liberties such as the right to vote to convicted criminals actually predates the criminal justice system (O'Keefe, 2010) and has been upheld by the Supreme Court in its interpretation of the Fourteenth Amendment (*Richardson v. Ramirez*, 1974).

Collateral consequences, on the other hand, are a more modern invention (O'Keefe, 2010). Beyond losing the right to vote, individuals convicted of a crime face a deluge of restrictions on employment, government benefit eligibility, driver's licenses, and adoption or foster parent privileges, among others (Whittle & Parker, 2014). These "secret sentences" (Chin & Holmes, 2002, p. 700) are separate from the direct consequences, or punishment, attached to a conviction. In 2007, various hearings across the country made it evident that (1) collateral consequences were both incredibly widespread and capable of affecting many areas of an ex-offender's life, and (2) it was nearly impossible to find a full accounting of all the possible collateral consequences that could be imposed upon conviction (Uggen & Stewart, 2014). It is estimated that an ex-offender may face as many as 50,000 possible collateral consequences (Laird, 2013).

Between disenfranchisement and the restrictions imposed through collateral consequences, the acceptance of a guilty plea can have far-reaching and often lifelong implications for an individual. Within roughly 97% of felony convictions resulting from guilty pleas (U.S. Department of Justice Executive Office for United States Attorneys, 2013), the issue of collateral consequences and felon disenfranchisement cannot be addressed without discussing pleas and plea bargaining.

This chapter will begin by describing the extent of the issue when a criminal record leads to disenfranchisement and the loss of other rights for vast segments of the population. From there, I will move into how plea bargains exacerbate the problem and whether there are appropriate safeguards in place, such as acknowledging the responsibility to communicate collateral consequences to the defendant and which party should assume that responsibility. And if the information is conveyed, will defendants actually take it into consideration when making their choice? Research is discussed that shows the process may be more complicated than is presently known.

The Scope of the Problem

The loss of the right to vote, as mentioned previously, predates the criminal justice system in the United States (O'Keefe, 2010), and the introduction of other civil restrictions came in with the adoption of the English common law traditions, which serve as the basis for our current criminal justice system (Chin, 2012). *Civil death*, in its most archaic form, basically indicated that an individual was considered deceased, insofar as the rules of society. This was a limitation on or removal of not just one's rights and privileges but also property and possessions. When a felony conviction meant an automatic death sentence, imposing these sanctions was a common-sense procedure, but some states still have "civil death" on the books for those convicted of life without the possibility of parole (e.g., New York and Rhode Island; Chin, 2012). While many states abandoned the practice and courts voiced disdain throughout the twentieth century, the existence of felon disenfranchisement (and the increase in statutes imposing collateral consequences, as discussed in the next section) indicates that the practice is alive and well, albeit under a different name. We may not treat convicted prisoners like they are civilly "dead" insofar as society is concerned, but the burdens imposed communicate a very similar sentiment.

Effects of Disenfranchisement

The rates of felon disenfranchisement in this country are staggering. A 2016 report from The Sentencing Project estimates that, currently, 6.1 million Americans are disenfranchised due to felony convictions (Uggen, Larson, & Shannon, 2016). Loss of the right to vote is not contingent on the type of felony crime or conviction, but instead is automatically imposed, regardless of situation (Burmilla, 2017; though the specifics of the limit vary by jurisdiction, as will be discussed). The effects of this cannot be understated. For example, Florida, a notorious "swing state," accounts for roughly 27% of disenfranchised individuals nationwide—about 1.5 million people. In a state with just over 20 million residents, that is a significant segment of the population. And in fact, some research suggests that had Florida's disenfranchised voters turned out at the state-estimated voting rate (27.2%) for the 2000 elections, Al Gore would have won the state of Florida—and thus the presidential election—by at least 80,000 votes (Uggen & Manza, 2002).

Disenfranchising such significant portions of the population does more than just drastically change the composition of elected parties (Uggen & Manza, 2002). Preventing those with criminal records from voting can contribute to an increased focus on crime control by those who are elected, spurring increases in our current rates of mass incarceration, which then leads to more disenfranchised citizens (Mungan, 2017). And, like much of the application of the criminal justice system, disenfranchisement occurs in a racially biased manner. As of 2016, roughly 7.4% of African Americans in this country are currently disenfranchised—four times the number of the rest of the population, even though African Americans only constitute about 13% of voting-age citizens (Uggen et al., 2016). In Florida, Kentucky, Tennessee, and Virginia, over 20% of voting-age African Americans are disenfranchised. Projecting these trends out, roughly 30% of African American men will lose the right to vote at some point in their lifetime (Fellner & Mauer, 1998).

Currently, only two states (Vermont and Maine) do not employ disenfranchisement—all other jurisdictions in the United States practice it at some level (Burmilla, 2017). While most jurisdictions have an automatic end date to restriction of voting rights, 10 states (such as Florida) disallow ex-felons from voting even after the completion of their sentence. As sentencing expert Marc Mauer (1999) pointed out, "an 18-year-old first offender convicted of writing a bad check in Florida or Virginia who successfully completes a sentence to probation loses the right to vote for life" (p. 186). And the United States stands virtually alone (compared to other democratic nations) in the employment of strict disenfranchisement of its citizens *after* sentence completion (Manza & Uggen, 2006). Some nations disenfranchise those currently incarcerated, but many countries are even moving away from that practice and are now allowing incarcerated individuals to continue to exercise their right to vote (Uggen & Manza, 2002).

With the history of "civil death" and the rates of disenfranchisement that are practiced in the United States, it is clear we do not see convicted felons as equal members of our society. It should be of little surprise, then, that we do not stop at simply removing the right to vote.

Effects of Collateral Consequences

Trends show that the imposition and enactment of collateral consequences began to decrease around the middle of the twentieth century, and continued to decline until the early 1980s (Travis, 2002). In the 1980s and 1990s, an increased focus on crime control policies, coupled with concern over making communities safe from convicted sex offenders, led to a reversal in the trend and a new focus on stripping rights from the "morally questionable." Sex offender registries were the main fuel behind the increase in civil restrictions and regulations (O'Keefe, 2010). The 1994 Jacob Wetterling Crimes Against Children Registration Act and its subsequent revision in 2006, the Adam Walsh Child Protection and Safety Act, made it a requirement for states to track individuals convicted of sex offenses and created community notification systems. These have been expanded to include restrictions on employment and residency (both where one may live and who else can occupy that residence). These registries apply to any sex offense convictions in any state, and are retroactive—as O'Keefe (2010) notes, even if you pleaded guilty (or "no contest") and served your entire sentence prior to the enactment of the Walsh Act, you will need to register as a sex offender.

Another troubling aspect of collateral consequences is that they need not be tied to a conviction. Many jurisdictions impose the restrictions simply upon arrest or suspicion of criminal activity (Ewald, 2012). Arrests can lead to the loss of parental rights or to an unpaid suspension from work, for example (Uggen & Stewart, 2014). New York City's implementation of its Narcotics Eviction Program (NEP) not only encourages landlords to evict individuals suspected of having ties to narcotics but assists them in the process and may impose fines on those landlords if they impede the eviction in any way (Levy, 2008). All that is required to instigate the NEP process is a search warrant; if the probable cause exists for a warrant, individuals can face eviction. And the restrictions reach beyond the offender. Consider the individuals represented in the Supreme Court case, *HUD v. Rucker* (2002). Here, in a unanimous decision, the Supreme Court upheld the eviction of four senior citizens from public housing because their grandchildren had been caught smoking pot in the parking lot or nearby neighborhoods or with drug paraphernalia in their possession (Levy, 2008).

Informal Collateral Consequences

Some researchers and scholars point out that the informal collateral consequences can be just as devastating as the formal consequences that I have discussed up to this point, including such things as the social stigma of a criminal record (Love, Roberts, & Klingele, 2016). For example, even if collateral consequences related to employment bans or licensures did not exist, an ex-felon may still have a difficult time landing a job. Background checks have become increasingly easy and commonplace for employers, volunteer organizations, and schools to perform. Organizations may have a fear of dealing with a potentially "risky" population or they may simply want to avoid the negative publicity associated with hiring convicted criminals.

One often-cited empirical study (Pager, 2003) trained two pairs of young men in the Milwaukee area (one African American, one white), and after controlling for factors affecting physical appearance and presentation, had them apply for various low-skill positions with "help wanted" postings. Half of the time the actors posed as someone with a criminal history on their record (i.e., his work history included a job in a correctional facility and he used a parole officer as a reference), and half of the time they did not (i.e., his work history had a similar low-skill job to that from the correctional facility). Pager looked at callback rates and found that, beyond strong race effects, those individuals with a criminal history were significantly less likely to receive a callback. For the white actors, the rate of callback dropped from 34% to 17%; for the black actors, the rate dropped from 14% to 5%. Note that the white applicant with a record receiving a more favorable response than the minority applicant without a record was replicated in a New York City study comparing callback rates for both black and Latino applicants to those of their white counterparts (Pager, Western, & Bonikowski, 2009). A similar study conducted in Minnesota (Uggen, Vuolo, Lageson, Ruhland, & Whitman, 2014) found that callback rates for white applicants and black applicants were reduced by 10% and 15%, respectively, when the applicant had just a minor arrest (no conviction) on their record. This stigma, combined with the impositions imposed by bans on employment licensures and work with specific populations, equates to an estimated 30–40% annual earning deficit for offenders released from incarceration (Western, 2006).

Public Support of Civil Restrictions

When it comes to employment, there may be real, logical restrictions imposed for specific jobs directly related to an individual's past conviction (e.g., hiring a former burglar to be a locksmith; Petersen, 2015). Employers may also be concerned with the possibility that an ex-offender will be a less stable employee (i.e., more likely to quit), show lower moral character, or put the company at risk for negligence suits—but none of these factors are supported in the research (Petersen, 2015). This begs the question: What sort of collateral consequences does the public support?

Looking specifically at disenfranchisement, Pinaire, Heumann, and Bilotta (2003) conducted a public survey to assess attitudes toward felons and ex-felons. While the vast majority of individuals surveyed felt that permanent disenfranchisement was not appropriate (over 80%), most individuals did believe that losing the right to vote while incarcerated, while on parole/probation, or both was appropriate. Interestingly, the researchers found a divided sample on the question of whether felons have too many (45.1%) or enough/too few (45.7%) rights. What we do not know from this study is whether or not the public is actually educated on what rights felons do or do not have. For example, some research on sentencing shows that individuals commonly believe that defendants "get off" or are given too light a sentence, but when given the opportunity to choose what they feel is a just sentence for a crime, individuals often choose a sentence that is actually below the mandatory minimums or common sentences employed (Roberts & Doob, 1989; Stalans & Diamond, 1990). It seems that the stereotypes the public may employ are those extreme circumstances that tend to receive press coverage specifically *because* they are abnormally lenient. The same may be true when it comes to perceptions of the rights afforded to ex-felons: The public may focus on publicized cases of ex-felons recidivating and feel that the individual must have been afforded too much freedom or that more restrictions would have kept the individual in line.

In an attempt to delve deeper into the public's reasoning, Heumann, Pinaire, and Clark (2005) conducted focus groups with the public, discussing the rights afforded to ex-felons. Perhaps not surprisingly, the public showed very little awareness of disenfranchisement or other collateral consequences imposed on individuals convicted of a crime. They also voiced surprise that these consequences were not tied to specific crimes but distributed virtually identically across all felony convictions. There was a sense that "some felons" deserved these additional sanctions (e.g., those charged with violent offenses), but support for blanket policies was uncommon.

My own research has shown a similar trend. In one study (Edkins & Dervan, 2018), both college students and participants recruited from an online survey site (MTurk—an online recruitment tool) showed some support for the imposition of collateral consequences. Participants were given examples of real collateral consequences, grouped into three categories (employment-related, government benefits, and individual rights), and rated the consequences on a 6-point Likert scale, from "This should not be banned at all" to "Should be a lifetime ban." Individuals were most comfortable with imposing restrictions on employment (e.g., ineligible to serve as a police officer or firefighter) and somewhat less so with restrictions on benefits (e.g., ineligible to receive food stamps or reside in public housing) or individual rights (e.g., ineligible to vote or adopt a child). The mean scores for the employment restrictions fell between support for a 2- to 4-year ban and a 5- to 9-year ban. The other two categories had means reflecting support for bans lasting between 1 year and 2 to 4 years. It seems that there is support that ex-felons should not be reintroduced as full citizens immediately upon release, but that they should, eventually, regain the same rights.

Plea Bargaining's Contribution

In the Supreme Court's landmark decision upholding the use of plea bargaining (*Brady v. United States*, 1970), the court also recognized the importance of the assistance of counsel during the plea bargaining process. The requirement that pleas be made knowingly and voluntarily was interpreted to mean that the defendant must be informed of the *direct* consequences of pleading guilty. Defense attorneys have consistently been held to a standard dictating that they make direct consequences known to their client, and the plea colloquy (where the defendant enters his or her plea before a judge) must outline the sanctions that will be imposed (Lang, 2012). What is missing from this discussion—and what lower courts have deemed outside the responsibility of defense counsel or any other party to the process (e.g., prosecutor, judge, etc.)—is informing the defendant of collateral consequences.

Communication of Collateral Consequences

Prior to the Supreme Court's decision in *Padilla v. Kentucky* (2010; see Chapter 1 and Chapter 3 for more details on the *Padilla* case), collateral consequences of convictions did not have to be communicated to defendants. This "collateral consequences rule" (Roberts, 2009, p. 124; Lang, 2012, p. 955) was practiced by lower courts since the *Brady* (1970) decision and is the reason collateral consequences have been referred to as the "secret sentence" (Chin & Holmes, 2002, p. 700). As one assessment reports, court rulings prior to *Padilla* in 11 federal circuits, 30 states, and the District of Columbia absolved defense attorneys of the requirement to communicate collateral consequences associated with a plea bargain (Chin & Holmes, 2002). The "rule," as practiced, kept defendants in the dark as to the collateral consequences attached to their convictions, and kept defense attorneys from being censured for failing to inform the defendants of the consequences. In *Padilla* (2010), the Supreme Court recognized that Jose Padilla's lawyers' advice to accept a plea, without proper understanding of the implications the plea would have on Jose's status as a permanent legal resident (i.e., automatic deportation), did not satisfy the *Strickland* (1984) standards for effective assistance of counsel and was therefore in violation of the Sixth Amendment (see Chapter 3 for a more in-depth discussion of the *Strickland* standard). Here the court decided that the specific collateral consequence of deportation was severe enough to warrant its necessary communication to the client.

Still, the recognition of the import of collateral consequences in *Padilla* (2010) does not mean that the collateral consequences rule is dead. Lang (2012) published a review of how lower courts are reacting to the *Padilla* decision (i.e., whether they are holding that *Padilla* covers deportation consequences only or whether they are extending the decision to other collateral consequences). At the time of the review, 24 cases had addressed whether or not *Padilla* extends to other collateral consequences: 9 held that it could be extended (e.g., notifications regarding sex offender registration, loss of pension, parole eligibility, etc.), and the other 15 cases held that it does not (e.g., enhanced penalties, sex offender registration, parole eligibility, etc.). The disagreement suggests the Supreme Court will likely need to clarify *Padilla's* reach. And, in fact, since the *Padilla* decision, a survey of prosecutors in the five states with the largest number of incarcerated non-citizens showed that the majority of the prosecutor offices did not have a written policy regarding the communication of immigration consequences to defendants entering into a guilty plea (Eagly, 2013).

A recent survey of state statutes and court rules shows that 24 states make no mention of required collateral consequences that need to be communicated to defendants upon entry of a guilty plea (Zottoli et al., 2018). The remaining jurisdictions that mention collateral consequences during plea entry focus on sex offender registries, immigration and deportation consequences, and possible future sentence enhancements (e.g., for three-strikes laws or "career criminal" considerations)—a handful of jurisdictions also require that defendants be informed that the guilty plea could make them ineligible to own a firearm (often restricted to domestic violence convictions). Indeed, recognition of the growing number of (and concern over) collateral consequences has led to multiple congressional hearings (Ewald, 2012) and to the creation of the American Bar Association's National Inventory of Collateral Consequences of Conviction database (https://niccc.csgjusticecenter.org/map/), funded by the National Institute of Justice. Here, literally tens of thousands of possible collateral consequences have been catalogued, representing each state, the District of Columbia, and the federal government. In effect, this could make the communication of *possible* collateral consequences to the defendant much easier, but unless the consequence is written into the statute as mandatory and automatic, each jurisdiction is going to differ on whether or not the particular consequence is imposed, and if an individual relocates, new or different collateral consequences will become relevant (Jain, 2016). The question still remains of who should communicate these consequences to the defendant.

While the Supreme Court has extended ineffective assistance of counsel claims to envelop the plea bargaining process (*Lafler v. Cooper,* 2012; *Missouri v. Frye,* 2012) and has noted that collateral consequences such as deportation upon conviction should be informed to the defendant and could actually serve a purpose in the plea negotiation process (*Padilla v. Kentucky,* 2010; *Vartelas v. Holder,* 2012), other lower court rulings have stated that Sixth Amendment ineffective assistance claims cannot occur if the defense attorney does not *explicitly ask* the defendant about his or her immigration status (Lang, 2012). This is consistent with previous ineffective assistance rulings that state a defense attorney can only be held in the wrong if he or she gives misinformation or misrepresents a point of law (Roberts, 2009), leading to the conclusion that completely avoiding the topic of collateral consequences may be a better choice than inadvertently omitting or misrepresenting the imposition of a particular consequence. Silence is also in the best interest of the prosecutor (Roberts, 2009). If, during the plea bargaining process, the prosecutor is unsure as to whether a defendant has been informed by his or her counsel about potential collateral consequences attached to the plea deal, the prosecutor may choose to remain quiet, knowing that courts have not held collateral consequence information as part of the prosecutor's duty and believing that communicating information about the consequences may lead to the defendant changing his or her mind and deciding to proceed to trial.

Many courts are also deciding that as long as information is contained in the plea colloquy, ineffective assistance claims cannot be made (Lang, 2012). Judge Frederic Block, the justice discussed at the beginning of the chapter, concluded that both the defense attorney and the prosecutor have a duty to consider the consequences and bring them to attention of the defendant and to the court (*U.S. v. Nesbeth*, 2016). In addition, Block opined that the Probation Department should also include collateral consequences in all presentence reports, and noted that the National Inventory of Collateral Consequences of Conviction has made this task achievable.

One extensive survey conducted with various legal-system players in the state of Ohio sought to address the question of who should inform defendants of collateral consequences (Frank, Travis, Reitler, Goulette, & Flesher, 2009). The authors surveyed over 900 individuals: judges (*N* = 153), prosecutors (*N* = 200), defense attorneys (*N* = 332), and probation and parole officers (*N* = 205), asking about their perceptions and opinions regarding the hundreds of possible collateral consequences a conviction in Ohio could initiate. The majority of individuals believed that defendants should be informed of these consequences and, overwhelmingly, the judge was mentioned as the party that should communicate the sanctions to the defendant. The defense attorney was a close second, but the plea hearing/plea colloquy seemed to be the common response for when and where collateral consequence information should be imparted.

It is possible that a more authoritative figure, such as a judge, informing the defendant of the collateral consequences of conviction might increase the importance and influence of these considerations in the defendant's decision-making process. But, there is a very real possibility that this information may have *less* of an effect coming from a judge if the information is not provided until the plea colloquy stage (i.e., the point in the case where the judge decides the factual basis for the charges and the defendant allocutes to the charges). Once defendants have personally committed to pleading guilty—a difficult choice to make—psychological research would suggest they would begin to engage in *dissonance reduction* (Festinger, 1957), downplaying the attractiveness of the alternative (proceeding to trial). Any new information after this point, such as a judge discussing the collateral consequences of the plea deal at the plea colloquy, will likely be downplayed, or possibly even ignored, by the defendant, rather than fully weighed in the decision (Lang, 2012).

Also, the belief that the judge should be responsible for the conveying the information certainly does not reflect how the system currently operates. A survey of 282 state trial court judges across the United States indicates that upward of 40% state that they rarely or never discuss collateral consequences with defendants during sentencing or plea hearings (Ewald & Smith, 2008). When judges were asked whether or not it was their responsibility to inform defendants, about 36% agreed that it was; the other 64% felt the onus was not on them. While roughly 90% of judges agreed that defendants need to know about the consequences, almost all (97%) felt that the informing was the defense attorney's responsibility.

Bargaining with Collateral Consequences

A very real concern in the plea bargaining literature is the enormous amount of prosecutorial discretion that plea bargaining allows (e.g., Bibas, 2004). As discussed in Chapter 4 of this volume, prosecutors may introduce personal biases or motivations, and the unfettered discretion means that the plea negotiations never see the light of day; there is no record of the process or the back-and-forth that goes into the discussions. There is the very real possibility that introducing collateral consequences into the equation only *increases* this discretion, while still keeping the process secret (Jain, 2016).

Similar to charge bargaining or sentence bargaining, utilizing collateral consequences in plea negotiations can increase the likelihood of a defendant accepting a plea (Jain, 2016). For example, prosecutors can offer to invoke charges with less serious collateral consequences (e.g., avoiding a sex offender registry) in return for a guilty plea. Additionally, prosecutors can approach these consequences as a way to apply retribution without having to exact the expenses necessary to investigate the possibility of additional criminal charges or more severe charges. In this manner, employing charges with collateral consequences attached ensures a stiffer punishment is administered without the prosecutor's office expending any additional resources. Increasing discretion—as we have seen in previous sections of this volume—can lead to increased opportunities for individual biases to creep into the decision-making process. We know that prosecutors are significantly more likely to pursue charges with mandatory minimums attached for minority defendants than they are with white defendants (Starr & Rehavi, 2013). If this is the case, perhaps prosecutors are also more likely to file charges that result in harsh collateral sanctions for minorities. Research would need to investigate this possibility.

Some states are opting to avoid issues that may arise with prosecutorial discretion related to collateral consequences by requiring prosecutors to address any heavy-handed consequences directly and consider them as part of the sanction the guilty plea would impose (Eagly, 2017). This is because immigration consequences, such as deportation, can be more serious of a concern for a defendant than a prison sentence. California now requires that prosecutors pursue charges against non-citizens in such a way as to avoid consequences like deportation, insofar as the crime will allow (A.B. 1343, 2015). Defense attorneys in the state are also required to ensure that the topic of immigration consequences is broached with prosecutors during plea negotiations.

Effect of Communicating Consequences

Regardless of whose responsibility it is to convey information about collateral consequences, an important question to ask is whether this information makes a difference to defendants when deciding to take a plea or go to trial. One school of thought is that knowledge of the collateral consequences would make defendants less likely to enter into a plea deal. Based on his own anecdotal experience, one prosecutor noted that automatic collateral consequences attached to convictions make defendants much less likely to cooperate and more likely to take their cases to trial (Johnson, 2001).

The judges surveyed in the Ewald and Smith (2008) paper were divided on the possible effect of communicating these consequences. Some echoed Johnson's (2001) concerns that knowledge would impede bargaining, but many felt that collateral consequences information would not have any effect on the plea decision. Since rates of recidivism are already very high, individuals entering into the criminal justice system may have already had these civil sanctions imposed on them, and another criminal (felony) conviction would not change their current lack of access to employment or benefits (Ewald & Smith, 2008). Frank et al.'s (2009) survey of criminal justice actors reported that the majority of individuals did not believe the information would lead to an increase in trials. A study looking at pretrial detention and its effects on plea bargains quoted one attorney as stating, "They plead guilty to get out; that happens a lot. The thought of collateral consequences is the furthest thing from their minds—they just want to get out" (Sacks & Ackerman, 2012, p. 273). Is this true, or will the communication of consequences change a defendant's attitude toward accepting a plea deal?

As discussed in previous chapters, the decision-making inherent in the plea bargain process is complex and multifaceted, but little research has directly investigated the impact of collateral consequences on plea bargaining. Focusing on a defendant's evaluation of a plea offer, what we have is a defendant weighing a certain, negative outcome (accepting a plea of guilty and its accompanying sanction) against an uncertain outcome that could be positive (acquittal at trial) or significantly more negative (a more punitive sanction if found guilty at trial). Decision-making under risk and uncertainty, and in particular Khaneman and Tversky's (1983) prospect theory, can offer some predictions. Prospect theory is especially relevant because it allows consideration of the defendant's starting point on the subsequent decision. The starting point can affect how the "deal" outlined in the plea bargain is seen—importantly, as a gain or a loss. If an individual is currently in pretrial detention, many times the acceptance of a plea deal can mean freedom. Compared to an individual awaiting trial on the outside, the "loss" of a conviction for those detained pretrial could actually be a gain relative to their current standing, not to mention the fact that the collateral consequences are *future* consequences; release from pretrial detention is immediate.

The idea behind *temporal discounting* (Ainslie, 1975) is that we tend to put less weight on a future outcome, simply because it is in the future. Immediate consequences weigh heavier and have a larger impact on our decisions. Pleading guilty moves an individual out of the "limbo" stage of awaiting for trial, and allows the person to begin serving their sentence/probation (as well as to possibly be released from pretrial detention) and to move on with their lives. Many of the collateral consequences will not be implemented for months or even possibly years. Defendants may have a difficult time truly weighing the impact of these consequences on their lives.

In a recent study, a colleague and I investigated the impact of informing individuals of collateral consequences on their decisions to accept a plea deal for a fictitious crime (Edkins & Dervan, 2018). In an initial exploratory vignette study using college students for our sample, we found that in situations where pretrial detention was part of the equation (and the plea deal allowed for release plus probation), plea deals were overwhelmingly accepted, regardless of the collateral consequences imposed. Students were asked to place themselves in the shoes of individuals who were charged with a crime and to decide whether or not to accept a plea bargain. In the conditions depicting collateral consequences combined with pretrial detention, one vignette described a student held in pretrial detention who, upon a criminal conviction, would no longer be able to get student loans for school; another depicted an unemployed individual held in pretrial detention who resided in public housing and relied on food stamps—both of which the person would have to forfeit upon a criminal conviction. In both situations, participants preferred to plead guilty (even if they had been told they were innocent of the charge). Overall, 50.3% pleaded guilty in the student scenario and 67.1% pleaded guilty in the unemployed scenario; when they saw the collateral consequences attached to the conviction, the rates of pleading guilty were 53% and 65.5%, respectively. The only condition that showed a trend toward a consideration of the collateral consequences was the vignette depicting a nurse who was *not* in pretrial detention and who would lose her nursing license upon conviction. Here, presentation of collateral consequences reduced guilty plea rates from 51.5% to 39.1% (the difference approached significance).

A follow-up study on U.S. adults (using MTurk) employed a single vignette and manipulated defendant guilt, pretrial detention, and the presentation of collateral consequences (Edkins & Dervan, 2018). Participants considered the scenario presented and again indicated whether they would choose to plead guilty (i.e., accept the "deal" offered by the prosecutor) or take their case to trial. We found similar effects to those in the first study: Knowledge of the collateral consequences did not affect decisions to plead. Playing the role of an individual guilty of the accused offense was the main predictor—as would be expected—but an interesting finding was that pretrial detention actually affected "innocent" participants more so than "guilty" ones. When detained and offered freedom for a plea, the plea rates for innocent individuals were significantly higher than when the same individuals were awaiting trial on the outside. The weight of the immediate overshadowed all else—not just collateral consequences, but even actual guilt.

When we examined the factors that predicted guilty pleas, guilt was the strongest predictor, but the second most important factor was a desire to put the matter behind them—to get the process over with (Edkins & Dervan, 2018). Again, the immediate outweighs the distant future, supporting the theory of temporal discounting. When we educated all participants about the collateral consequences at the end of the study and asked if they felt knowledge prior to the plea would have affected their decisions, over 80% said that it would not have.

These findings are concerning, because they suggest that these very real, very important restrictions cannot be fully appreciated during the plea bargaining process. And some of the suggestions by legal-system players to make information about collateral consequences the task of the judge (Frank et al., 2009), presumably during the sentencing hearing, would not help these considerations. By this point, defendants' decisions have been made and it is not clear that the defendant would feel as though he or she *could* change their mind during this hearing (Lang, 2012). The long history of social science research suggests that once people have committed to a decision, future information to change that decision is often discounted or downplayed (Festinger, 1957).

Moving Collateral Consequences Research Forward

No one denies the potential life-altering nature of the non-penal sanctions imposed on acceptance of a guilty plea or a conviction at trial. What social scientists should be concerned with is how we can adequately convey the information in a manner that *will* be taken into consideration when deciding on a plea. How we can alter the system to make consideration of these consequences easier on the part of the defendant and more prominent on the part of the attorneys doing the bargaining?

A former felon, turned criminologist, discussed his experiences with collateral consequences:

> When I pled guilty to crimes in the 1990s, I did so understanding that there would be punishment. I pled guilty understanding that I would have to serve several years in prison and would likely be on parole afterward. I did not, however, plead guilty expecting to serve a life sentence, with opportunities denied for events that occurred when I was in my teens and early 20s. And this leaves me with a very simple, yet very disturbing question: Will my punishment ever be over? (Oliver, 2010, p. 450)

Oliver's question epitomizes the situation: Individuals serve their time, yet their punishment is not over. The fact that the justice system has become a system of pleas necessarily means that the system has also become overrun with people fighting their way through imposed employment restrictions, limits to government benefits, and restrictions on civil rights. So how can social science help address the problem?

First, we need more studies discussing the actual and real impact of these consequences on stigma and limits to earnings showing direct links from the collateral consequences to the negative effects. Experimental research in this area can contribute to the current research looking at felons and employment and the impact on recidivism. We know that employed ex-felons are significantly less likely to recidivate than their unemployed counterparts (Visher, Debus, & Yahner, 2008), and we know that criminal records hamper employment (Pager et al., 2009). Empirical research can help pinpoint the specific attitudes or reasons that may make employers hesitant to hire an ex-felon and provide a starting point for introducing various "treatments" to see what factors could increase employers' willingness to take a chance on an individual with a record.

Second, requiring prosecutors and defense attorneys to acknowledge the impact of collateral consequences when considering plea bargains can bring these sanctions out of the shadows and into the light, treating them as the serious punishments that they are. Related to the first point, social scientists can evaluate public opinion around including collateral consequences in the punishment of offenses. Quite likely, individuals will see these as powerful sanctions, and with this fuel, prosecutors can feel free to consider them as part of the defendant's "sentence." The policies mentioned in California with noncitizen defendants are an excellent start. Researchers can determine whether or not there is public support for such policies, and how just sanctions with collateral consequences considered are seen compared to those that simply focus on sentences.

Third, if we are to influence the defendant's decision-making process, one way to make future consequences weightier (or at least to have them considered with the true weight they possess, compared to the immediate consequences) would be to make those consequences occur immediately or to make them much more salient. Experimental research can look at the effects of increasing the focus on the collateral consequences, highlighting them in such a way as to make the impact very clear for each individual and his or her particular circumstance, as well as manipulating when the consequences go into effect and explaining the exact implications and how life will change when they do go into effect. We may never be able to make these future consequences as weighty as something like immediate release from pretrial detention, but we can determine ways for the defendant to acknowledge their true weight in the consideration of accepting a plea bargain.

Conclusion

In 2011, then Attorney General Eric Holder wrote a letter to all state attorneys general asking them to survey their collateral consequences in order to remove those that may be too burdensome without actually providing additional public safety. While changes at the state and federal levels have been slow, this is something that needs to stay on the radar. The United States imprisons its citizens at a rate higher than any other country in the world (Gottschalk, 2006), with more than 100 million people possessing an arrest or criminal record (U.S. Department of Justice, 2009). It may be easy for us to think in terms of "us" versus "them" when discussing people with criminal convictions, but with more than 600,000 individuals—almost all of whom pleaded guilty—being released from custody or supervision *every year* (Heumann et al., 2005), there really is no "them"—it is all "us."

References

A.B. 1343, Cal. Reg. Sess. (2015) (enacted).

Adam Walsh Child Protection and Safety Act (2006), H.R. 4472, 109th Congress.

Ainslie, G. (1975). Specious reward: A behavioral theory of impulsiveness and impulse control. *Psychological Bulletin, 82*, 463–496. doi: 10.1037/h0076860

Bibas, S. (2004). Plea bargaining outside the shadow of trial. *Harvard Law Review, 117*, 2463–2547. doi: 10.2307/4093404

Brady v. United States, 397 U.S. 742 (1970).

Burmilla, E. M. (2017). Voter turnout, felon disenfranchisement and partisan outcomes in presidential elections, 1988–2012. *Social Justice Research, 30*, 72–88. doi: 10.1007/s11211-017-0277-2

Chin, G. J. (2002). Race, the War on Drugs, and the collateral consequences of criminal conviction. *Journal of Gender, Race & Justice, 6*, 253–275. doi: 10.2139/ssrn.390109

Chin, G. J. (2012). The new civil death: Rethinking punishment in the era of mass conviction. *University of Pennsylvania Law Review, 160*, 1789–1833.

Chin, G. J., & Holmes, R. W. (2002). Effective assistance of counsel and the consequences of guilty pleas. *Cornell Law Review, 87*, 697–742.

Eagly, I. V. (2013). Criminal justice for noncitizens: An analysis of variation in local enforcement. *New York University Law Review, 88*, 1126–1223.

Eagly, I. V. (2017). Criminal justice in an era of mass deportation: Reforms from California. *New Criminal Law Review, 20*, 12–38.

Edkins, V. A., & Dervan, L. E. (2018). Freedom now or a future later: Pitting the lasting implications of collateral consequences against pretrial detention in decisions to plead guilty. *Psychology, Public Policy, and the Law, 24*, 204–215.

Ewald, A. C. (2012). Collateral consequences in the American states. *Social Science Quarterly, 93*, 211–247. doi: 10.1111/j.1540-6237.2011.00831.x

Ewald, A. C., & Smith, M. (2008). Collateral consequences of criminal convictions in American courts: The view from the state bench. *Justice System Journal, 29*, 145–165.

Fellner, J., & Mauer, M. (1998). *Losing the vote: The impact of felony disenfranchisement laws in the United States*. Washington, DC: The Sentencing Project. Available at http://sentencingproject.org.

Festinger, L. (1957). *A theory of cognitive dissonance*. Redwood, CA: Stanford University Press.

Frank, J., Travis, L. F., Reitler, A., Goulette, N., & Flesher, W. (2009). *Collateral consequences of criminal conviction in Ohio. Research Report to the Ohio Office of Criminal Justice Services*. Retrieved from https://www.uc.edu/content/dam/uc/ccjr/docs/reports/Collateral%20Consequences%20Final%20Report.pdf

Gottschalk, M. (2006). *The prison and the gallows: The politics of mass incarceration in America*. New York: Cambridge University Press.
Heumann, M., Pinaire, B. K., & Clark, T. (2005). Beyond the sentence: Public perceptions of collateral consequences for felony offenders. *Criminal Law Bulletin*, *41*, 24–46.
Holder, E. H. (April 18, 2011). *Letter to state attorneys general* Retrieved from http://www.national reentryresourcecenter.org/documents/0000/1088/Reentry_Council_AG_Letter.pdf
HUD v. Rucker, 535 U.S. 125, 130 (2002).
Jacob Wetterling Crimes Against Children Registration Act (1994), H.R. 324, 103rd Congress.
Jain, E. (2016). Prosecuting collateral consequences. *Georgetown Law Journal*, *104*, 1197–1244.
Johnson, R. M. A. (2001). Collateral consequences. *Criminal Justice*, *16*, 32–33.
Kahneman, D., & Tversky, A. (1983). Choices, values, and frames. *American Psychologist*, *39*, 341–350. doi: 10.1037/0003-066X.39.4.341
Lafler v. Cooper, 132 S. Ct. 1376 (2012).
Laird, L. (June, 2013). Ex-offenders face tens of thousands of legal restrictions, bias and limits on their rights. *ABA Journal*. Retrieved from http://www.abajournal.com/magazine/article/ex-offenders_face_tens_of_thousands_of_legal_restrictions
Lang, D. M. (2012). *Padilla v. Kentucky*: The effect of plea colloquy warning on defendants' ability to bring successful *Padilla* claims. *Yale Law Journal*, *121*, 944–997.
Levy, S. D. (2008). The collateral consequences of seeking order through disorder: New York's Narcotics Eviction Program. *Harvard Civil Rights-Civil Liberties Law Review*, *43*, 539–580.
Love, M. C., Roberts, J., & Klingele, C. (2016). *Collateral consequences of conviction: Law, policy, and practice*. 2016 edition. Washington, DC: NACDL Press.
Manza, J., & Uggen, C. (2006). *Locked out: Felon disenfranchisement and American democracy*. New York: Oxford University Press.
Mauer, M. (1999). *Race to incarcerate*. New York: The New Press.
Missouri v. Frye, 132 S. Ct. 1399 (2012).
Mungan, M. C. (2017). Over-incarceration and disenfranchisement. *Public Choice*, *172*(3-4), 377–395. doi: 10.1007/s11127-017-0448-6
Neyfakh, L. (2016, May). In a remarkable decision, federal judge lays out all the ways our justice system hurts ex-cons. *Slate Magazine*. Retrieved from http://www.slate.com/blogs/the_slatest/2016/05/25/frederic_block_federal_judge_speaks_out_against_collateral_consequences.html
O'Keefe, K. (2010). Two wrongs make a wrong: A challenge to plea bargaining and collateral consequence statutes through their integration. *Journal of Criminal Law and Criminology*, *100*, 243–276.
Oliver, B. E. (2010). My sentence is over but will my punishment ever end? *Dialectical Anthropology*, *34*, 447–451. doi: 10.1007/s10624-010-9165-y
Padilla v. Kentucky, 559 U.S. 356 (2010).
Pager, D. (2003). The mark of a criminal record. *American Journal of Sociology*, *108*, 937–975. doi: 10.1086/374403

Pager, D., Western, B., & Bonikowski, B. (2009). Discrimination in a low-wage labor market: A field experiment. *American Sociological Review, 74*, 777–799. doi: 10.1177/000312240907400505
Peterson, I. B. (2015). Toward true fair-choice hiring: Balancing stakeholder interests and reality in regulating criminal background checks. *Texas Law Review, 94*, 175–203.
Pinaire, B., Heumann, M., & Bilotta, L. (2003). Barred from the vote: Public attitudes toward the disenfranchisement of felons. *Fordham Urban Law Journal, 30*, 1519–1550.
Richardson v. Ramirez, 418 U.S. 24 (1974).
Roberts, J. (2009). Ignorance is effectively bliss: Collateral consequences, silence, and misinformation in the guilty-plea process. *Iowa Law Review, 95*, 119–194.
Roberts, J. V., & Doob, A. N. (1989). Sentencing and public opinion: Taking false shadows for true substances. *Osgood Hall Law Journal, 27*, 491–515.
Sacks, M., & Ackerman, A. R. (2012). Pretrial detention and guilty pleas: If they cannot afford bail they must be guilty. *Criminal Justice Studies, 25*, 265–278. http://dx.doi.org/10.1080/1478601X.2012.705536
Stalans, L. J., & Diamond, S. S. (1990). Formation and change in lay evaluations of criminal sentencing. *Law and Human Behavior, 14*, 199–214. http://dx.doi.org/10.1007/BF01352749
Starr, S. B., & Rehavi, M. M. (2013). Mandatory sentencing and racial disparity: Assessing the role of prosecutors and the effects of Booker. *Yale Law Journal, 123*, 2–38.
Strickland v. Washington, 466 U.S. 668 (1984).
Travis, J. (2002). Invisible punishment: An instrument of social exclusion. In M. Mauer & M. Chesney-Lind (Eds.), *Invisible punishment: The collateral consequences of mass imprisonment*. New York: The New Press.
Uggen, C., Larson, R., & Shannon, S. (2016). *6 million lost voters: State-level estimates of felony disenfranchisement*. Washington, DC: The Sentencing Project. Retrieved from http://www.sentencingproject.org/publications/6-million-lost-voters-state-level-estimates-felony-disenfranchisement-2016/
Uggen, C., & Manza, J. (2002). Democratic contraction? Political consequences of felon disenfranchisement in the United States. *American Sociological Review, 67*, 777–803. doi: 10.2307/3088970
Uggen, C., & Stewart, R. (2014). Piling on: Collateral consequences and community supervision. *Minnesota Law Review, 99*, 1871–1910.
Uggen, C., Vuolo, M., Lageson, S., Ruhland, E., & Whitman, H. K. (2014). The edge of stigma: An experimental audit of the effects of low-level criminal records on employment. *Criminology, 52*, 627–654. doi: 10.1111/1745-9125.12051
U.S. Department of Justice Executive Office for United States Attorneys. (2013). *United States attorneys' annual statistic report: Fiscal report 2013*. Retrieved from https://www.justice.gov/sites/default/files/usao/legacy/2014/09/22/13statrpt.pdf
U.S. Department of Justice. (2009). *Survey of state criminal history information systems, 2008*. Washington, DC: Bureau of Justice Statistics, U.S. Department of Justice. Retrieved from https://www.ncjrs.gov/pdffiles1/bjs/grants/228661.pdf
U.S. v. Nesbeth, 43 F. Supp. 239 (E.D. NY 2016).
Vartelas v. Holder 132 S. Ct. 1479 (2012).

Visher, C. A., Debus, S., & Yahner, J. (2008). *Employment after prison: A longitudinal study of releases in three states (Justice Policy Center Research Report)*. Washington, DC: The Urban Institute.

Western, B. (2006). *Punishment and inequality in America*. New York: Russell Sage Foundation.

Wetterling Act § 170101 (f) (1) (2006).

Whittle, T. N., & Parker, K. F. (2014). Public ideology, minority threat, and felony collateral sanctions: A state-level analysis. *Criminal Justice Review*, *39*, 432–454. doi: 10.1177/0734016814543352

Zottoli, T. M., Dartary-Kapur, T., Edkins, V. A., Redlich, A., King, C., Dervan, L. E., & Tahan, E. (2018). State of the states: A survey of procedural and administrative rules governing the guilty plea process in the United States. Manuscript under review.

Conclusion

Moving Forward in a System of Pleas

Allison D. Redlich and Vanessa A. Edkins

This volume has gathered together research from multiple disciplines, integrated into one overall picture of the current state of our justice system. The system of pleas that defendants inhabit means that while plea bargaining is thoroughly entrenched in our present-day notion of justice, the law has not caught up. Only in the last 5 to 7 years have the courts started to rule that constitutional protections traditionally tied to trials also pertain to plea bargains and offers. We have the research to contribute to the current movement in policy initiatives. Increasing awareness of cognitive biases and of faulty decision-making tendencies, for example, is part of this, as is increasing the understanding of how race, age, mental status, and innocence play a role in decisions. But we also need to address the sentencing disparities created through these pleas, the issue of pretrial detention and its undue influence on plea decisions, and how we can reduce limitations imposed on individuals convicted of crimes and the increasing disenfranchisement created through this system of pleas. Social science has much to offer at this new frontier of the system of pleas.

In this concluding chapter of the book, our goal is twofold. First we highlight two major themes that cut across the chapters. Although there were many possible themes to choose among, we focus here on innocence and plea decision-making. Our second goal is to summarize chapter authors' suggestions for future research—that is, to delineate what the next generation of plea-related scholarship may look like, so that scholars and legal decision-makers alike may continue to move forward.

Themes in a System of Pleas

This volume includes three main sections in which authors review (1) the system of pleas and its players (defendants, defense attorneys, and prosecutors),

(2) influences on plea decision-making (defendant race, juvenile defendants, and innocence), and (3) results of the system of pleas (sentencing disparities, mass incarceration, and collateral consequences). Moreover, the chapters were written by authors from varying disciplinary perspectives, including psychology, sociology/criminology, public policy, economics, and legal scholarship. Despite the diversity of topics and disciplines, several prominent themes emerged. While we focus on only two (innocence and plea decision-making) here, others include individual differences (e.g., in risk seeking, race, age, levels of understanding) and disparities in outcomes.

Innocence with a Capital *I*

Nearly all of the chapters in this volume have touched on the concept of innocence. Presumably those who study and practice guilty pleas would agree that the overwhelming majority of entered guilty pleas are made by factually guilty defendants. That is, most of the 97% of the millions of misdemeanor and felony defendants who plead guilty every year are probably guilty. But that minority of defendants who are innocent—a minority whose size remains unknown and perhaps unknowable (is it 1% or 10% of pleas?)—has seemingly captured the fascination of scholars. As of February 2018 and as noted by Wilford and Khairalla in Chapter 7, there are only 399 known exonerations of persons wrongly convicted by false guilty pleas (National Registry of Exonerations, n.d.). When we consider the large numbers of defendants who have pleaded guilty since 1989 (the year the National Registry uses as their starting point), 399 is like a teaspoon of water in all five oceans combined.[1]

Of course, the entire chapter by Wilford and Khairalla was dedicated to the nexus of defendant innocence and guilty pleas. In Chapter 7, they reviewed the different types of false guilty pleas, the prevalence of such pleas, and the different methods (self-reported, lab-recorded, documented) used to examine them. They also discussed the rationales underlying false guilty pleas and the individual factors that tend to positively correlate with them, such as race (see also Chapter 5) and young age (see also Chapter 6). But beyond Wilford and Khairalla's chapter, other authors also wrangled with the construct of innocence. In the chapter introducing this volume, Dervan (Chapter 1) notes that the Supreme Court's view (*Brady v. United States*, 1970) that innocents do not plead guilty, at least not with great frequency, is outdated and ultimately allows for the system of pleas and related incentives that can, at times, encourage innocent people to plead guilty. Dervan also points out that some of today's Supreme Court justices have relied on this outdated precedent and have not kept pace

[1] Most scholars agree that this number of known false guilty pleas is a gross underestimate. There are systematic reasons (e.g., often waived right to appeal; leniency associated with pleas that results in no or little incarceration time) that confound the uncovering of false guilty pleas (see Redlich, 2010).

with the innocence scholarship. Bushway, in discussing defendant plea decision-making (Chapter 2), addressed how the predominant theory of plea decision-making, the shadow of trial, cannot always explain why innocent defendants plead guilty. That is, whereas some innocent defendants anticipate the probability of conviction at trial and act accordingly, lab-based experiments have found that innocent defendants often have other salient considerations (e.g., Tor, Gazal-Ayal, & Garcia, 2010). Henderson, in her chapter on defense attorneys and guilty pleas (Chapter 3), included an entire section on "advising the innocent client" wherein she discussed how innocents' risk-seeking preferences and unrealistic levels of optimism make a difficult situation even more difficult. In Chapter 4, McCannon did not write in depth about innocence but did mention prosecutors' motivation to avoid false positives, or innocent defendants being convicted by plea or by trial.

In Sections 2 and 3 of this volume, we continued to see innocence as a common theme. In Chapter 5, on race, Johnson and Richardson highlighted that the majority of exonerations identified to date are of minority defendants. In addition, of the 399 known false guilty pleas, 66% were made by minorities (National Registry of Exonerations, n.d.). Redlich, Zottoli, and Daftary-Kapur (Chapter 6) noted how youth are likely to be at heightened risk for false guilty pleas in both juvenile and criminal courts. And finally, in Chapter 9, Edkins discussed new research in which she and a colleague manipulated guilt/innocence and type of collateral consequences. Neither guilty nor innocent participants were affected by the longer-term collateral consequences of pleading guilty, but the innocent participants were particularly affected by the short-term gain of being released from detention. Adding to Hester's writing in Chapter 8 on sentencing disparities and mass incarceration, if 10% of defendants are innocent and only guilty defendants were incarcerated, then we could reduce jail and prison populations by 10%, a meaningful decrease.

In sum, the innocence of defendants deciding to plead guilty has been a pressing concern among social scientists and legal scholars. What is less clear is whether the law itself and those who practice the law are as concerned with the possibility of innocents entering into guilty pleas. Whereas convictions by trial are, in theory, intended to have separated out the guilty from the innocent, convictions by plea cannot say the same.

Plea Decision-Making

Decisions surrounding the guilty plea are a broad theme but one touched on in all of the chapters. Most notably, the shadow-of-the-trial model was discussed or at least mentioned in seven of the nine chapters. That this model emerged as common theme is somewhat tautological. The publication of Bibas' seminal 2004 *Harvard Law Review* article introduced the shadow model to many social scientists who now study pleas and has served as inspiration to empirically test the arguments Bibas put forth (e.g., Bushway, Redlich, & Norris, 2014).

Thus, in summarizing the extant literature, chapter authors had little choice but to address the shadow model (an argument that also applies to the innocence theme in the book).

In brief, the shadow model is a rational actor model that "establishes the maximum value of the potential plea or, alternatively, the minimally acceptable discount. This minimally acceptable discount is driven by the expected value of the trial outcome, which is the anticipated trial outcome discounted by the probability of being convicted at trial" (Bushway, Chapter 2, p. 24). In the majority of chapters that addressed the shadow model, attempts were made to demonstrate how the theory is less than comprehensive. For example, both Bushway (Chapter 2) and Wilford and Khairalla (Chapter 7) pointed out that the shadow theory does not account for innocent defendants, who have been shown to not act in accord with the model. Further, McCannon (Chapter 4) explained how the simplistic version of the shadow model makes several assumptions, including that the costs of pleading guilty are zero, that the preferences of the prosecutor and defendant are linear, and about the exact mechanisms of the bargaining itself. Johnson and Richardson (Chapter 5) astutely pointed out that "few discussions of the shadow model explicitly focus on racial disparities" (p. 88). Indeed, being a rational actor model, the shadow model does not account for defendant race, even though (unfortunately) race has been shown to influence trial outcomes (e.g., see Devine, Clayton, Dunford, Seying, & Pryce, 2001) and defenders' plea advisements to clients (Edkins, 2011). Finally, Henderson (Chapter 3) devoted an entire section in her chapter expanding the shadow model, recognizing its simplicity as McCannon did. Relevant to her topic—defense attorneys—Henderson argued that defenders are ill equipped to accurately estimate the value of a plea and the likelihood of an acquittal at trial because of informational deficits. Overall, as Bibas (2004) so cogently argued, the shadow-of-trial model falls short in explaining plea decision-making, as there are numerous practical, individual, and structural aspects that are not taken into account.

Beyond discussion of the shadow model, other chapters focused on different aspects of plea decision-making. For example, Johnson and Richardson (Chapter 5) touched on how defendant risk proclivities and perceptions of fairness in relation to defendant race influence the decision to plead guilty. Redlich, Zottoli, and Daftary-Kapur (Chapter 6) reviewed the literature on whether plea decisions by juvenile defendants are entered knowingly, intelligently, and voluntarily, in addition to examining the circumstances surrounding and the rationales underlying the decisions. And in line with the structure of this volume, Edkins (Chapter 9) discussed the consequences of plea decisions, focusing on disenfranchisement and other collateral outcomes. Edkins also addressed how defendants in deciding to plead guilty seem to care little about these longer-term consequences but rather focus on the short-term gains, such as getting out of jail.

Finally, whereas most of the chapters discussed decision-making by individual actors, such as defendants (Bushway), prosecutors (McCannon), and defense attorneys (Henderson), Hester (Chapter 8) took more of a systems approach. Hester does not deal with plea decision-making per se but does, in a sense, explain how the plea bargaining system itself promotes sentencing disparities, or the large discounts between the plea and trial-conviction sentences, that then serve as (almost irresistible) inducements to people in their plea decision-making. Hester also explains how these sentencing disparities, which often manifest as suspended sentences or probation, ultimately result in longer incarceration terms (i.e., through probation violations) and thus fuel the U.S. mass incarceration problem.

Overall, social scientists are often concerned with the how and why of decision-making. As such, a common theme in the chapters here and in the summarized literature on guilty pleas is the myriad aspects surrounding plea decisions. Whereas the shadow model is often described as the predominant theory of plea decision-making, this description is often followed by statements about the theory's limitations or about the dearth of empirical testing of the theory.

Moving Forward in a System of Pleas

In each of the chapters, we asked authors to opine on future directions. In this section, we synthesize authors' suggestions, noting common themes when appropriate. In many ways, delineating what next to explore in plea-related scholarship and how (i.e., methodologies) was one of the primary aims of the volume. Whereas the summarized literature that appears in each chapter on the topics addressed (e.g., defendants, defense attorneys, innocence) are important contributions toward integrating what has already been learned (sometimes only preliminarily), the suggested directions forward are arguably even more important contributions to consider. In short, it was our hope that this volume serves as a key resource for current and future scholars of guilty pleas.

As mentioned, Chapter 1, written by Dervan, provided the historical backdrop of the rise of guilty pleas in the United States. Within this context, Dervan reviewed the new—and recent—era of guilty plea jurisprudence by discussing U.S. Supreme Court cases since 2010. In 2017, the Supreme Court heard two important plea cases, *Lee v. U.S.*, and *Class v. U.S.* Both cases and the assumptions inherent in the majority and minority opinions raise important empirical questions. For example, as pointed out by Dervan, Justice Thomas' dissent in *Lee* assumes that guilty pleas are "generally reliable" in that innocent defendants do not (or very rarely) plead guilty. Creating research that tests these assumptions will be an important endeavor. As noted by Zottoli and Edkins (2018), "it is only with knowledge of existing law that we can develop ecologically valid research that can make a real contribution to policy discourse" (p. 1). This sentiment is especially true when studying pleas.

In Chapter 2, Bushway provides several suggested pathways forward. First, he calls for increased efforts to define and estimate the size of plea discounts. In large part, the size of the plea discount, or the distance between plea and trial-conviction sentence, is believed to be the primary driver behind false and/or involuntary guilty pleas. Second, Bushway urges researchers to move beyond experimental lab studies to understand false guilty pleas. At the same time, however, he also calls for continued experimentation that serves as an analogy to the courtroom workgroup and negotiations that involve all the pertinent actors. Henderson, in Chapter 3, also emphasizes the need to study plea *negotiations*. She poses questions that have gone unanswered: "What influences the 'give and take' in [plea] decisions (e.g., reciprocity within the courtroom workgroup)? Does prosecutorial overcharging exacerbate the issues related to fair negotiation? Does overestimation influence these decisions?" (p. 192). Too little research has been conducted on the role of the defense attorney in advising and negotiating pleas. More than 40 years ago, Alschuler (1975) published his seminal articles on defense attorneys (one in a series) and guilty pleas. We would encourage researchers to examine what has and has not changed from his observations.

Like Bushway and Henderson, McCannon (Chapter 4) picks up on the need to more clearly understand plea discounts and the negotiation process, particularly the role of prosecutors. According to McCannon, the motivations of prosecutors in relation to plea bargaining, and the institutional framework in which they operate, are not well understood but essential to our understanding of this process. He also stresses the need for a unifying framework to guide the systematic analysis of plea decision-making, with the express need to balance generalizability, precision, and flexibility.

In Chapter 5, Johnson and Richardson rightly point out that a uniform definition of plea bargaining is lacking. That is, scholars, many of whom are from unique disciplines, operationalize the concept differently, thereby making it harder to draw generalizations and reach conclusions. Moreover, they posit that "[m]ost plea bargaining research relies on simplistic outcome measures, such as whether or not any charge reduction occurs, without delving into finer distinctions that often distinguish the overall quality of a plea deal" (p. 95). Thus, like other authors in this volume, Johnson and Richardson note the lack of research on the negotiation process and the variety of concessions that prosecutors have at their disposal to leverage plea deals. Johnson and Richardson call for increased quality of and access to data—data collected by the courts for administrative purposes as well as data collected by independent investigators. And finally, specific to race, the focus of their chapter, they note the dearth of research on minorities other than African American, including Latino/as, Asians, and Native Americans.

In Chapter 6, Redlich, Zottoli, and Daftary-Kapur encourage researchers to examine formal decision-making models that incorporate group and individual differences, such as those that account for different models of processing and developmental decision-making. They also suggest deeper examinations, which use a variety of methods, of factors beyond probability of conviction that impinge on plea decision-making. Finally, whereas an understanding of the knowingness of plea decision-making is taking shape, studies on the voluntary nature of these decisions are few and far between. With juveniles in particular, concerns about their ability to make voluntary decisions in plea bargaining should be at the forefront.

Wilford and Khairalla begin their "Future Directions" section of Chapter 7 with a simple statement: "We still know relatively little about the decision to plead guilty; we know even less about the decision to plead guilty falsely" (p. 145). To help fill these gaps, they suggest adopting a commonly used framework that has been instrumental in shaping eyewitness research—system and estimator variables (Wells, 1978). These are variables that are (system) and are not (estimator) under the control of the criminal justice system. Defendants' actual innocence is an estimator variable, as this cannot be modified but the system's response to innocent defendants can be (e.g., limiting the size of plea discounts, videotaping negotiations). More research into both of these types of variables can help to elucidate why and under what circumstances innocent defendants plead guilty. Wilford and Khairalla also stress the need to study individual difference factors in false guilty plea decisions, such as age and race.

Echoing Johnson and Richardson (Chapter 5) and Wilford and Khairalla (Chapter 7), Hester, in Chapter 8, highlights the role of racial minorities in the consequences of our system of pleas. In particular, Hester explains that, because racial minorities receive the brunt of sentencing disparities and mass incarceration, increased insight into preventing and treating the deleterious effects of these outcomes (and the policies that lead to them) is key. Moreover, Hester asks if "the plea–trial punishment gap is justifiable." He also asks: "Are current plea sentences sufficient for utilitarian outcomes like deterrence and incapacitation?" "Are there . . . certain types of offenders or certain types of higher-level targets that [plea] discounts should be tailored toward?" "Should there be more guidance, and less prosecutorial discretion, in applying substantial assistance discounts?" And, finally, are the nearly one in five defendants who receive a substantial departure leading toward the conviction of a violent offender? To our knowledge, these questions have not been addressed by social scientists or legal scholars, but we agree with Hester that they are important to answer.

In Chapter 9, which is focused on collateral consequences, Edkins raises three good avenues for future research. First is to conduct more studies—in the field and in the lab—on the direct and indirect consequences that convicted offenders actually face, in terms of both tangible (e.g., loss of employment opportunities) and intangible costs (e.g., experiencing stigma). Second is to require prosecutors and defense attorneys to consider collateral consequences when offering and advising plea deals. The third is to determine how to make this information salient and meaningful to defendants who are deciding whether or not to plead. Research studies examining the public support for and effects of such requirements would be helpful in determining the best ways to make this an impactful policy.

Conclusion

In proposing this book to potential publishers, we concluded that *A System of Pleas: Social Science's Contributions to the Real Legal System* was without competition in the field. While there have been books published on plea bargains (e.g., Fisher, 2004; Heumann, 1978; Lippke, 2011), they were not written by social scientists, for social scientists, or they predated the majority of science. After completion of the book, we are confident—and, quite frankly, ecstatic—that this volume constitutes a real contribution to the scholarship on guilty pleas and to the real legal system. In this conclusion chapter, we have highlighted some common themes and summarized potential paths for future directions. It is our sincere hope that the readers of this book will initiate or continue researching guilty pleas, the main mechanism of conviction in the United States and abroad.

References

Alschuler, A. W. (1975). The defense attorney's role in plea bargaining. *Yale Law Journal, 84*(6), 1179–1315. doi: 10.2307/795498

Bibas, S. (2004). Plea bargaining outside the shadow of trial. *Harvard Law Review, 117*, 2463–2547.

Brady v. United States, 397 U.S. 742 (1970).

Bushway S. D., Redlich A. D., & Norris R. J. (2014). An explicit test of plea bargaining in the "shadow of the trial." *Criminology 52*, 723–754. doi: 10.1111/1745-9125.12054

Class v. United States, 583 U.S. __ (2018).

Devine, D. J., Clayton, L. D., Dunford, B. D., Seying, R., & Pryce, J. (2001). Jury decision-making: 45 years of empirical research. *Psychology, Public Policy, and Law, 7*, 622–727.

Edkins, V. A. (2011). Defense attorney plea recommendations and client race: Does zealous representation apply equally to all? *Law and Human Behavior, 35*, 413–425. doi: 10.1007/s10979-010-9254-0

Fisher, G. (2004). *Plea bargaining's triumph: A history of plea bargaining in America.* Stanford, CA: Stanford University Press.

Heumann, M. (1978). *Plea bargaining: The experiences of prosecutors, judges, and defense attorneys.* Chicago: University of Chicago Press.

Lee v. United States, 582 U.S., 137 S. Ct. 1958 (2017).

Lippke, R. L. (2011). *The ethics of plea bargaining.* New York: Oxford University Press.

National Registry of Exonerations. (n.d.). Available at, http://www.law.umich.edu/special/exoneration/Pages/about.aspx

Redlich, A. D. (2010). False confessions and false guilty pleas: Similarities and differences. In G. D. Lassiter & C. Meissner (Eds.), *Interrogations and confessions: Current research, practice and policy* (pp. 49–66). Washington, DC: APA Books.

Tor, A., Gazal-Ayal, O., & Garcia, S. M. (2010). Fairness and the willingness to accept plea bargain offers. *Journal of Empirical Legal Studies*, *7*(1), 97–116.

Wells, G. L. (1978). Applied eyewitness-testimony research: System variables and estimator variables. *Journal of Personality and Social Psychology*, *36*, 1546–1557.

Zottoli, T., & Edkins, V. A. (2018). Ignorance of the law can no longer be a defense for researchers. In C. M. King (Ed.), *American psychology—Law Society Newsletter*. Retrieved from http://ap-ls.wildapricot.org/resources/EmailTemplates/2018_02%20February%20AP-LS%20Newsletter/LegalUpdateFeb2018.pdf

Index

www.ingramcontent.com/pod-product-compliance
Ingram Content Group UK Ltd.
Pitfield, Milton Keynes, MK11 3LW, UK
UKHW022024150926
475595UK00013B/270

9 780190 689247